D0536445

MICROSOFT® OFFICE OUTLOOK® 2007
QuickSteps

MARTY MATTHEWS

CAROLE MATTHEWS

BOBBI SANDBERG

McGraw Hill

New York Chicago San Francisco
Lisbon London Madrid Mexico City
Milan New Delhi San Juan
Seoul Singapore Sydney Toronto

The McGraw·Hill Companies

Cataloging-in-Publication Data is on file with the Library of Congress

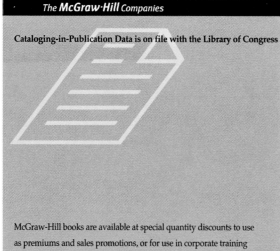

MICROSOFT® OFFICE OUTLOOK® 2007 QUICKSTEPS

234567890 CCI CCI 01987

ISBN-13: 978-0-07-226373-2
ISBN-10:   0-07-226373-3

SPONSORING EDITOR / Roger Stewart

EDITORIAL SUPERVISOR / Patty Mon

PROJECT MANAGER / Vasundhara Sawhney

ACQUISITIONS COORDINATOR / Carly Stapleton

SERIES CREATORS AND EDITORS / Marty and Carole Matthews

TECHNICAL EDITOR / John Cronan

COPY EDITOR / Lisa McCoy

PROOFREADER / Raina Trivedi

INDEXER / Robert Swanson

PRODUCTION SUPERVISOR / Jim Kussow

COMPOSITION / International Typesetting and Composition

ILLUSTRATION / International Typesetting and Composition

ART DIRECTOR, COVER / Jeff Weeks

COVER DESIGN / Pattie Lee

SERIES DESIGN / Bailey Cunningham

About the Authors

Marty and **Carole Matthews** have used computers for over 30 years, from some of the early mainframe computers to recent personal computers. They have done this as programmers, systems analysts, managers, and company executives. As a result, they have first-hand knowledge of not only how to program and use a computer, but also how to make the best use of all that can be done with a computer.

Over 27 years ago Marty and Carole wrote their first computer book on how to buy mini-computers. Over 23 years ago they began writing books as a major part of their occupation. In the intervening years they have written over 70 books including ones on desktop publishing, web publishing, Microsoft Office, and Microsoft operating systems from MS-DOS through Windows Vista. Recent books published by McGraw-Hill include *Windows Vista QuickSteps, Microsoft Office PowerPoint 2007 QuickSteps, and QuickSteps to Winning Business Presentations.*

Marty and Carole live on an island in Puget Sound where, on the rare moments when they can look up from their computers, they look west across seven miles of water and the main shipping channel to the snow-capped Olympic Mountains.

Bobbi Sandberg has been involved with computers and accounting for five decades. Her extensive background combined with her ability to explain complex concepts in plain language has made her a popular instructor, speaker, and consultant. Bobbi has been a CPA and was a geek long before it was popular. She is the co-author of *Quicken 2007 Personal Finance Software QuickSteps.* Currently semi-retired, she lives on an island surrounded by deer, chipmunks, trees—and at last count, 23 computers in various stages of operation.

Contents at a Glance

Contents

3   Chapter 3   **Creating and Sending E-mail** 41

4   Chapter 4   **Managing Contacts** 67

5

6

7 Chapter 7   Using a Journal and Making Notes 141

8 Chapter 8   Managing Files and Folders 157

Acknowledgments

This book is a team effort of truly talented people. Among them are:

Lisa McCoy, copy editor, added to the readability and understandability of the book while always being a joy to work with. Thanks, Lisa!

Patty Mon and **Vasundhara Sawhney**, project editors, greased the wheels and straightened the track to make a very smooth production process. Thanks, Patty and Vasundhara!

Roger Stewart, sponsoring editor, believed in us enough to sell the series, and continues to stand behind us as we go through the second edition. Thanks, Roger!

Introduction

QuickSteps books are recipe books for computer users. They answer the question "how do I…" by providing a quick set of steps to accomplish the most common tasks with a particular operating system or application.

The sets of steps are the central focus of the book. QuickSteps and QuickFacts sidebars show how to quickly perform many small functions or tasks that support the primary functions or better understand some nuisance of that function. Notes, Tips, and Cautions augment the steps, and are presented in a separate column to not interrupt the flow of the steps. The introductions are minimal and other narrative is kept brief. Numerous full-color illustrations and figures, many with callouts, support the steps.

QuickSteps books are organized by function and the tasks needed to perform that function. Each function is a chapter. Each task, or "How To," contains the steps needed for accomplishing the function along with the relevant Notes, Tips, Cautions, and screenshots. You can easily find the tasks you want to perform through:

- The table of contents, which lists the functional areas (chapters) and tasks in the order they are presented

- A How To list of tasks on the opening page of each chapter

- The index, which provides an alphabetical list of the terms that are used to describe the functions and tasks

- Color-coded tabs for each chapter or functional area with an index to the tabs in the Contents At a Glance (just before the Table of Contents)

Conventions Used in this Book

Microsoft Office Outlook 2007 QuickSteps uses several conventions designed to make the book easier for you to follow. Among these are

- A 🔍 or a 🪐 in the table of contents or the How To list in each chapter references a QuickSteps or QuickFacts sidebar in a chapter.

- **Bold type** is used for words or objects on the screen that you are to do something with, like "…click the **Office Button** and click **Save As**."

- *Italic type* is used for a word or phrase that is being defined or otherwise deserves special emphasis.

- <u>Underlined type</u> is used for text that you are to type from the keyboard.

- SMALL CAPITAL LETTERS are used for keys on the keyboard such as ENTER and SHIFT.

- When you are expected to enter a command, you are told to press the key(s). If you are to enter text or numbers, you are told to type them.

How to...

Chapter 1
Stepping into Outlook

When someone mentions Outlook, the first thought is generally the sending and receiving of e-mail. Outlook does handle e-mail quite competently, but it also does a lot more, including managing contacts, scheduling activities, tracking tasks, keeping a journal, and using notes. Outlook also provides the means to collaborate with others, it can be used with and from other applications, and can link to and synch up with both a team Web site using Windows SharePoint Services, and with a PDA (personal digital assistant).

In this chapter you will familiarize yourself with Outlook; see how to start and leave it; use the windows, panes, ribbons, toolbars and menus in Outlook; learn how to get help; and find out how to customize Outlook.

Start Outlook

How you start Outlook depends on how it was installed and what has happened to it since its installation. In this section you'll see a way to start

![Start menu showing Windows programs and Microsoft Office Outlook 2007 highlighted]

Figure 1-1: The foolproof way to start Outlook is through the Start menu.

NOTE

If you have been running Outlook Express and then install Outlook, you may get a message when you run the Outlook 2007 Startup Wizard asking if you want to upgrade from Outlook Express and if you want to import your Outlook Express messages and addresses. See "Upgrade from Outlook Express" later in this chapter.

Outlook and some alternatives, you'll see how to use the Startup Wizard and how to upgrade from Outlook Express. You'll also see how to exit Outlook.

Use the Start Menu to Start Outlook

If there are no other icons for or shortcuts to Outlook available on your desktop, you can always start Outlook using the Start menu.

1. Start your computer if it is not already running, and log on to Windows if necessary.

2. Click **Start**. Click **All Programs**, click **Microsoft Office**, and click **Microsoft Office Outlook 2007**, as shown in Figure 1-1.

Use the Startup Wizard

The first time you start Outlook on either a new computer with Office 2007 or a new installation of Office 2007, the Outlook 2007 Startup Wizard will open. You'll see an Outlook 2007 Startup screen and a smaller Configuring Outlook message box.

1. Click **Next**. Accept the default response of **Yes** to configure an e-mail account, and click **Next**.

2. Type your name, e-mail address, and password. Then retype the password. Click **Next**.

3. E-mail configuring will take several minutes. When it finishes, click **Next**.

4. When it has finished, you will see a dialog box showing the steps that were taken and the results, as shown in Figure 1-2. Click **Finish**. The wizard will close and Outlook will open. See "Explore Outlook" later in this chapter.

5. You will be asked if you want Outlook and Microsoft Internet Explorer to synchronize the RSS (Real Simple Syndication) lists (Web sites that you subscribe to that will be automatically downloaded, such as CNN) and make them available in Outlook as well as Internet Explorer and other places, such as on the Windows Vista sidebar. Make the selection that is relevant for you.

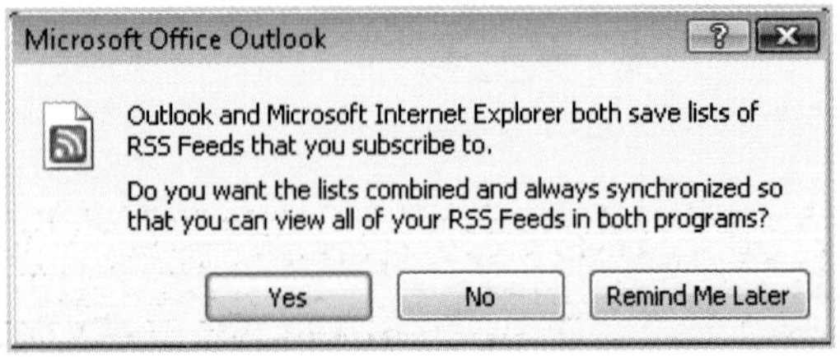

> **Microsoft Office Outlook**
>
> Outlook and Microsoft Internet Explorer both save lists of RSS Feeds that you subscribe to.
>
> Do you want the lists combined and always synchronized so that you can view all of your RSS Feeds in both programs?
>
> [Yes] [No] [Remind Me Later]

TIP

A *protocol* is an industry standard that is widely accepted and used by many organizations to perform a function, like exchanging e-mail.

QUICKSTEPS

STARTING OUTLOOK IN OTHER WAYS

In addition to using All Programs on the Start menu, there are several other ways to start Outlook.

USE THE START MENU

The upper-left area of the Start menu has a permanent place for your e-mail program. If Outlook is the default e-mail program on your computer, it will automatically be placed on the Start menu. If it isn't there, you can change that.

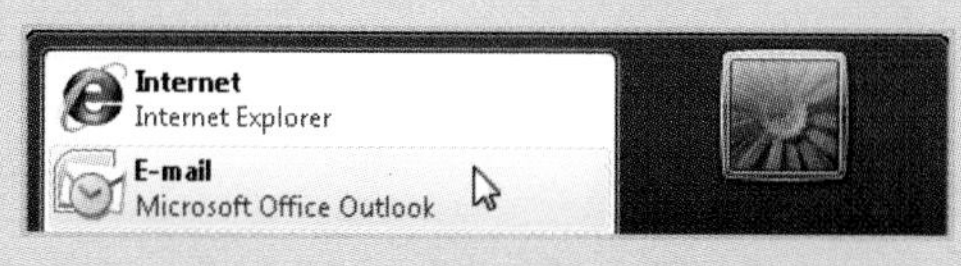

1. Right-click **Start** and click **Properties**. If it is not already selected, click **Start Menu**, and then click **Customize**.

2. Next to the E-mail Link check box (which should be selected) at the bottom of the dialog box, click the down arrow, and click **Microsoft Office Outlook** from the menu.

   | Open |
   | Explore |
   | Search... |
   | SnagIt ▸ |
   | Properties |
   | Open All Users |
   | Explore All Users |

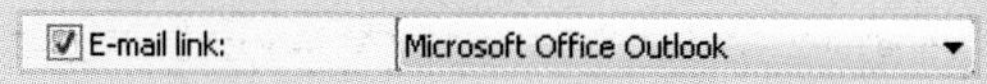

   ☑ E-mail link: Microsoft Office Outlook   ▾

3. Click **OK** twice to close both dialog boxes.

Continued . . .

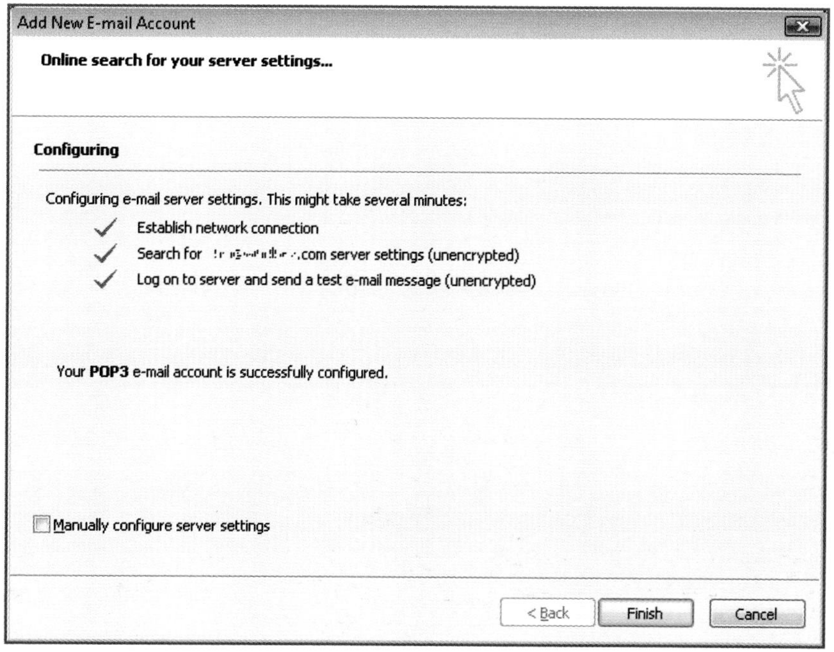

Add New E-mail Account

Online search for your server settings...

Configuring

Configuring e-mail server settings. This might take several minutes:

✓ Establish network connection
✓ Search for 'r ⱨⱤⱳⱤ꜀ꜞⱦⱦⱬ .com server settings (unencrypted)
✓ Log on to server and send a test e-mail message (unencrypted)

Your **POP3** e-mail account is successfully configured.

☐ Manually configure server settings

< Back   Finish   Cancel

Figure 1-2: You will see when your e-mail setup has successfully completed.

Upgrade from Outlook Express

If you have been using Outlook Express and you install Office 2007, when the Outlook 2007 Startup Wizard runs, you may be asked if you want to upgrade from Outlook Express. If you choose to upgrade, you will be asked if you want to import your Outlook Express messages and addresses. Click **Yes,** and you will see the progress as the files are being imported and will get a summary upon completion.

If you have been using Outlook Express and were not asked by the Outlook 2007 Startup Wizard if you want to upgrade, you can still import your Outlook Express files into Outlook.

1. Start **Outlook** in one of the ways described earlier in this chapter.

2. Click the **File** menu, and click **Import And Export**.

QUICKSTEPS

STARTING OUTLOOK IN OTHER WAYS *(Continued)*

CREATE A SHORTCUT TO START OUTLOOK

An easy way to start Outlook is to create a shortcut icon on the desktop, and then to use it to start the program.

Click **Start**, click **All Programs**, click **Microsoft Office**, right-click **Microsoft Office Outlook 2007**, click **Send To**, and click **Desktop (Create Shortcut)**.

Send To	▶	Compressed (zipped) Folder
		Desktop (create shortcut)
		Documents

USE THE QUICK LAUNCH TOOLBAR

If the Quick Launch toolbar was turned on when you installed Office 2007, then an Outlook icon was placed on the Quick Launch toolbar. If your Quick Launch toolbar was not on, open it and put an Outlook icon there.

1. To display the toolbar, right-click a blank area of the taskbar, click **Toolbars**, and click **Quick Launch**.

2. Click **Start**, click **All Programs,** click **Microsoft Office**, and drag **Microsoft Office Outlook 2007** to the position you want on the Quick Launch toolbar.

TIP

You can save the Import Summary report by clicking **Save In Inbox**.

3. Click **Import Internet Mail And Addresses**, and click **Next**.

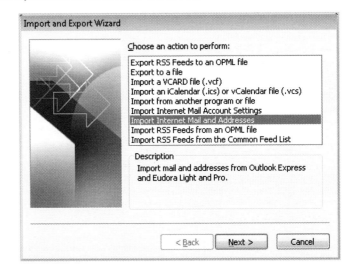

4. Click **Outlook Express** and make sure that the **Import Mail**, **Import Address Book**, and **Import Rules** check boxes are all selected, as shown in Figure 1-3.

5. Click **Next**, choose how you want to handle duplicates, and then click **Finish**.

Figure 1-3: You can choose the source of your imported mail, address book, and import rules.

NOTE

If you want to import Outlook Express or Windows Mail files from another computer, locate the files by starting the program on the other computer, click the **Tools** menu, choose **Options**, click the **Advanced** tab (the Maintenance tab in Outlook Express), click the **Maintenance** button (skip this in Outlook Express), and click **Store Folder**. Drag across the entire address line, press CTRL+C, and click **OK** to close the Store Location dialog box. Then click **Start**, click **Computer**, click the computer icon at the left end of the Address bar, press CTRL+V to copy the contents into the address bar, and click the **Go To** button or press ENTER. This will show you the Outlook Express files. Copy these files to the new computer, import them into Outlook Express on that computer, and then use the instructions under "Upgrade from Outlook Express" to import the files into Outlook.

Store Location   ☒

Your personal message store is located in the following folder:

C:\Users\Owner\AppData\Local\Microsoft\Windows Mail

[Change...]   [OK]   [Cancel]

You will be told the progress as the files are being imported and will get a summary upon completion.

Exit Outlook

When you are done using Outlook, you can exit the program.

- Click the **File** menu, and click **Exit**.

  –Or–

- Click **Close** on the right of the title bar.   [x]

  –Or–

- Press **ALT+F4**.

Explore Outlook

Outlook uses a wide assortment of windows, toolbars, menus, and special features to accomplish its functions. Much of this book explores how to find and use all of those items. In this section you'll see the most common features of the default Outlook window, including the parts of the window, the buttons on the principal toolbars, and the major menus. Also, you'll see how to use the Navigation pane and Outlook Today.

Explore the Outlook Window

The Outlook window takes on a different appearance depending on the function you want Outlook to perform. The initial view when you first start Outlook is for handling mail, as shown in Figure 1-4. However, this view changes as soon as you start to do anything else, even create e-mail, as you'll see in this chapter. Other functions are described in their corresponding chapters. The principal features of the Outlook window are described in Table 1-1.

Change Views

The view you will have on the main Outlook window can be changed, depending on what you want to see. Typically, as shown earlier in Figure 1-4, you will see

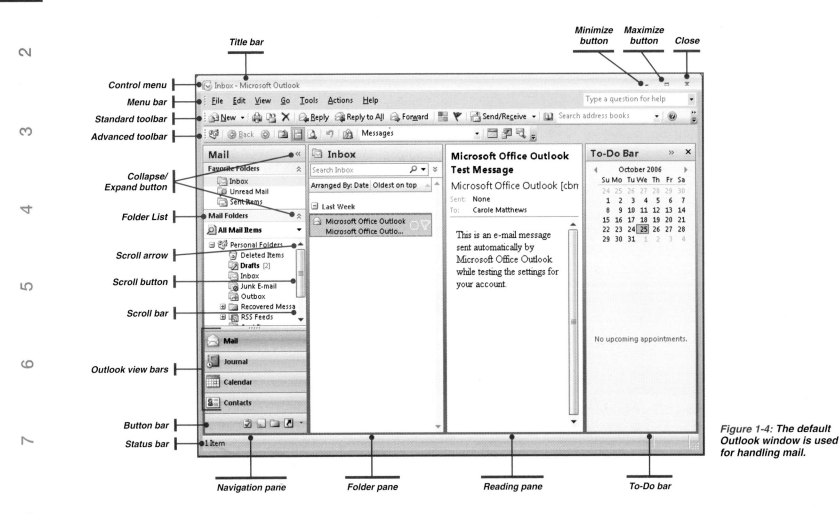

Title bar

Minimize button

Maximize button

Close

Control menu

Menu bar

Standard toolbar

Advanced toolbar

Collapse/ Expand button

Folder List

Scroll arrow

Scroll button

Scroll bar

Outlook view bars

Button bar

Status bar

Navigation pane

Folder pane

Reading pane

To-Do bar

Figure 1-4: The default Outlook window is used for handling mail.

the Navigation pane, Folder pane, Reading pane, and To-Do Bar. You may change these by clicking another view on the Outlook view bar or, you can:

Click the **View** menu, and select the pane or bar you want to change. Select the appropriate option from the menu.

OUTLOOK FEATURES	DESCRIPTION
Title bar	Name of the open folder; contains the controls for the window.
Menu bar	Contains the primary controls for Outlook.
Standard toolbar	Changes to contain the controls needed for the open folder.
Advanced toolbar	Provides additional controls to those on the Standard toolbar.
Minimize button	Minimizes the window to an icon on the taskbar.
Maximize button	Maximizes the window to fill the screen. When maximized, this becomes the Restore button; clicking it returns the window to its previous size.
Close	Exits Outlook and closes the window.
Collapse/Expand button	Collapses or expands the current list box, whatever it might contain.
Scroll arrow	Moves the contents of the pane in the direction of the arrow.
Scroll button	Moves the contents of the pane in the direction it is dragged.
Scroll bar	Moves the contents of the pane in the direction it is clicked.
Navigation pane	Contains the means for selecting what you want to do and look at.
Reading pane	Displays the contents of the selected message in the open folder.
Folder pane	Displays the contents of the selected folder.
To-Do Bar	Contains the current month's calendar and appointments for the day.
Folder List	Contains the folders within the selected view.
Outlook view bars	Provides selection of the various views.
Control menu	Contains controls for the window itself.
Status bar	Displays information about what is selected.

Table 1-1: Principal Features of the Outlook Window

Display the Advanced Toolbar

By default, the Advanced toolbar is not displayed. You can display it at any time, however.

1. In the initial Outlook view, click the **View** menu and click **Toolbars**. The Toolbars menu will be displayed.

2. Click the **Advanced** toolbar. A check mark appears next to it, and the toolbar is displayed on the screen.

TIP

Another way to display a toolbar is to click the **Tools** menu, click **Customize**, and click the **Toolbars** tab. Click the check box next to the Advanced toolbar, and click **Close**.

USING OUTLOOK TOOLBARS

SEE WHAT A TOOL DOES

Hold the mouse pointer over the tool. A *ScreenTip* will appear, telling you what the tool does.

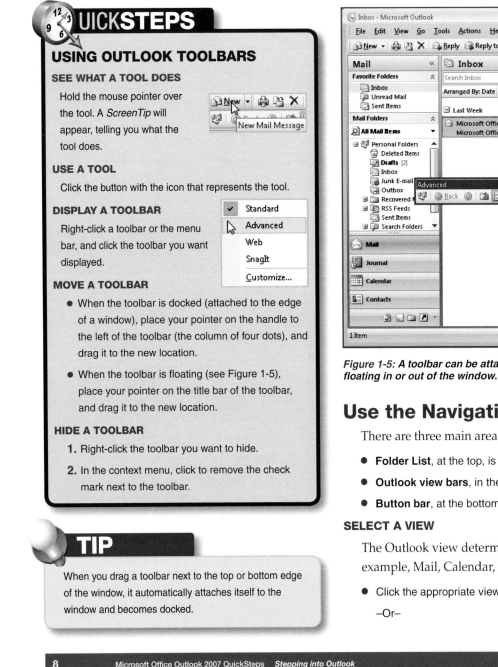

USE A TOOL

Click the button with the icon that represents the tool.

DISPLAY A TOOLBAR

Right-click a toolbar or the menu bar, and click the toolbar you want displayed.

MOVE A TOOLBAR

- When the toolbar is docked (attached to the edge of a window), place your pointer on the handle to the left of the toolbar (the column of four dots), and drag it to the new location.
- When the toolbar is floating (see Figure 1-5), place your pointer on the title bar of the toolbar, and drag it to the new location.

HIDE A TOOLBAR

1. Right-click the toolbar you want to hide.
2. In the context menu, click to remove the check mark next to the toolbar.

TIP

When you drag a toolbar next to the top or bottom edge of the window, it automatically attaches itself to the window and becomes docked.

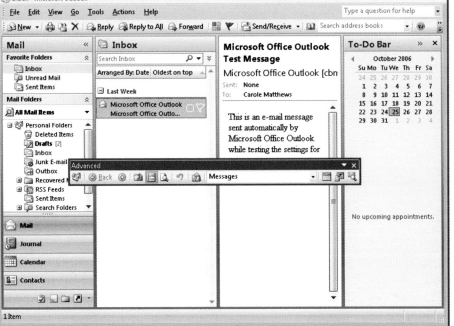

Figure 1-5: A toolbar can be attached to any edge of the Outlook window, or it can be floating in or out of the window.

Use the Navigation Pane

There are three main areas of the Navigation pane, as shown in Figure 1-6:

- **Folder List**, at the top, is where you can select the folder you want to open.
- **Outlook view bars**, in the middle, are where you can select the view in which to work.
- **Button bar**, at the bottom, lets you access views not available in the view bars.

SELECT A VIEW

The Outlook view determines which area of Outlook you will work in—for example, Mail, Calendar, or Contacts. To select a view:

- Click the appropriate view bar.

    –Or–

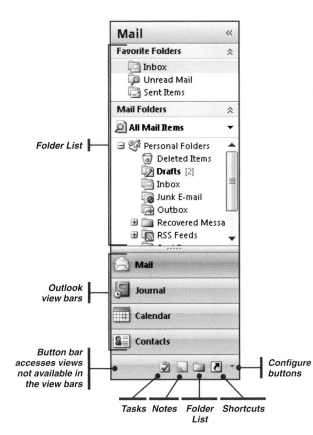

Folder List

Outlook
view bars

Button bar
accesses views
not available in
the view bars

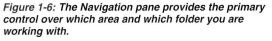

Configure
buttons

Tasks Notes Folder Shortcuts
List

Figure 1-6: The Navigation pane provides the primary
control over which area and which folder you are
working with.

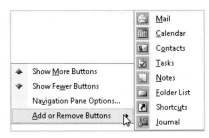

• Click the appropriate button in the button bar, see Figure 1-6.

–Or–

• Click the **Go** menu, and then click the desired view.

OPEN A FOLDER

The folder that is open determines which specific documents you will work on,
for example, incoming messages in the Inbox folder or notes in the Notes folder.
To open a folder:

• Click the appropriate folder in the Folder List.

–Or–

• Click the related view in the view bar, button in the Button bar, or view in the Go menu.

DISPLAY VIEW BARS

The number of view bars displayed depends on the size of the Outlook window
and the size of the area dedicated to the view bars. To change the number of
view bars displayed:

• Drag the bottom window border up or down.

–Or–

• Drag the handle between the top view bar and the bottom
of the Folder List.

DISPLAY BUTTONS

The buttons in the button bar are just an extension of view bars. When you
reduce the number of view bars, the options become buttons on the button bar.
To change the buttons on the button bar, in addition to changing the number of
view bars that are displayed:

1. Click the **Configure button** on the right of the button bar.

2. Click **Add Or Remove Buttons**, and then click the button you want to add or remove.

REORDER NAVIGATION PANE BUTTONS

To change the buttons or the order of the button in the Navigation Pane:

1. Click the **Tools** menu, and click **Options**.

QUICKSTEPS

USING MENUS

Menus are the foundational means of control in Outlook. Many, if not most, of the menu options are also on toolbars or some other control. When you can't find a control, however, look at the menus.

OPEN A MENU WITH THE MOUSE

Click the menu.

OPEN A MENU WITH THE KEYBOARD

Press **ALT+** the underlined letter in the menu name. For example, press **ALT+F** to open the File menu. [File]

OPEN A SUBMENU

A number of menu options have a right-pointing arrow on their right indicating that there is a submenu associated with that option. To open the submenu:

Move the mouse pointer to the menu option with a submenu, and the submenu will open.

File	Edit	View	Go	Tools	Actions	Help		
New					Mail Message			Ctrl+N
Open					Post in This Folder			Ctrl+Shift+S

2. Click the **Other** tab, and under Outlook Panes, click **Navigation Pane**. The Navigation Pane Options dialog box will open.

3. Highlight a button, and click **Move Up** or **Move Down** to reorder the list. Click **OK** twice.

CLOSE THE NAVIGATION PANE

If you need more room to display a folder and its contents, you can close the Navigation pane:

- Click the **View** menu, and click **Navigation Pane**.

  –Or–

- Click the **Collapse** button at the top of the Navigation pane to reduce its size. (Click it again (now the Expand button) to restore the Navigation pane to its regular size.

Mail	«
Favorite Folders	

Use Outlook Today

Outlook Today gives you a summary of the information in Outlook for the current day. You can see a summary of your messages, your appointments and meetings, and the tasks you are slated to do, as shown in Figure 1-7.

OPEN OUTLOOK TODAY

If the Advanced toolbar is open, click the **Outlook Today** icon. (If it is not open, click **View**, click **Toolbars**, and click **Advanced** so that a check mark is in the check box.)

CHANGE OUTLOOK TODAY

Click **Customize Outlook Today** in the upper-right corner of the Outlook Today folder. Customize Outlook Today will open, as shown in Figure 1-8.

Customize Outlook Today

MAKE OUTLOOK TODAY YOUR DEFAULT PAGE

To display Outlook Today by default when you open Outlook:

1. In the Customize Outlook Today pane, opposite Startup, click **When Starting, Go Directly To Outlook Today**.

2. Click **Save Changes**.

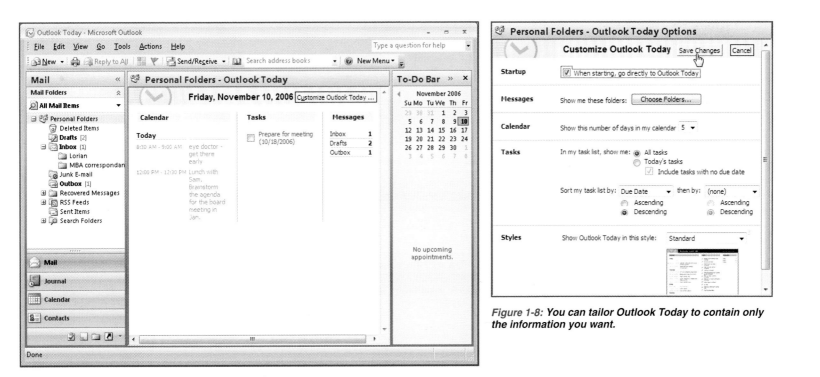

Figure 1-8: *You can tailor Outlook Today to contain only the information you want.*

Figure 1-7: *Outlook Today provides a summary of information for the current day, such as appointments and tasks.*

Customize the To-Do Bar

To customize the To-Do Bar and determine what is displayed in it:

1. Click the **View** menu, click **To-Do Bar**, and click **Options** in the flyout menu.

2. Click the check boxes next to the options you want.

3. Click **OK**.

Get Help

Microsoft provides substantial assistance to Outlook users. Outlook tailors much of the assistance offered, depending on whether you are working online or offline. If you are offline, you will get quick but more limited help. If you are or can be online, it will be slower, but more comprehensive.

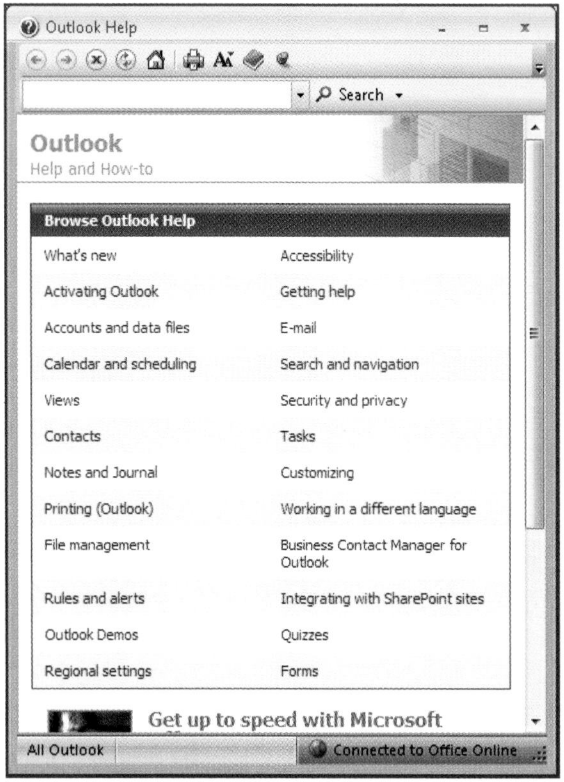

Figure 1-9: The Outlook Help pane provides links to several avenues of online and offline assistance.

Obtain Help

You can obtain help in Outlook using one of the following techniques.

DISPLAY OUTLOOK HELP

The Outlook Help pane, shown in Figure 1-9, provides links to several assistance tools and forums, including a table of contents, access to downloads, contact information, and late-breaking news on Outlook. To display the Outlook Help task pane:

- Click the **Help** menu, and click **Microsoft Office Outlook Help**.

  –Or–

- Click the **Microsoft Office Outlook Help** icon 🔘 on the Standard toolbar.

  –Or–

- Press **F1**.

ASK A QUESTION

You can quickly ask a question about Outlook directly from the menu bar without using the Outlook Help task pane.

1. Type your question in the **Type A Question For Help** text box on the right of the menu bar. `Type a question for help  ▾`
2. Press **ENTER**. The Outlook Help dialog box will appear, as you can see in Figure 1-10. Click one of the search results, and Microsoft Office Outlook Help will open and display the requested information.

Find a Message

No matter how many messages your e-mail folders contain, Outlook can help you find a specific one. You can perform instant searches for large sized files, related messages, or messages from a particular sender. You can further qualify the search by having Outlook search only certain folders, or by specifying content for which you're searching.

PERFORM INSTANT SEARCHES

Click in the search text box in the Inbox Folder pane (or which ever folder you want to search in) and type the text for which you want to search.

Figure 1-10: From the Outlook Help dialog box, you can search both online and offline Help, as well as other sources.

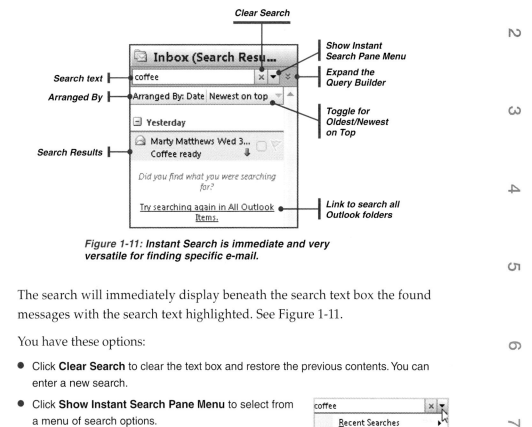

Figure 1-11: Instant Search is immediate and very versatile for finding specific e-mail.

The search will immediately display beneath the search text box the found messages with the search text highlighted. See Figure 1-11.

You have these options:

● Click **Clear Search** to clear the text box and restore the previous contents. You can enter a new search.

● Click **Show Instant Search Pane Menu** to select from a menu of search options.

● Click **Expand the Query Builder** to refine and add other search criteria.

● Click **Arranged By** to change the order for search results from the context menu.

● Click **Oldest/Youngest On Top** to toggle the date ascending/descending sequence.

● Click **Try Searching Again In All Outlook Items** to expand the search to additional folders.

EXPLORE ADVANCED SEARCHES

In addition to the Instant Search found on the Folder Pane, you can also use the menu system to perform other, more advanced searches.

```
Tools   Actions   Help
    Send/Receive                    ▶   ⟐ ▼ | 📄 Send/Receive ▼ | 🔖 Search addre:
    Instant Search                  ▶   🔎  Instant Search              Ctrl+E
📖  Address Book...    Ctrl+Shift+B      ⩔  Expand the Query Builder   Ctrl+Alt+W
📇  Organize                         🔍  Search All Mail Items        Ctrl+Alt+A
📑  Rules and Alerts...               🔍  Indexing Status...
    Mailbox Cleanup...               📄  Search Options...
🗑  Empty "Deleted Items" Folder        Advanced Find...             Ctrl+Shift+F
    Forms                         ▶      Related Messages...
    Macro                         ▶      Messages from Sender...
    Account Settings...
    Trust Center...
    Customize...
    Options...
```

```
🔍 Advanced Find                                              _  □  X
  File   Edit   View   Tools
  Look for: Messages            ▼   In:  Inbox              Browse...
   Messages | More Choices | Advanced |                     Find Now
    Search for the word(s):                        ▼         Stop
                  In:  subject field only          ▼        New Search
       From...
       Sent To...
    ☐ Where I am:   the only person on the To line    ▼       🔍
            Time:  none    ▼    anytime              ▼
```

NOTE

Reference tools provided with Outlook, such as a thesaurus, are available with Outlook message windows, but not from the main Outlook window.

1. Click the **Tools** menu, and click **Instant Search**. The flyout menu contains the following options for conducting a search:
   - **Instant Search** displays a search pane so that you can search for a phrase in the selected folder. Instant Search builds an index to search.
   - **Expand The Query Builder** displays a search pane where you can build detailed search criteria.
   - **Search All Mail Items** searches all mail items based on the detailed criteria set in the Search pane.
   - **Indexing Status** reports on an indexing function performed by Outlook and returns a status. This must show that all indexing is complete before Instant Search can be relied upon.
   - **Search Options** displays the Search Options dialog box, where you can set options for indexing files and indexing during searches, displaying search results faster and in color, searching deleted items, and, in the Instant Search, including only a selected folder or all folders.
   - **Advanced Find** displays the Advanced Find dialog box where search criteria can include even more detail.
   - **Related Messages** searches for messages related to the selected one.
   - **Messages From Sender** searches for messages from selected senders.

2. Click your choice and type the information needed. Click OK if needed. (If your choice of option does not require a dialog box, you will not need to click OK.)

CHANGE SEARCH OPTIONS

To change some of the search defaults, use the Search Options dialog box, shown in Figure 1-12.

1. Click **Tools**, click **Instant Search**, and click **Search Options** in the sub menu. The Search Options is displayed.

2. Under **Indexing** select the data files to be indexed (so that searches can be faster), and if you choose, deselect the default to display a message if the indexing is incomplete for a selected file. If this message is displayed, it tells you that the indexing is still in process and that results will be incomplete.

3. Under **Search**, you can determine whether you want to change the defaults to display results as you type the search text, to limit the number of results so that the searches are faster, or to highlight the search text in results and change the highlight color.

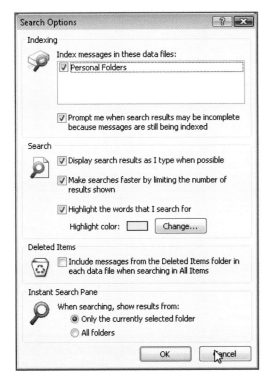

Figure 1-12: *In the Search Options dialog box, you can change search defaults that assist you during your search activity.*

NOTE

Ways of setting preferences in each of the major areas—Mail, Calendar, Tasks, Contacts, and Notes—are discussed in the chapters that pertain to those subjects. Here, you'll see how to set general preferences for e-mail.

4. Under **Deleted Items**, click the option to include messages in the Deleted Items folder in the data files being searched.

5. Under **Instant Search Pane** choose between searching the currently selected folder (the default), or all folders in the Instant Search feature.

6. Click **OK**.

Customize Outlook

Outlook provides a number of ways to customize both how it looks and how it operates. Some of these ways to customize have already been discussed in this chapter; others will be discussed in later chapters. In this section, you'll see how to set general preferences, how to customize the toolbars and menus, how to create a user profile, and how to update Outlook.

Customize Outlook Toolbars

You can customize a toolbar by adding commands or menus to an existing toolbar or by creating a new toolbar and adding commands or menus to that.

ADD COMMANDS TO THE TOOLBAR

If you find the buttons on the toolbars are not as convenient as you would like, or if you frequently use a feature that is not on one of the toolbars, you can rearrange the buttons or add buttons to a toolbar.

1. Click the **Tools** menu, click **Customize**, and click the **Commands** tab.

2. Under Categories, select the category where the command will be found.

3. Under Commands, find the command, and drag it from the dialog box to the location on the toolbar where you want it (see Figure 1-13).

4. Click **Close** when you are finished.

CREATE A CUSTOM TOOLBAR

You can create a custom toolbar with the commands on it that you use most frequently, avoid displaying several toolbars, and make more open space for Outlook's primary functions of mail, calendar, tasks, and so on.

NOTE

Setting up multiple users in Windows is different from setting up multiple Outlook user accounts. Each Windows user has a unique Outlook user profile with his or her folders and files. The multiple Outlook user accounts discussed in this chapter are for a single Windows user.

NOTE

Setting up security for Outlook is covered in Chapter 8.

NOTE

As you drag the command from the dialog box to the toolbar, it will initially drag a small rectangle containing an "X," signifying that it can't be placed where it is. The rectangle will change into a plus sign, signifying a copy, when the pointer is over the toolbars, and then into an I-beam icon over other individual icons. This I-beam icon marks the insertion point where the command icon will be inserted between the adjoining icons in the toolbar.

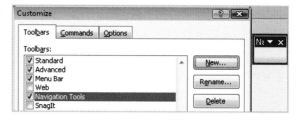

Figure 1-13: You can drag commands from a number of categories, both to existing and to new toolbars.

1. Click the **Tools** menu, click **Customize**, and click the **Toolbars** tab.

2. Click **New**. The New Toolbar dialog box appears.

3. Enter the name of the new toolbar, and click **OK**.
   A small toolbar will appear on the screen with the first few letters of its name in the title bar and its name added to the list of toolbars in the Customize dialog box.

4. Use the steps in the preceding "Add Commands to the Toolbar" section to populate the toolbar with the commands you want.

QUICKSTEPS

SETTING PREFERENCES

Setting preferences allows you to adapt Outlook to your needs and work style. The Options dialog box provides access to these settings.

Click the **Tools** menu, and click **Options** to open the Options dialog box.

OMIT ORIGINAL TEXT IN REPLIES

1. Click the **Preferences** tab, and click the **E-mail Options** button to open the E-mail Options dialog box, shown in Figure 1-14. [E-mail Options...]

2. Under On Replies And Forwards, beneath When Replying To A Message, click the text box down arrow.

3. Click **Do Not Include Original Message** from the menu.

4. Review the other options and make any changes.

5. Click OK twice to close the two E-mail Options dialog boxes.

MAKE OUTLOOK THE DEFAULT E-MAIL PROGRAM

1. In the Options dialog box, click the **Other** tab.

2. In the General area, select the **Make Outlook The Default Program For E-mail, Contacts, And Calendar** check box.

   ☑ Make Outlook the default program for E-mail, Contacts, and Calendar.

3. Click **OK** to close the Options dialog box.

SET BEGINNING FOLDER VIEW

1. In the Options dialog box, on the Other tab, click the **Advanced Options** button (see Figure 1-15).

Continued . . .

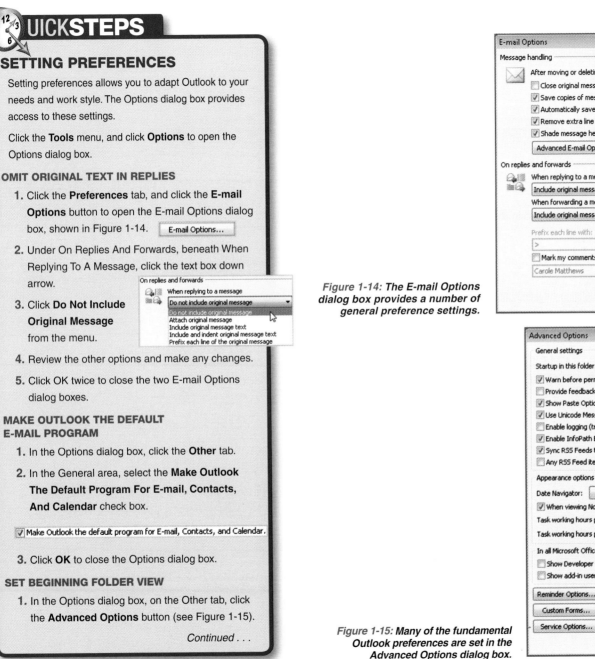

Figure 1-14: The E-mail Options dialog box provides a number of general preference settings.

Figure 1-15: Many of the fundamental Outlook preferences are set in the Advanced Options dialog box.

QUICKSTEPS

SETTING PREFERENCES (Continued)

2. Click **Browse** next to Startup In This Folder, and the Select Folder dialog box appears.

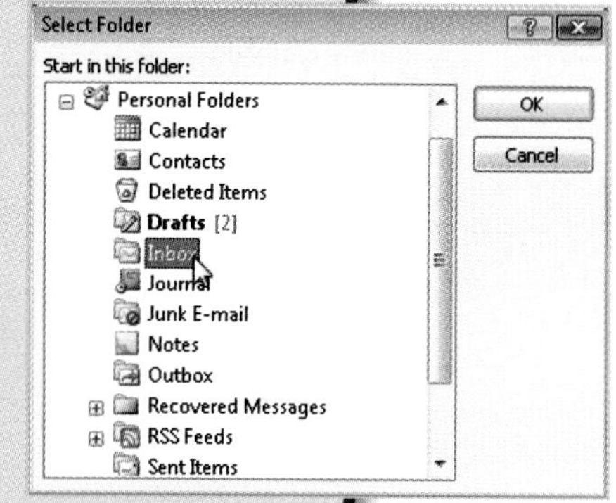

3. Click the folder you want displayed at startup.

4. Review the other options and make any changes you want.

5. Click **OK** three times to close all the dialog boxes.

Select Folder

Start in this folder:

- Personal Folders
  - Calendar
  - Contacts
  - Deleted Items
  - **Drafts** [2]
  - Inbox
  - Journal
  - Junk E-mail
  - Notes
  - Outbox
  - Recovered Messages
  - RSS Feeds
  - Sent Items

[OK] [Cancel]

ADD A NEW E-MAIL ACCOUNT

1. In the Options dialog box, on the **Mail Setup** tab, click the **E-mail Accounts** button. The Account Settings dialog box appears, as shown in Figure 1-16. [E-mail Accounts...]

2. Click **New**. The Add New E-mail Account Wizard is displayed.

   a. Choose the type of e-mail service you have, and click **Next**.

   b. Type the new name, e-mail address, and password. Click **Next**.

   c. An online search will be made to verify your settings with your server. Click **Next**.

3. When the settings have been confirmed, click **Finish**.

4. Click **Close** to close the Account Settings dialog box, and then click **OK** to close the Options dialog box.

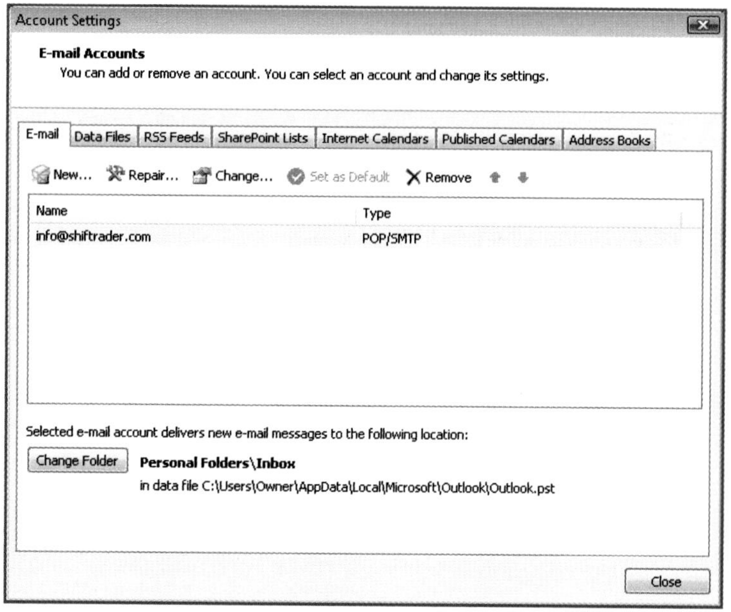

Account Settings

E-mail Accounts
You can add or remove an account. You can select an account and change its settings.

| E-mail | Data Files | RSS Feeds | SharePoint Lists | Internet Calendars | Published Calendars | Address Books |

New... | Repair... | Change... | Set as Default | X Remove | ↑ ↓

Name	Type
info@shifttrader.com	POP/SMTP

Selected e-mail account delivers new e-mail messages to the following location:

[Change Folder] **Personal Folders\Inbox**
in data file C:\Users\Owner\AppData\Local\Microsoft\Outlook\Outlook.pst

[Close]

Figure 1-16: You can add, repair, change, or remove new e-mail accounts and change the folder where e-mail messages are stored.

DRAG A MENU TO A TOOLBAR

Outlook provides several menus that you can add to a custom or existing toolbar.

1. Click the **Tools** menu, click **Customize**, and click the **Commands** tab.

2. Select **Menu Bar** from the Categories list.

3. Drag the menu you want to the destination toolbar. See "Add Commands to the Toolbar," earlier in this chapter, for steps on how to move commands.

DELETE A TOOLBAR

You can delete only custom toolbars that you created.

1. Click the **Tools** menu, click **Customize**, and click the **Toolbars** tab.

2. Click the check box next to the toolbar you want to delete.

3. Click **Delete**. You will be asked if you really want to delete the toolbar.

4. Click **OK** and click **Close**.

> **TIP**
>
> Don't worry about making a mistake and placing something where you don't want it. You can always click **Reset Menu And Toolbar Usage Data** on the Options tab of the Customize menu to restore the menus and toolbars to their default settings.

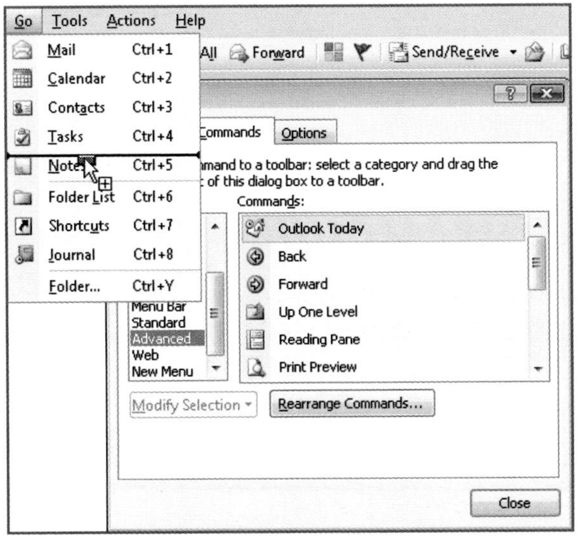

Figure 1-17: ***An obvious additional menu option is the addition of Outlook Today to the Go menu.***

Customize Outlook Menus

Customizing a menu is similar to customizing a toolbar. It can be done by adding commands to an existing menu or by creating a new menu and adding commands to it.

ADD COMMANDS TO A MENU

If you find that the options on a menu don't meet your needs or work style, or if you frequently use a feature that is not on one of the menus, you can rearrange the options or add commands to become new options on a menu.

1. Click the **Tools** menu, click **Customize**, and click the **Commands** tab.
2. Under Categories, select the category where the command will be found.
3. Under Commands, find the command you want, and drag it from the dialog box to the location on the menu where you want it, as shown in Figure 1-17.
4. Click **Close** when you are finished.

CREATE A CUSTOM MENU

You can create a custom menu with the options on it that you most frequently use.

1. Click the **Tools** menu, click **Customize**, and click the **Commands** tab.
2. Under Categories, click **New Menu**. Under Commands, drag **New Menu** to the menu bar at the location where you want it. 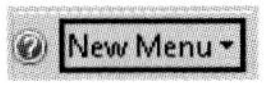

3. Right-click the new menu. Opposite Name, enter the name of the new menu, and press ENTER.
4. Use the steps in "Add Commands to a Menu" to build the menu with the commands you want.

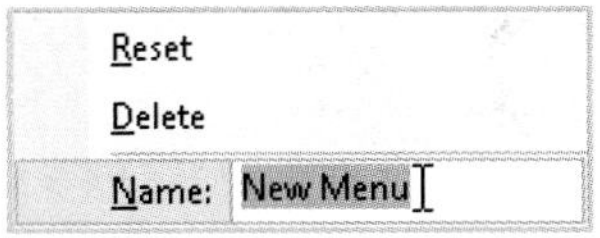

DELETE A MENU

You can delete only custom menus that you created.

1. Click the **Tools** menu, click **Customize**, and click the **Commands** tab.
2. Drag the menu off the menu bar and out of the window.
3. Click **Close**.

DISPLAY COMMON COMMANDS IN MENUS

You can cause the menus to display the most common commands you use first, and then expand to include all commands. This makes your most commonly used commands more accessible.

1. Click the **Tools** menu, click **Customize**, and click the **Options** tab.
2. Clear the **Always Show Full Menus** check box.
3. Click the **Show Full Menus After A Short Delay** check box.
4. Click **Close**.

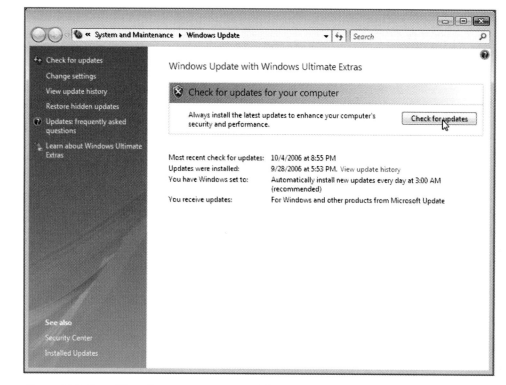

Figure 1-18: *One of the primary reasons to check for and download Office and Outlook updates is to get needed security patches.*

Update Outlook

Periodically, Microsoft comes out with updates for Office and Outlook. You can check for available updates and download and install them from the Microsoft Web site.

1. Click the **Help** menu, and click **Check For Updates**. Your Web browser will start, and the Windows Update window will open (see Figure 1-18).
2. Click the **Check For Updates** button.
3. Follow the instructions that you are given. Your system will be checked for any necessary updates, and you will be given the opportunity to download and install them.
4. When you have downloaded the updates you want, close your Web browser.

Chapter 2

Receiving and Handling E-mail

Most people get Outlook so that they can send and receive e-mail. For anyone who has Internet access, e-mail has essentially replaced letter writing. As great as e-mail is, however, it's possible to get overwhelmed by the amount of mail that arrives—much of it *spam*, or anonymously mass-mailed junk. In this chapter, you'll learn how to create e-mail accounts, receive e-mail, and deal with the messages that come in.

Set Up E-mail

The Internet provides a global pipeline through which e-mail flows; therefore, you need a connection that lets you tap into that pipeline. Both local and national Internet service providers (ISPs) offer e-mail with their Internet connections. At your work or business, you may have an e-mail account over a local area network (LAN) that also connects to the Internet. You can also obtain e-mail accounts on the Internet that are independent of the connection. You can access these Internet accounts (Hotmail, for example) from anywhere in the world. These three ways of accessing Internet e-mail—ISPs, corporate connections, and Internet e-mail—use different types of e-mail systems:

- **POP3** (Post Office Protocol 3), used by ISPs, retrieves e-mail from a dedicated mail server, and is usually combined with SMTP (Simple Mail Transfer Protocol) to send e-mail from a separate server.
- **MAPI** (Messaging Application Programming Interface) lets businesses handle e-mail on Microsoft Exchange Servers and LANs.
- **HTTP** (Hypertext Transfer Protocol) transfers information from servers on the World Wide Web to browsers (that's why your browser's address line starts with "http://") and is used with Hotmail and other Internet mail accounts.

Get Online

Whether you choose dial-up or a high-speed service like DSL (digital subscriber line) or cable Internet, getting online requires hardware, software, and some system configuration. It's possible that everything you need is already installed or that your computer came with extra disks for getting online. First, find an ISP:

- **Get a recommendation** from satisfied friends.
- **Look in the** yellow pages under "Internet Service Providers" or "Internet Access Providers."
- **Look on your computer**. Many computer manufacturers include software from nationwide Internet providers, such as AOL, EarthLink, and others.

If you find what you want in an Internet provider already on your computer, double-click the provider's icon, or click the link and follow the instructions. If you have a disk that came with your computer or from an ISP, pop it in and follow the instructions. If you use a local provider, their tech support people will usually walk you through the entire setup process on the phone.

Get a Hotmail Account

Hotmail, one of many Internet-based HTTP services, is free, and you can access it from any Internet connection in the world, so you don't even need to own a computer. The easiest way to set up Hotmail is to get a Microsoft Passport account just for Hotmail—even if you already have one using your ISP e-mail address (see Figure 2-1).

TIP

To find out where your e-mail data files are named and located, click **Tools** in the initial Outlook window, click **Options**, and on the Options dialog box, click **Data Files**. On the Data Files tab, you will see the name and location of the Personal Folders.

| E-mail | Data Files | RSS Feeds | SharePoint Lists | Internet Calendars | Published Calendars | Address Books |

🔩 Add... | 📝 Settings... | ✓ Set as Default | ✗ Remove | 📁 Open Folder...

Name	Filename		Comment
Personal Folders	Outlook.pst in C:\Users\Owner\AppData\Local\Microsoft\Outlook		Default

2

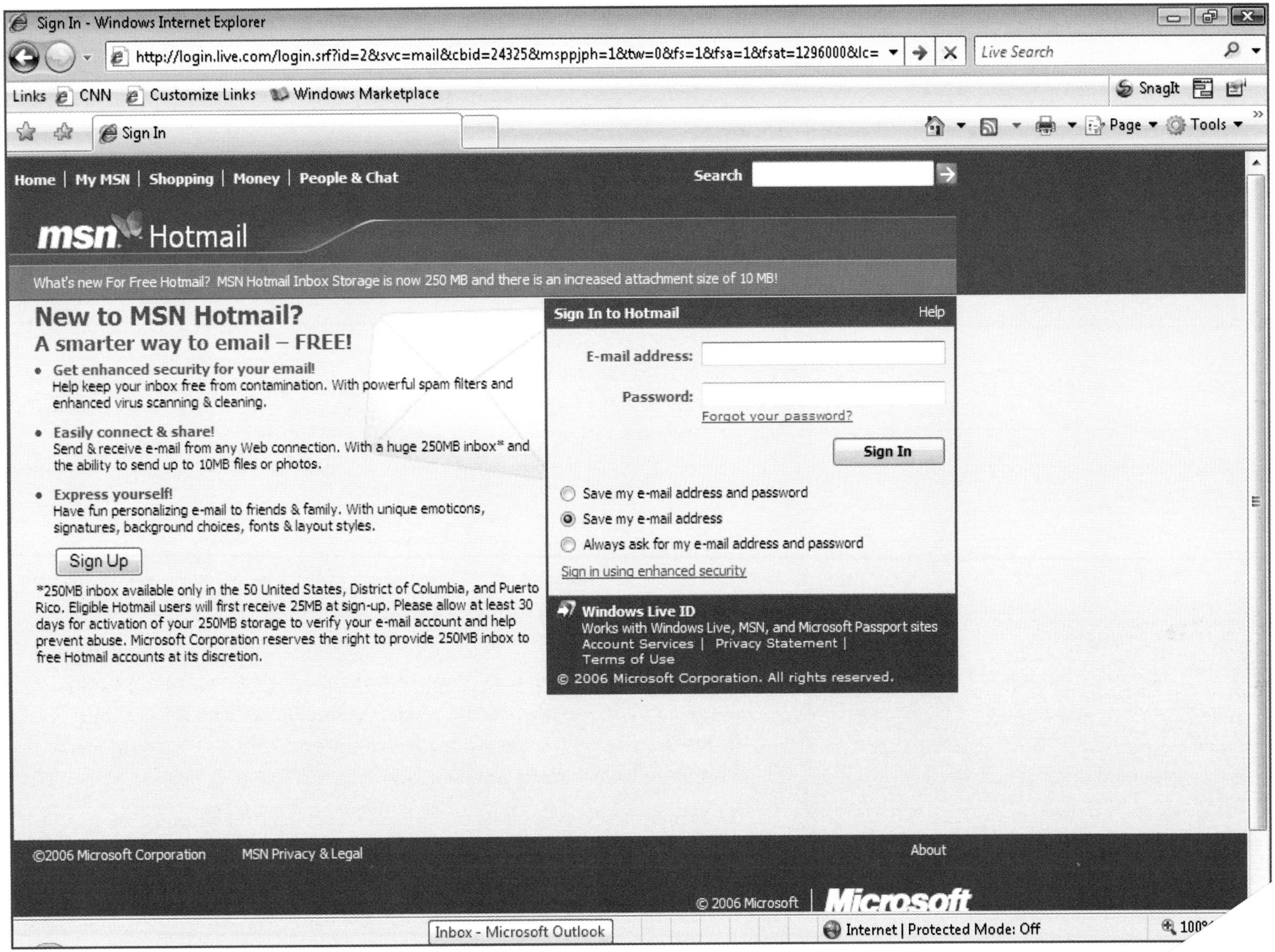

Figure 2-1: The Microsoft Passport account lets you remember a single user name and password to log on to many secure Web sites.

To get a Hotmail account, you must already have a way to get on the Internet, and the instructions here assume you can do that.

QUICKFACTS

COLLECTING ACCOUNT INFORMATION

The information needed to install an e-mail account in Outlook depends on the type of e-mail you choose.

ISP ACCOUNTS

- **Type of server:** POP3 or IMAP
- **E-mail address**
- **User name**
- **Password**
- **Incoming mail server name**
- **Outgoing mail server name**

HTTP ACCOUNTS (LIKE HOTMAIL)

Type of server: HTTP

E-mail address: Microsoft Live ID or other user ID

User name

Password

Your mail service Internet address, if not Hotmail or MSN, which are provided

TIP

To remove an e-mail account, click **Tools** and click **Account Settings** to open the Account Settings dialog box. Click the account to select it, and then click **Remove**. Click **Yes** to confirm the removal of the account, and click **Close**.

SET UP HOTMAIL

1. Click **Start**, click **Internet**, and/or follow any steps needed for you to open your Internet browser and get on the Internet. In your browser's address bar, type www.hotmail.com, and press **ENTER**.

2. Ignore the Microsoft Passport Sign-In box, and click the Sign Up button. Click the e-mail solution that is right for you. You may select a free service or one for an annual or monthly price.

3. Fill in every field on the registration form. For the Windows Live ID, enter the name you want for the account, leaving out the "@hotmail.com" part. You can click Check Availability to check whether the ID you want is available. You'll have to read and accept the Windows Live Service Agreement and the Privacy Statement. Click I **Accept**.

4. Scroll your way through a few pages of pitches, selecting any items you want delivered to your Inbox, until you can click **Continue**. You will see information about the mailbox usage and your current messages. At this point, your Hotmail account has been created.

Install Accounts in Outlook

Once you have an e-mail account, you need to tell Outlook where to find the server that stores your mail. As you proceed through the E-mail Accounts Wizard, you will need some information about the account. See the QuickFacts "Collecting Account Information" for the information you'll need to enter. When you have the information handy:

1. Open Outlook, click **Tools**, and click **Account Settings**. The Account Settings dialog box appears.

2. Click **New**, and The Add New E-Mail Account wizard starts. This short wizard will lead you through the process of configuring an account in Outlook. Continue as detailed in Chapter 1 on how to work through the steps.

If you like where the old Preview pane was located in earlier versions of Outlook, you can place the Reading pane beneath the Folder pane: Click the **View** menu, point at **Reading Pane**, and click **Bottom**. (You can also turn it off.)

Receive E-mail

With at least one e-mail account installed in Outlook, you're ready to receive mail. Everything is done from the Outlook Mail folder, shown in Figure 2-2. Be sure to share your e-mail address with the friends you'd like to hear from.

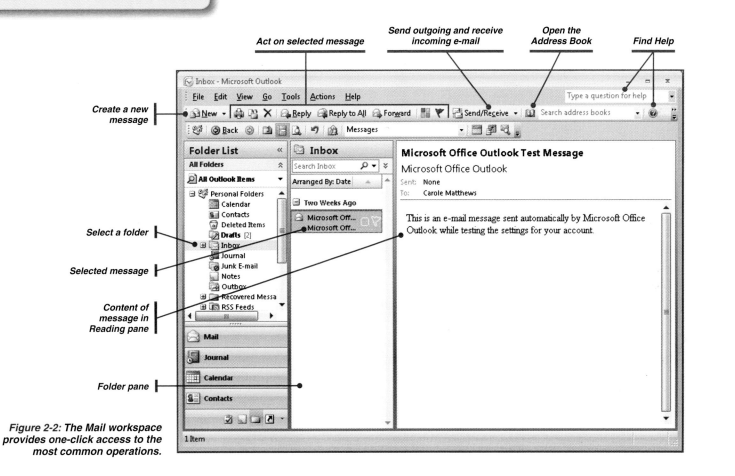

Act on selected message

Send outgoing and receive incoming e-mail

Open the Address Book

Find Help

Create a new message

Select a folder

Selected message

Content of message in Reading pane

Folder pane

Figure 2-2: The Mail workspace provides one-click access to the most common operations.

NOTE

If you don't see the Send/Receive button on your toolbar, click **Toolbar Options** at the right end of the toolbar, and click the **Send/Receive** button you see there. After you do that once, it will appear in its normal place.

TIP

You can download messages from a particular e-mail provider, if you prefer. Click **Tools**, point to **Send/Receive**, click the desired account, and click **Inbox**.

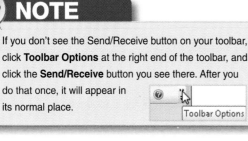

Figure 2-3: The Options dialog box is where you can customize many Outlook processes.

Check for E-mail

Once you are set up, it's easy to download mail.

1. Make sure you're connected to the Internet or can be automatically connected, and that **Mail** is selected in the Outlook Navigation pane.

2. Click **Send/Receive** on the toolbar. `Send/Receive ▾`

3. If it is not already open, click the **Inbox** icon in the Navigation pane, and watch the mail come in. `Inbox`

RECEIVE E-MAIL AUTOMATICALLY

Not only can Outlook periodically check your e-mail provider for you, but it can also do it automatically. Desktop alerts are subtle, given the way they quietly fade in and out.

1. Click **Tools** and click **Options**.

2. Click the **Mail Setup** tab, shown in Figure 2-3, and click **Send/Receive**.

3. Under the section Setting For Group, check **Schedule An Automatic Send/Receive Every**, type or click the spinner to enter the number of minutes to elapse between checking, and click **Close**.

> Setting for group "All Accounts"
> ☑ Include this group in send/receive (F9).
> ☑ Schedule an automatic send/receive every 30 ⇅ minutes.
> ☐ Perform an automatic send/receive when exiting.

4. If you also want to create a desktop alert telling you when mail arrives, click the **Preferences** tab, click **E-mail Options**, and click **Advanced E-mail Options**. Check **Display A New Mail Desktop Alert**, and click **OK** twice.

> ☑ Display a New Mail Desktop Alert (default Inbox only)

5. Click **OK** to close the Options dialog box.

Read E-mail

Besides being easy to obtain, e-mail messages are effortless to open and read. There are two ways to view the body of the message:

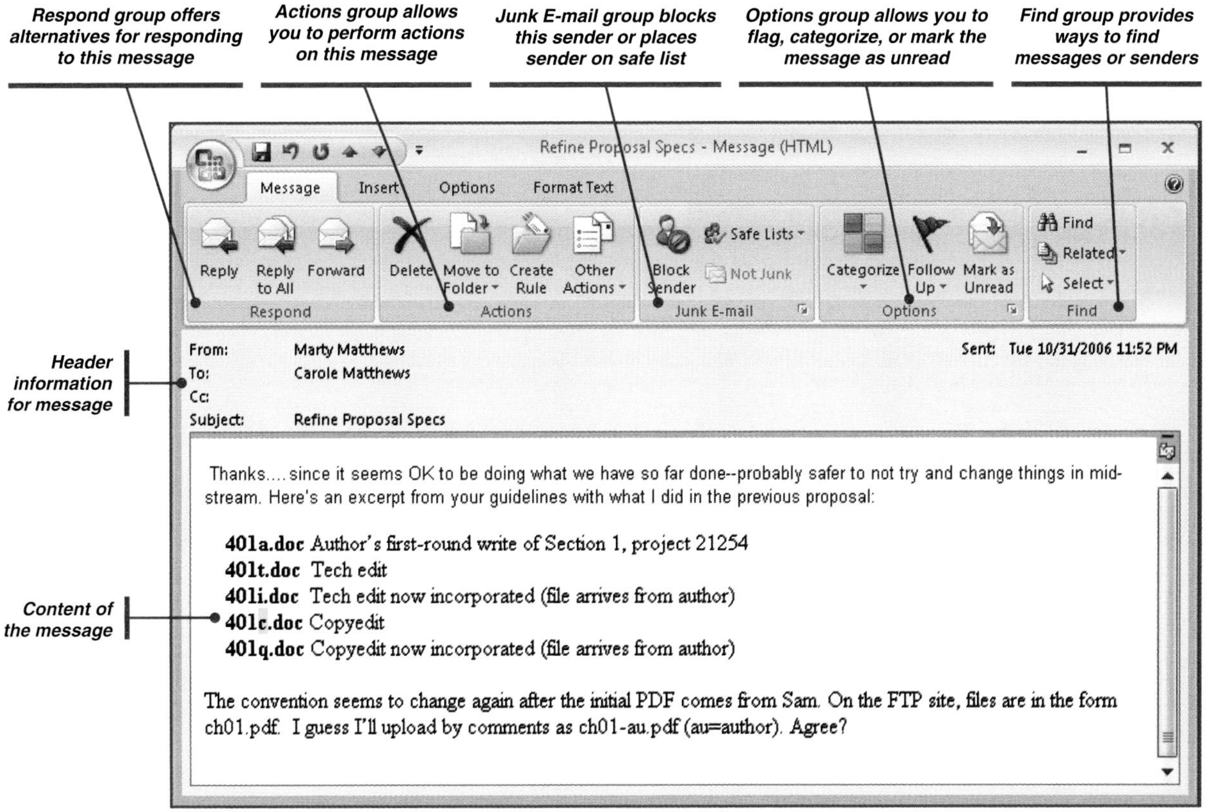

Respond group offers alternatives for responding to this message

Actions group allows you to perform actions on this message

Junk E-mail group blocks this sender or places sender on safe list

Options group allows you to flag, categorize, or mark the message as unread

Find group provides ways to find messages or senders

Refine Proposal Specs - Message (HTML)

Message   Insert   Options   Format Text

Reply   Reply to All   Forward   Delete   Move to Folder ▾   Create Rule   Other Actions ▾   Block Sender   Safe Lists ▾   Not Junk   Categorize ▾   Follow Up ▾   Mark as Unread   Find   Related ▾   Select ▾

Respond   Actions   Junk E-mail   Options   Find

Header information for message

From: Marty Matthews   Sent: Tue 10/31/2006 11:52 PM
To: Carole Matthews
Cc:
Subject: Refine Proposal Specs

Content of the message

Thanks…. since it seems OK to be doing what we have so far done--probably safer to not try and change things in mid-stream. Here's an excerpt from your guidelines with what I did in the previous proposal:

401a.doc Author's first-round write of Section 1, project 21254
401t.doc Tech edit
401i.doc Tech edit now incorporated (file arrives from author)
401c.doc Copyedit
401q.doc Copyedit now incorporated (file arrives from author)

The convention seems to change again after the initial PDF comes from Sam. On the FTP site, files are in the form ch01.pdf. I guess I'll upload by comments as ch01-au.pdf (au=author). Agree?

Figure 2-4: An e-mail message window contains all the information and tools you need to respond.

- Double-click the message and read it in the window that opens, as shown in Figure 2-4.

  –Or–

- Click the message and read it in the Reading pane, scrolling as needed.

Of course, you can also control which accounts you check, what kinds of e-mail you let in, and how it is presented to you.

Download Sender and Subject Information Only

If you are inundated with e-mail, or if messages contain really large files (like lots of photos), you might want to choose among your messages for specific ones to download to Outlook. You can save time downloading e-mail, especially with large files—which you may want to download at a later time. This only works on your POP server e-mail (not on HTTP server e-mail, such as Hotmail). First, you instruct Outlook to download only the headers, and then you mark the headers for which you want to download the messages.

RECEIVE HEADERS MANUALLY

1. Click **Inbox** (or whatever folder you prefer).

2. Click the **Send/Receive** down arrow on the toolbar, click the account for which you want to download the headers, and click **Download** *foldername* **Headers**.

   –Or–

   Click the **Tools** menu, point at **Send/Receive**, click the account for which you want to download headers, and click **Download** *foldername* **Headers**.

The headers, assuming you have e-mail waiting to be downloaded, will be downloaded to your selected folder. It will have an identifying icon:

MARK HEADERS TO DOWNLOAD, COPY, OR DELETE

1. Right-click a header-only message in the folder to open the context menu.

   –Or–

   Double-click a header-only message in the Inbox folder to open the Remote Item Header dialog box.

2. In either case, click one of these options:

   ● **Open** displays the Remote Item Header dialog box, which allows you to unmark the header, mark it to be downloaded and/or copied on the server, or deleted.

   ● **Mark To Download Message(s)** downloads the whole message the next time you click Send/Receive.

   ● **Mark To Download Message Copy** downloads the whole message the next time and leaves the original on the server (this is handy when checking e-mail on the road).

   ● **Delete** removes the message from the server and from Outlook the next time you click Send/Receive.

3. Repeat the process for all headers, and click **Send/Receive** to perform the actions selected.

Inbox
Download Inbox Headers
Process Marked Headers

Remote Item Header

⚠ This item has not been retrieved from the server.
Do you want to:

● Unmark this header item
○ Mark to download this message
○ Mark to download this message and leave a copy on the server
○ Mark to delete this message from the server

OK   Cancel

Carole McIlhenny...
Fv

Open
Mark to Download Message(s)
Mark to Download Message Copy
× Delete

RECEIVE HEADERS AUTOMATICALLY

If you want to download only headers from your POP server accounts every time, you can set up Outlook to do so.

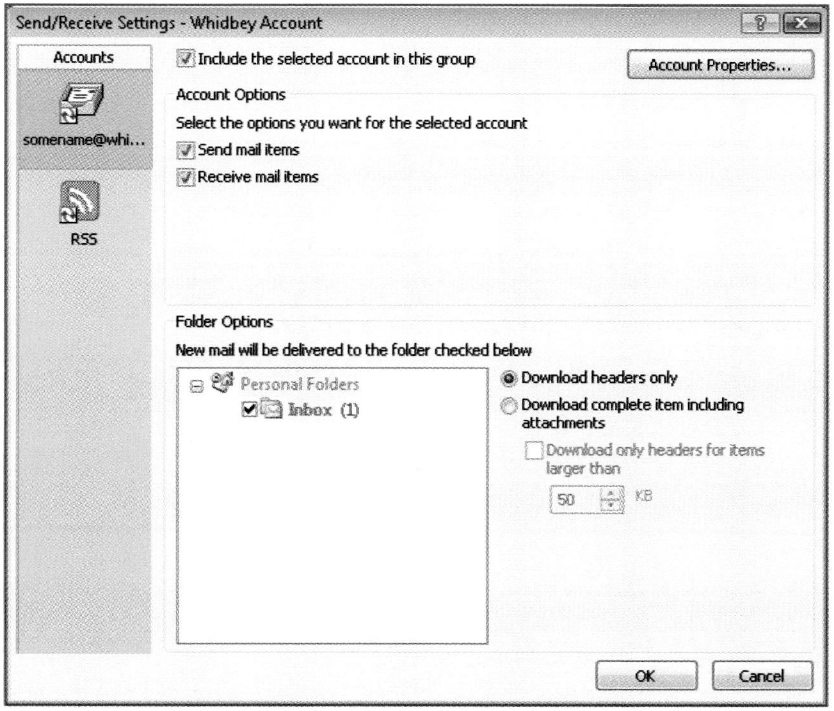

Send/Receive Settings - Whidbey Account

Accounts

somename@whi...

RSS

☑ Include the selected account in this group   Account Properties...

Account Options

Select the options you want for the selected account
☑ Send mail items
☑ Receive mail items

Folder Options

New mail will be delivered to the folder checked below

⊟ 📁 Personal Folders
  ☑ 📁 Inbox (1)

◉ Download headers only
○ Download complete item including attachments
  □ Download only headers for items larger than
  [50] KB

OK   Cancel

Figure 2-5: Outlook can be set up to download only headers for all messages.

1. Click the **Send/Receive** down arrow on the toolbar, point at **Send/Receive Settings**, and click **Define Send/Receive Groups**.

   –Or–

   Click the **Tools** menu, point at **Send/Receive**, point at **Send/Receive Settings**, and click **Define Send/Receive Groups**.

2. Make sure **All Accounts** is selected, and click **Edit**. All your e-mail accounts are listed on the left.

3. Click the desired POP account.

4. Under Folder Options, click **Download Headers Only**, as shown in Figure 2-5, click **OK**, and click **Close**.

PROCESS HEADERS

When your headers have been marked, you can download them.

1. Click the **Send/Receive** down arrow.

2. Click **Process All Marked Headers** or **Process Marked Headers In This Folder**.

Process All Marked Headers
Process Marked Headers in This Folder

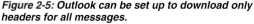

NOTE

The *domain* in a person's e-mail address is the part of the address after "@." In an Internet address (URL, or uniform resource locator) the domain is the part after the "http://www"—for example, "whidbey.net" (a local ISP) or "loc.gov" (the Library of Congress Web site).

Filter Junk Mail

Outlook can automatically filter out a lot of annoying spam before you ever see it, and it can set aside suspicious-looking messages in a Junk E-mail folder. It does this in two ways: by analyzing message content based on a protection level you choose, and by having you identify good and bad senders.

Outlook also prevents pictures and sounds from being downloaded into messages that contain HTML formatting. Up to now, savvy spammers have

FILTERING OUT SPAM

Begin by setting the options for the Junk E-mail folder.

1. Click the **Tools** menu, and click **Options**.

2. Click the **Preferences** tab, and click the **Junk E-mail** button.

SELECT A LEVEL OF PROTECTION

Click the **Options** tab, and click the desired level of protection.

BUILD ADDRESS LISTS

The Safe Senders, Blocked Senders, and Safe Recipients tabs let you manually create lists of e-mail addresses and domain names.

For each entry, click **Add**, type the information, and click **OK** twice.

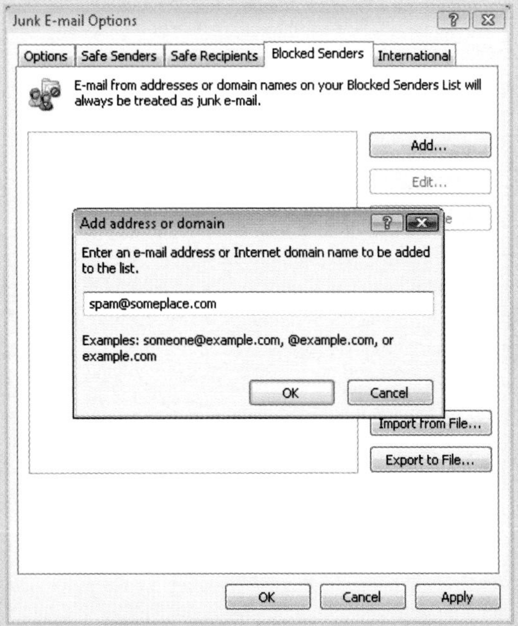

Junk E-mail Options

Options | Safe Senders | Safe Recipients | Blocked Senders | International

E-mail from addresses or domain names on your Blocked Senders List will always be treated as junk e-mail.

Add...

Edit...

Add address or domain

Enter an e-mail address or Internet domain name to be added to the list.

spam@someplace.com

Examples: someone@example.com, @example.com, or example.com

OK   Cancel

Import from File...

Export to File...

OK   Cancel   Apply

Continued . . .

been able to design messages that only download images when you open or preview the message. They plant *Web beacons* in the messages, which tell their server that they have reached a valid address so that they can send you even more junk. Outlook blocks both the external content, as shown in Figure 2-6, and the beacon, unless you tell it to unblock it.

CHOOSE A PROTECTION LEVEL

The amount of junk e-mail you receive suggests the level of protection you need. By default, Outlook sets the level at Low, but you might decide that

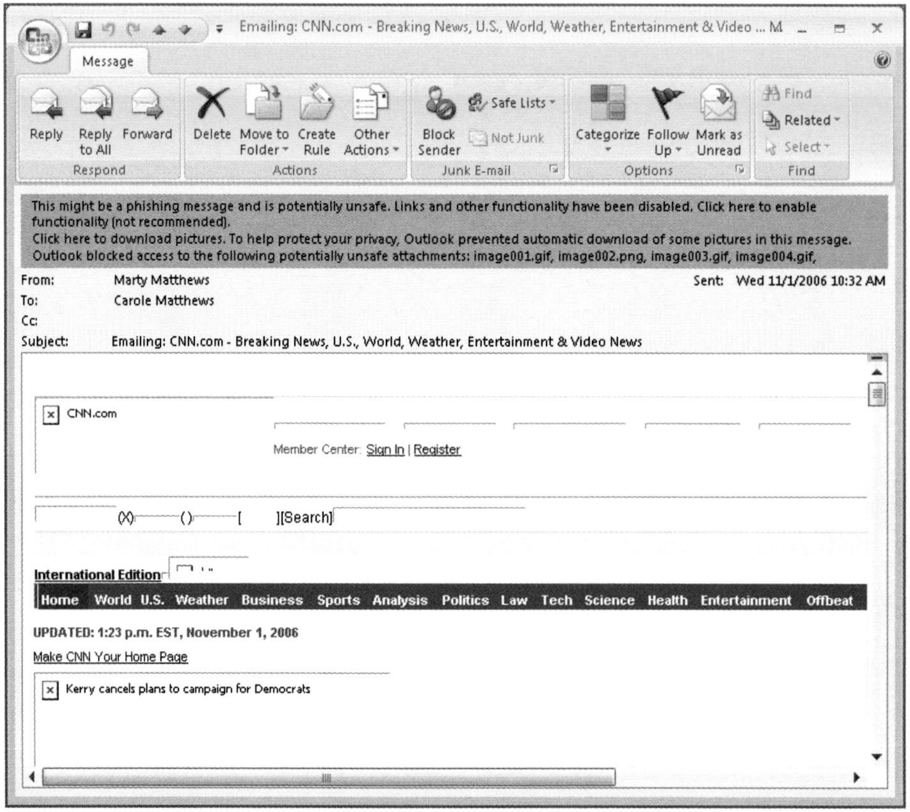

Message

Reply | Reply to All | Forward | Delete | Move to Folder | Create Rule | Other Actions | Block Sender | Safe Lists | Not Junk | Categorize | Follow Up | Mark as Unread | Find | Related | Select

Respond | Actions | Junk E-mail | Options | Find

This might be a phishing message and is potentially unsafe. Links and other functionality have been disabled. Click here to enable functionality (not recommended).
Click here to download pictures. To help protect your privacy, Outlook prevented automatic download of some pictures in this message.
Outlook blocked access to the following potentially unsafe attachments: image001.gif, image002.png, image003.gif, image004.gif,

From: Marty Matthews   Sent: Wed 11/1/2006 10:32 AM
To: Carole Matthews
Cc:
Subject: Emailing: CNN.com - Breaking News, U.S., World, Weather, Entertainment & Video News

CNN.com

Member Center: Sign In | Register

(XX)———()———[   ][Search]

International Edition
Home   World   U.S.   Weather   Business   Sports   Analysis   Politics   Law   Tech   Science   Health   Entertainment   Offbeat

UPDATED: 1:23 p.m. EST, November 1, 2006
Make CNN Your Home Page

Kerry cancels plans to campaign for Democrats

Figure 2-6: Blocking image and sound files protects your computer, but you can easily unblock a message by clicking in its top banner.

QUICKSTEPS

FILTERING OUT SPAM (Continued)

UPDATE LISTS QUICKLY

Sender and recipient addresses can be added quickly to the Safe Senders, Blocked Senders, and Safe Recipients lists from an Outlook folder.

1. Right-click a message whose sender you want to put on a list.

2. Point at Junk E-mail, and click the appropriate option.

UNBLOCK PICTURE DOWNLOADS

By default, picture downloads are blocked to speed up the downloading of e-mail. To change that for specific items:

- For a **single opened message**, click **Click Here To Download Pictures** in the information bar at the top of the message.

- For **all mail from the source of the open message**, right-click a blocked item, point at **Junk E-mail**, and click **Add Sender's Domain To Safe Senders List**.

- For **all HTML mail** (not recommended), click the **Tools** menu, click **Trust Center**, click the **Automatic Download** option on the left, and clear the **Don't Download Pictures Automatically In HTML E-Mail Messages Or RSS Items** check box. Click **OK**.

NOTE

One easy way to reduce the junk e-mail you get is to *avoid* replying to any suspicious message. If you reply and tell them to go away, they learn that they reached a valid address, which they will hit again and again.

another option would work better for you. Table 2-1 shows some considerations in choosing a level.

To set the protection level:

1. Click **Tools**, click **Options**, and click the **Junk E-mail** button.

2. Beneath Choose The Level Of Junk E-mail Protection You Want, click the desired protection level. See Table 2-1 for explanations.

OPTION	RESULT	PROS	CONS
No Automatic Filtering	Only mail from blocked senders goes to the Junk E-mail folder.	You have total control.	Your Inbox could be stuffed; you or others might see unsolicited pornography.
Low (default)	Outlook scans messages for offensive language and indications of unsolicited commercial mailings.	The worst of the junk gets caught.	Some canny spammers will still find ways around the protections.
High	Pretty much all the junk e-mail gets caught.	Considerably fewer rude shocks in the Inbox.	Some regular mail will inadvertently get sent to the junk folder.
Safe Lists Only	Only mail from Safe Senders and Safe Recipients lists goes to the Inbox.	Complete protection.	Lots of friendly mail will be junked.
Permanently Delete Suspected Junk E-Mail Instead Of Moving It To The Junk E-Mail Folder	Filtered junk mail never gets onto your computer.	You never have to inspect the Junk E-Mail folder.	Unless you chose the No Automatic Filtering option, you are sure to lose some friendly mail.

Table 2-1: Junk E-mail Protection Levels

ADD ADDRESSES TO FILTER LISTS

The four other tabs in the Junk E-mail Options window provide a means for you to specifically identify good and bad e-mailers:

- **Safe Senders** specifies e-mail senders from whom you always want to receive messages. This list automatically contains your contacts, so Outlook never identifies their messages as junk, no matter how silly their jokes are. If you subscribe to a newsgroup or some other mass mailing, you might need to specifically add it to the list.

- **Safe Recipients** ensures that mailing lists you subscribe to treat you as a safe sender when you contribute messages to the list.

- **Blocked Senders** sends messages from specified senders straight to the Junk E-mail folder. It's especially useful to add obnoxious domains to this list so that no address from that source makes it to your Inbox.

- **International** allows you to block international e-mails by foreign domain codes or by language.

Handle E-mail Messages

E-mail has a way of building up fast. Outlook lets you sort your messages just about any way you want. You will learn all about managing folders in Chapter 8. For now, we'll consider ways to sort and mark messages so that they don't get lost in the crowd.

Mark Messages as Read or Unread

A message is marked as "read" after you have selected it so that its contents display in the Reading pane for a designated time (see "Change the Time for Being Read"). The header in the Folder list changes from boldface to plain type. A message can get lost in the pile if it's accidentally selected and you don't notice or forget about it. You can easily mark it as unread again by right-clicking the message and clicking **Mark As Unread**.

Change the Time for Being Read

To change the time that a message must be selected before it is marked as read:

Reading Pane

Reading Pane options

☐ Mark items as read when viewed in the Reading Pane

Wait [5] seconds before marking item as read

☑ Mark item as read when selection changes

☑ Single key reading using space bar

[OK] [Cancel]

1. Click **Tools**, click **Options**, and click the **Other** tab.

2. In the Outlook Panes area, click the **Reading Pane** button. The Reading Pane dialog box will appear.

3. Click one of these options:

   ● **Mark Items As Read When Viewed In The Reading Pane** allows you to set the number of seconds that a message must be selected before being marked as read.

   ● **Mark Item As Read When Selection Changes** marks the message as read as soon as the pointer selects another message in the Folder pane. This is the default setting.

4. Click **OK** to close the dialog box.

Flag Your Messages for Follow-up

You can place colored flags beside messages you want to do something with later. The flag will appear in the flag column of the Folder pane.

Select the message you want to flag, click the **Flag** button ▼ in the standard toolbar, and click the type of flag you want to insert.

–Or–

Right-click the flag column of the selected message, and on the context menu, click the type of flag you want to insert.

FINE-TUNE YOUR FLAGS

You can fine-tune the follow-up actions of the flags and specify that a reminder be made so that an e-mail message can be responded to in a timely manner.

1. In the Folder pane, right-click the flag column, and click **Add Reminder** or **Custom**.

   –Or–

You can scroll through a selected message by pressing **SPACEBAR**. To disable this feature, click **Tools**, click **Options**, click the **Other** tab, click the **Reading Pane** button, and clear the **Single Key Reading Using Space Bar** check box.

NOTE

If you want to insert a Today red flag beside a message, just click in the flag column. A red flag displays. Or you can press **INSERT** on the keyboard. (Press again to toggle between the Follow-Up red flag and a Complete check mark.)

To group all of your flagged messages, click **View**, click **Arrange By**, and click **Flag: Start Date** or **Flag: Due Date**.

Flag: Start Date
Flag: Due Date

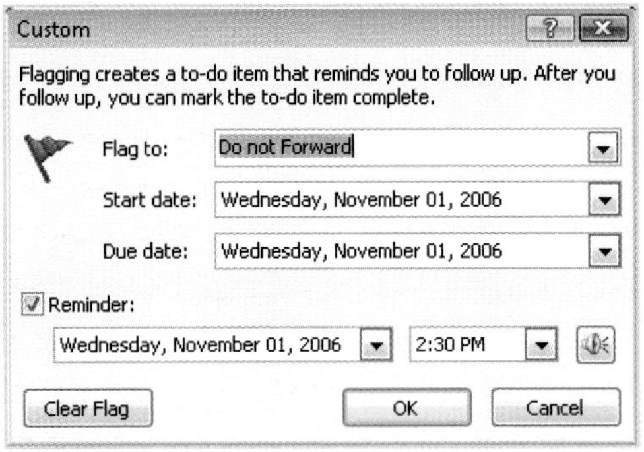

In the open message window, click the **Follow Up** button in the Options group on the toolbar, and click **Add Reminder** or **Custom**.

2. In the Custom dialog box, click the **Flag To** down arrow, and click an action.

3. Click the **Start Date** down arrow, and click a date to indicate when the message is to be flagged.

4. Click the **Due Date** down arrow, and click a date that indicates when the response to the e-mail is to be completed.

5. Click **Reminder** to place a check mark in the check box and to display the date when the reminder is to begin. Click the date down arrow, and click a date. Click the time down arrow, and click a time for the reminders to begin.

6. Click the **Sound** icon 🔊 to remove the default setting in which a sound file is played when the reminder displays on the screen.

7. Click **OK**.

8. At the designated time, a reminder will be displayed, as shown in Figure 2-7. To repeat the reminder, click the snooze down arrow, click an interval until the next sound, and then click **Snooze**.

NOTE

To remove a flag, or to indicate that the e-mail no longer needs to be handled, right-click the flag and click either **Clear Flag** or **Mark Complete**.

TIP

At times, you will receive e-mail tagged with an exclamation point to get your attention. If you disagree with the priority the sender gave it, right-click the message, click **Options**, and pick another level of importance. Click **Close**.

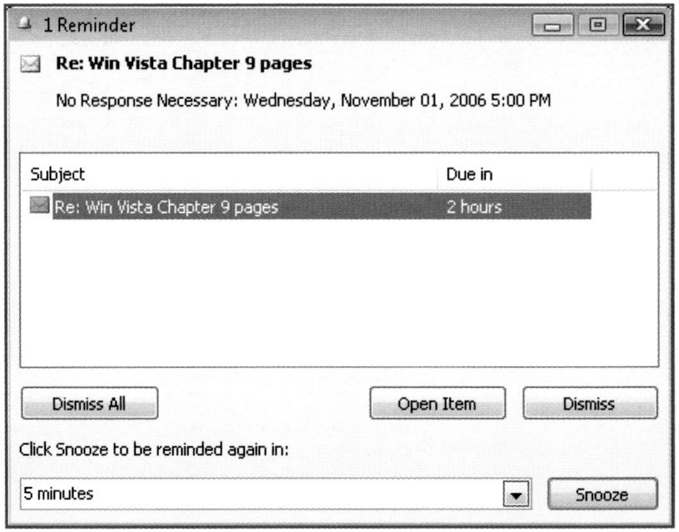

Figure 2-7: You can set a flag to display a reminder with a sound that alerts you that an important e-mail has not been handled.

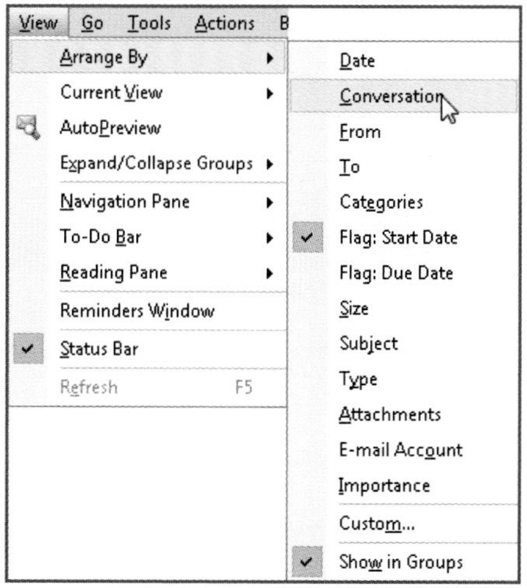

Arrange Messages in a Folder

Outlook contains 13 types of Inbox arrangements, as seen in Figure 2-8. You can have Outlook organize messages by the date they were sent, which Outlook uses by default; alphabetically by who sent them or by first word in the subject line; or by clustering those with attachments, colored flags you give them, or categories you created for your own use. Outlook can even group *conversations*, e-mail exchanges in which senders clicked Reply, thus preserving the subject line. To arrange messages:

1. Click **Inbox** or another specific mail folder in the navigation bar on the left side.

2. Click the **View** menu, point to **Arrange By**, and click one of the arrangements listed.

Figure 2-8: You can arrange the messages in a folder in many different ways to more easily find one message or to group messages in a meaningful way.

ADD COLORED CATEGORIES

Assigning categories to mail is one way of separating your messages by a colored code that you determine. You might categorize by project, priority, sender, etc. You determine what a color will mean when it is assigned to a message. Once your e-mail contains categories, it can be sorted and arranged so that you can find or track it more efficiently. The colors make the categories highly visible in lists. Mail is only one kind of item that you can categorize. You can assign categories to whatever you create in Outlook—tasks, appointments, contacts, notes, journal entries, and documents. You can also create new categories in the list.

1. Right-click a message (or other item), and click **Categorize**. The categories context menu opens, shown in Figure 2-9. (You can also click the **Categorize** button in the standard toolbar.)

2. Do one of the following:

   - Click **Create Category Search Folder** to create a folder that tracks all categorized e-mails. You can create a folder for all categories or for specific ones. When created, you can find this folder under Search Folders in the navigation pane's Folder list, and quickly scan your categorized and sorted e-mail.

NOTE

Whenever a menu displays the expansion arrow at the bottom of the list, pointing at it will expand the list.

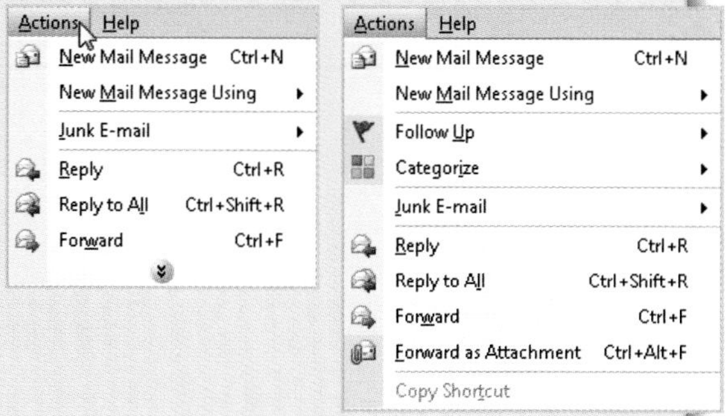

NOTE

A plus (+) or minus (–) sign to the left of an item indicates that you can expand or contract a list by clicking the sign.

Marty Matthews Wed 1...
Re: Win Vista Chapter ...

| Open |
| Print |
| Reply |
| Reply to All |
| Forward |
| Follow Up ▶ |
Categorize ▶	Clear All Categories
Mark as Unread	Create Category Search Folder...
Find All ▶	Blue Category
Create Rule...	Green Category
Junk E-mail ▶	Orange Category
✕ Delete	Red Category
Move to Folder...	Purple Category
Message Options...	Yellow Category
	All Categories...
	Set Quick Click...

Figure 2-9: The Categorize menu shows colors, which you can define as categories according to your needs.

TIP

You can reverse the sort of categories by clicking the sort bar at the top of the sorted item in the Folder pane. For example, if at first your sorted categories are at the bottom of the list, click the sort bar to place sorted categories at the top.

Arranged By: Categories Z on top

□ Red Category

Marty Matthews Wed 1...
Re: Win Vista Chapter ...

- Click a color category for the item.
- Click **All Categories** to assign more than one category to a name (or to edit a category—see "Edit a Category"). Click a color to select it (place a check mark in the check box), and then click **OK**.

Name
- ☑ Blue Category
- ☑ Green Category
- ☐ Orange Category
- ☑ Purple Category
- ☐ Red Category
- ☐ Yellow Category

3. View items sorted into categories by clicking the **View** menu, selecting **Arrange By**, and clicking **Categories**.

EDIT A CATEGORY

You can edit a category to change its name, its color, or assigned shortcut.

1. Right-click a message to be categorized, click **Categorize** from the context menu, and click **All Categories**.

2. Select from among these options:
   - To create a new category, click **New**. In the Add New Category dialog box, type a name; click the **Color** down arrow, and click a color; click the **Shortcut** key down arrow, and click a shortcut key if you want one. Click **OK**.
   - To rename a category, click a category, click **Rename**, and type the new name in the category name text box. ☑ Blue Category
   - To delete a category, click the category and click **Delete**.
   - To change the color, click the **Color** down arrow, and click a replacement color.
   - To assign a shortcut key, click the **Shortcut Key** down arrow, and click a shortcut key combination.

3. Click **OK** to close the Color Categories dialog box.

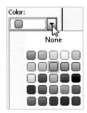

Make Up Your Own Rules

When it comes to sorting e-mail, you can make up the rules as you go along, and Outlook will follow them. Or you can pick from a list of predefined rules for common situations, like having Outlook send a message to your cell phone if you win an eBay auction or flagging all messages from your son at college for follow-up. (This only works for POP3 server accounts.)

1. With Mail selected, click the **Tools** menu, and click **Rules And Alerts**. The Rules And Alerts Wizard is displayed, as shown in Figure 2-10.

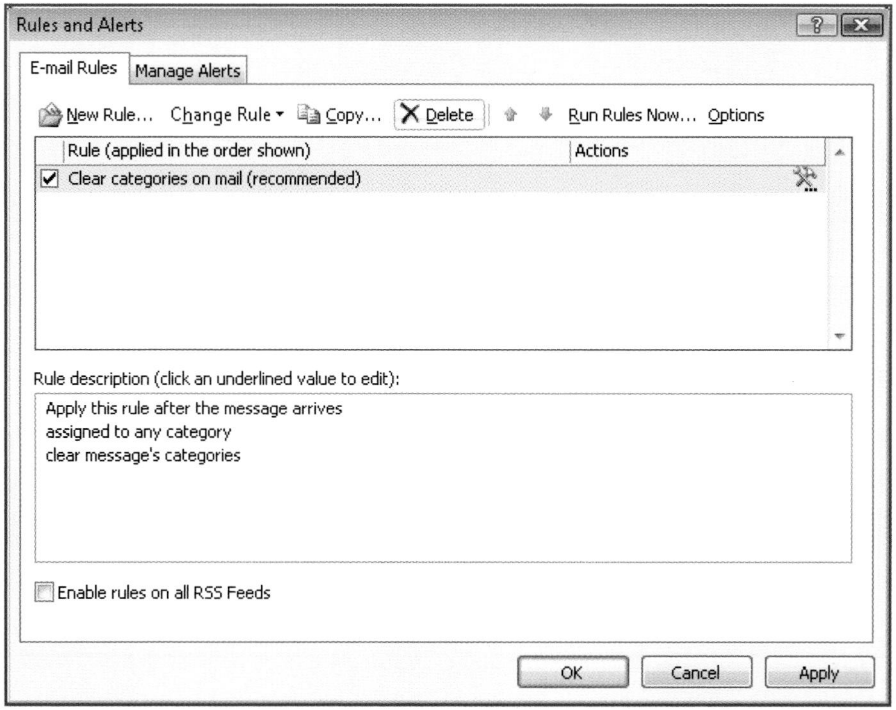

Rules and Alerts

E-mail Rules | Manage Alerts

New Rule... Change Rule ▾ Copy... ✕ Delete ⬆ ⬇ Run Rules Now... Options

Rule (applied in the order shown)	Actions
☑ Clear categories on mail (recommended)	🛠

Rule description (click an underlined value to edit):

Apply this rule after the message arrives
assigned to any category
clear message's categories

☐ Enable rules on all RSS Feeds

OK   Cancel   Apply

Figure 2-10: The Rules And Alerts Wizard is where you establish rules for handling e-mail, including being alerted to the arrival of e-mail.

2. Click **New Rule** and click one of the options in the list under Step 1 (it displays in the description box below Step 2) in one these categories:

- **Stay Organized** lets you manipulate e-mail in a variety of ways.
- **Stay Up To Date** alerts you when new mail arrives by displaying it in a special window, playing a sound, or alerting your mobile device.
- **Start From A Blank Rule** lets you build a completely custom rule for receiving or sending messages.

3. Click **Next**. Click all conditions under which you want the rule applied, clicking any underlined value and changing it as needed. The information is added to the scenario. Click **Next**.

4. Step through the wizard, selecting circumstances and actions, changing values as needed, and clicking **Next**.

5. Type a name for the rule where requested, click an option specifying when the rule goes into effect, click **Finish**, and click **OK**.

Delete Messages

Outlook creates two stages for deleting messages by providing a Delete folder, which holds all the things you deleted from other folders.

DELETE MESSAGES FROM THE INBOX

Start by clicking a message in the Inbox. Then perform one of the following actions:

- **Delete one message** by selecting a message and clicking **Delete** on the toolbar. ✕
- **Delete a block of messages** by clicking the first message, holding down SHIFT, clicking the last message (all the messages in between are selected as well), and clicking **Delete** on the toolbar.
- **Delete multiple noncontiguous messages** by pressing CTRL while clicking the messages you want to remove and then clicking **Delete** on the toolbar.

NOTE

Remember to delete the contents of the Sent folder on a regular basis. It can get huge.

QUICKSTEPS

MANIPULATING THE RULES

To get to the Rules And Alerts Wizard, click the **Rules And Alerts** button in the Advanced toolbar (or click **Tools** and click **Rules And Alerts**). The first page of the Rules And Alerts Wizard lists current rules under the names you gave them.

LEARN THE RULES

Select a rule in the list, and review it in the description pane below it.

CHANGE THE RULES

1. Click a rule in the list, click **Change Rule**, and click an action from the drop-down list.

   –Or–

   Double-click the rule to open the Rules And Alerts Wizard.

2. If you opened the wizard, change the contents as needed, click **Next**, click **Finish**, and click **OK**.

3. If you selected an option under Change Rules with an icon beside it, add any requested information or fill in any new underlined variable in the description, and click **OK** until the window is closed.

Continued . . .

Change Rule | Copy... | X Delete | ↑ ↓ |
- Edit Rule Settings...
- Rename Rule
- Display in the New Item Alert window
- Play a Sound...
- Move to Folder...
- Copy to Folder...
- Mark as High Priority
- Mark as Low Priority
- X Delete Message

EMPTY THE DELETED ITEMS FOLDER

1. Click the **Deleted Items** folder.

2. Choose one:

   ● Select files to be permanently deleted as you did earlier, click **Delete**, and click **Yes**.

   –Or–

   ● Press **CTRL+A** to select all items in the folder, click **Delete**, and click **Yes**.

   –Or–

   ● Right-click the **Deleted Items** folder, and click **Empty "Deleted Items" Folder**.

Manage Attachments

Messages that contain files, such as pictures and documents, display a paper clip icon in the second message line within the Folder pane to show that there's more to see. Attachments are listed in the message itself in the Reading pane, as shown in Figure 2-11. Since computer vandals like to broadcast debilitating viruses by way of attachments, you should be sure that you are dealing with a trusted source before you open any attachments. Also, it's important to have an up-to-date antivirus program running on your system, as well as any protection provided by your ISP. Make sure you have it, and keep your virus definitions up-to-date. If you are running Windows Vista, there are several Internet and e-mail protections built into it.

When a message comes in with an attachment, you can preview the attachment, open it, or save it first.

Marty Matthews 1:07 AM
Illustration

OPEN ATTACHMENTS

In the Reading pane:

● Double-click the attachment icon.

–Or–

● Right-click the attachment and click either **Preview** or **Open**.

SAVE ATTACHMENTS

If you have My Computer or Windows Explorer open to the folder where you want to save the attachment, you can drag the attachment there. Otherwise:

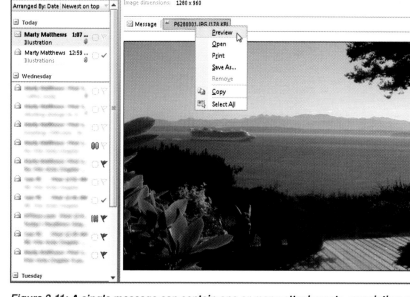

QUICKSTEPS

MANIPULATING THE RULES *(Continued)*

MAKE A SIMILAR RULE

1. Click a rule in the list, click **Copy**, accept the default folder or type a folder name to copy the rule to, and click **OK**. ☑ Copy of MBA

2. Double-click the copy.

3. Step through the wizard, changing settings as necessary and clicking **Next** as you go.

4. Give the rule a new name, and click **Finish**.

CANCEL A RULE

1. Select a rule in the list, and click **Delete**.

2. Click **Yes**.

REARRANGE THE RULES

You might want rules to be applied in a certain order.

1. Select a rule in the list that you want to move.

2. Click the **Move Up** or **Move Down** arrow until the rule resides where you want it in the sequence. ⬆ ⬇

BASE A RULE ON A MESSAGE

1. In the Mail Folder pane, right-click the message and click **Create Rule**.

2. Check the desired options in the Create Rule dialog box.

3. To use the more detailed specifications in the Rules And Alerts Wizard, click **Advanced Options**, step through the wizard (with information from the dialog box supplying some of the underlined values), click **Next** as needed, and then click **Finish**.

4. If using the Create Rule dialog box, click **OK** twice.

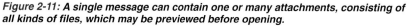

Figure 2-11: A single message can contain one or many attachments, consisting of all kinds of files, which may be previewed before opening.

1. Right-click the attachment icon, and click **Save As**.

2. Use the Save Attachment dialog box to navigate to the desired folder.

3. Type a name in the File Name text box, and click **Save**.

OPEN SAVED ATTACHMENTS

1. Navigate to the folder where you saved the file.

2. Double-click the file.

Print Messages

Occasionally, you might receive something that you want to print and pass around or save as a hard copy. Outlook lets you print in a hurry with the default print settings, or you can control certain parts of the process.

ARCHIVING MESSAGES

Archiving is for people who have a hard time throwing things away. Outlook is set up on a schedule, which you can see by clicking **Tools**, clicking **Options**, clicking the **Other** tab, and clicking **AutoArchive**.

The AutoArchive dialog box allows you to set the time interval between archive functions, when to delete old messages, the path to the archived file, and other settings.

By default, a dialog box appears, asking if you are ready to archive files; you can click **Yes** and be assured of finding the messages later. They are saved in a file structure that mirrors your Personal folders yet compresses the files and cleans up the Inbox. To open archived files, use one of these methods:

- Click ⊞ beside Archive Folders in the Navigation pane, and click a folder.

  –Or–

- Click the **File** menu, point to **Open**, click **Outlook Data File**, and click a file.

Either way, archived files, saved in .pst format, display in the Reading pane. You can search them to find the message you want.

AutoArchive

☑ Run AutoArchive every 14 ⏶⏷ days
☑ Prompt before AutoArchive runs
During AutoArchive:
   ☑ Delete expired items (e-mail folders only)
   ☑ Archive or delete old items
      ☑ Show archive folder in folder list
      Default folder settings for archiving
      Clean out items older than 6 ⏶⏷ Months ▼
      ◉ Move old items to:
      C:\Users\Owner\AppData\Local\Microsoft\Out Browse...
      ◯ Permanently delete old items
      [Apply these settings to all folders now]

To specify different archive settings for any folder, right-click on the folder and choose Properties, then go to the AutoArchive tab.

Retention policy
   The network administrator has not set retention policies.

[Retention Policy Information...]

[OK] [Cancel]

PRINT QUICKLY

Right-click the message or an attachment, and click **Print**.

CHOOSE PRINT SETTINGS

1. Select or open the message.

2. Click the **File** menu, and click **Print**. The Print dialog box appears.

Print

Printer
Name: ▼ [Properties]
Status:
Type:
Where: ☐ Print to file
Comment:

Print style
  Table Style [Page Setup...]
  Memo Style [Define Styles...]

Copies
Number of pages: All ▼
Number of copies: 1 ⏶⏷
☐ Collate copies

Print options
☐ Print attached files. Attachments will print to the default printer only.

[OK] [Cancel] [Preview]

3. Enter your preferences in the Print dialog box.

4. If desired, click **Properties**, select the layout or quality, and click **OK**.

5. Click **OK** to begin printing.

To select multiple attachments in an e-mail at one time to copy or save them, for instance, right-click one attachment and click **Select All**. Then right-click one of the selected attachments, and choose the activity.

How to...

- Create a Message
- Address a Message
- Understanding the Ribbon
- Use a Distribution List
- Add Carbon and Blind Copies
- Edit a Message
- Use Stationery
- Formatting Messages
- Including Hyperlinks
- Attach Files
- Sign Messages
- Using Signatures
- Use Digital Signatures
- Check Spelling
- Reply to Messages
- Forward Messages
- Set Message Priority
- Request Receipts
- Delay Delivery with a Rule
- Sending Messages

Chapter 3

Creating and Sending E-mail

As the saying goes, you have to send mail to get mail. The beauty of Outlook e-mail is that the messages are so easy to send and respond to that you can essentially carry on conversations. Outlook also makes it just as easy to send a message to one person or to 50, bedeck messages with fancy backgrounds known as *stationery,* insert links to Internet sites, include pictures—even add a distinctive signature. In this chapter you will learn how to create and enhance messages, as well as how to send copies, respond to others, and control how and when e-mail is sent.

Write Messages

Creating an e-mail message can be as simple as dispatching a note or as elaborate as designing a marketing poster. It's wise to get used to creating simple messages before making an art project of one. Without your having to impose any guidelines, however, Outlook is set to create an attractive basic e-mail message.

Create a Message

One click starts a message, and the only field you have to complete is the address of the recipient. Normally at least three fields are filled in before you send the message:

- **Recipient**   One or more e-mail addresses or names in your Address Book
- **Subject**   Words indicating the contents of the message (used by the Find tool in a search)
- **Message body**   Whatever you want to say to the recipient

To start a message:

With Outlook open and Mail selected in the navigation pane, click the **New** button on the standard toolbar. The new Message window opens, as shown in Figure 3-1.

Address a Message

Outlook is the lazy person's dream for addressing messages. Of course, the address itself is simple: *username@domain.suffix* (such as ".com"). Once you have entered names in the Contacts workspace, however, you can address your messages with almost no typing. (See Chapter 4 for a complete explanation of how to add contacts to the Address Book.) In this chapter we will focus on what happens to the e-mail itself. The following alternatives come into play as soon as you create a new message by clicking **New** on the toolbar.

TIP

To gain more working space, you can minimize the size of the ribbon. To do this, double-click the active tab name. Click it again to restore the size of the ribbon. You can also press **CTRL+F1** to toggle the size of the ribbon.

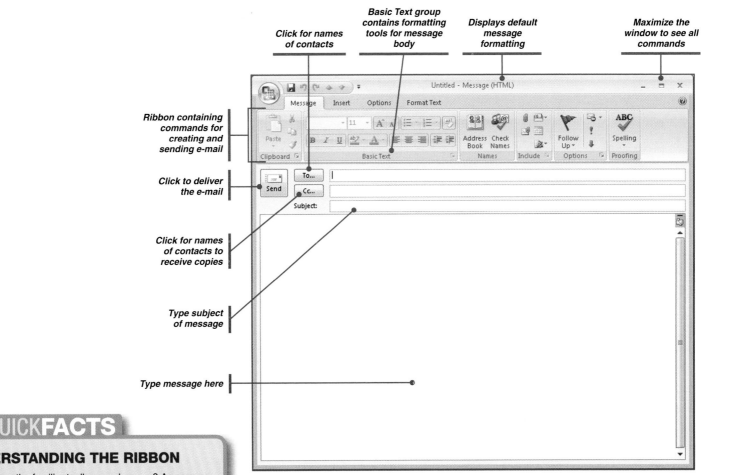

Click for names of contacts

Basic Text group contains formatting tools for message body

Displays default message formatting

Maximize the window to see all commands

Ribbon containing commands for creating and sending e-mail

Click to deliver the e-mail

Click for names of contacts to receive copies

Type subject of message

Type message here

Figure 3-1: The window for creating a message contains important differences from the one in which you read them.

TYPE THE ADDRESS

This is the most basic addressing technique. As soon as you click **New**, the cursor blinks in the To field on the message.

To...

QUICK**FACTS**

UNDERSTANDING THE RIBBON
(Continued)

The ribbon collects tools for a given function into *tabs*. For example, the Messages tab contains tools to work with messages, and the Insert tab contains tools to work with inserting objects into a message. The tabs organize the tools into *groups*. For example, the Basic Text group on the Messages tab provides the tools to work with text.

Each Office program has a default set of tabs with additional *contextual* tabs that appear as the context of your work changes. For instance, when you select an object, an *object Tools* tab appears with appropriate tools for working with the selected object. When the chart in Figure 3-2 is selected, the Chart Tools tabs are displayed—in this case, Design, Layout, and Format. These are tools that you can use with the selected chart, and when the object is unselected, the contextual tabs disappear.

Groups contain labeled buttons, such as the Address Book button in the Names group. Depending on the tool, you are then presented with additional options in the form of a list of commands, a dialog box or task pane, or galleries of choices that reflect what you'll see in your work. Groups that contain several more tools than can be displayed in the ribbon include a *Dialog Box Launcher* icon that takes you directly to these other choices in a dialog box or task pane. The ribbon also takes advantage of new Office 2007 features, including a live preview of many potential changes (for example, you can select text and see the text change as you point to various fonts in the Font list in the Basic Text group). See the accompanying sections and figures for more information on the ribbon and the other elements of the Outlook window.

- For **a single recipient**, type the address.
- For **multiple recipients**, type each address, separating them with semicolons (;).

SELECT FROM THE ADDRESS BOOK

1. Click **To**. The Select Names dialog box displays your Address Book.
2. Choose one of the following:

- Type the first letter of the recipient's name in the Name text box, or select a name from the list box, and double-click it in the list.
- Scroll through the list, and double-click the name you want.

3. For multiple names, choose one:
   - Type names with ; (semi-colon) separating names or e-mail addresses.
   - Repeat step 2 as needed until all desired names are listed in the To text box.
   - Hold down **CTRL** while you click all desired names, and then click **To**.

4. Click **OK**.

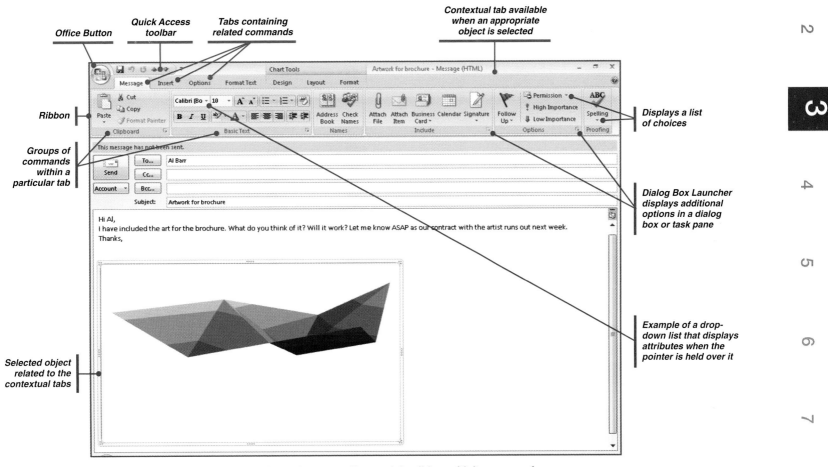

Office Button

Quick Access toolbar

Tabs containing related commands

Contextual tab available when an appropriate object is selected

Ribbon

Displays a list of choices

Groups of commands within a particular tab

Dialog Box Launcher displays additional options in a dialog box or task pane

Example of a drop-down list that displays attributes when the pointer is held over it

Selected object related to the contextual tabs

Figure 3-2: With the Office Button, Quick Access toolbar, and the ribbon with its groups of commands and tools, you can use Outlook's many features.

NOTE

Even if a name appears in your Address Book, the name won't be suggested with AutoComplete unless you have used it to send e-mail.

COMPLETE ADDRESSES AUTOMATICALLY

Outlook runs AutoComplete by default. As soon as you type the first letter of an address, Outlook begins searching for matches among names and addresses you've typed in the past.

You can turn off AutoComplete if you wish: In the initial Outlook window, click **Tools**, click **Options**, and click the **Preferences** tab. Then click the **E-mail Options** button, click **Advanced E-mail Options**, and clear the **Suggest Names While Completing To, Cc, And Bcc Fields** check box. Click **OK** three times to close.

> ☐ Suggest names while completing To, Cc, and Bcc fields
> ☑ Press CTRL+ENTER to send messages
>
> OK

TIP

You can also edit received messages. This can be handy when printing them. You might want to print only the final comment and eliminate the original message text in exchanges where participants replied a number of times.

1. Begin typing a name or address in the To field in the Message window. The closest name to what you have typed will be displayed in the Name list.

2. If the name you want appears in the list, press **DOWN ARROW** (if necessary) until the name is highlighted.

> Select Names: Contacts
>
> **Search:** ◉ Name only ○ More columns   **Address Book**
>
> al s| Go   Contacts
>
> Name   Display Name
> Al Soupa   Al Soupa (asoupa@aol.com)
> Alice Bergdofg   Alice Bergdorf (aliceb@hotmail.com)

3. Press **ENTER** to accept the address. The name displays, a semicolon follows it, and the cursor blinks where the next name would appear.

4. If you wish to add another recipient, begin typing another name (it will replace the highlighted text you previously typed), and repeat the process as needed.

5. Press **TAB** to go to the next desired field.

Use a Distribution List

As you group your contacts into distribution lists (see Chapter 4), you will have an even quicker way to add multiple addresses to messages. Use any of the preceding procedures, and enter or select the name of the distribution list as it appears in the Address Book. When you send it, the message will go to everyone on the list.

Add Carbon and Blind Copies

You may never have seen a real carbon copy, but Outlook keeps the concept alive by way of this feature located just below the To field in the new Message window. Persons who receive a message with their e-mail address in the *Cc* (carbon copy) line understand that they are not the primary recipients—they got the message as an FYI (for your information), and all other recipients can see that they got it (see Figure 3-3). A *Bcc* (blind carbon copy) hides addresses entered in that line from anyone else who receives the message.

> Select Names: Contacts
>
> **Search:** ◉ Name only ○ More columns   **Address Book**
>
> | Go   Contacts
>
> Name   Display Name
> Adco Studies Group   Adco Studies Group
> Adult Forum   Adult Forum
> Al Bar   Al Bar (al@aol.com)

Click to find the Show Bcc button in the Fields group

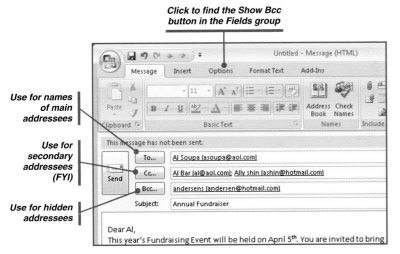

Use for names of main addressees

Use for secondary addressees (FYI)

Use for hidden addressees

Figure 3-3: The way a message is delivered suggests different roles for the various recipients.

INCLUDE OR REMOVE BCC ON NEW MESSAGES

1. On the Message window, click the **Options** tab.

2. In the Fields group, click **Show Bcc** to toggle the Bcc field on and off.

ADDRESS THE COPIES

Type addresses in the Cc and Bcc fields completely or with the aid of AutoComplete. You can also use the Address Book: click **Cc** or **Bcc** in the Message window, scroll through the names, and double-click the name(s) in the Address Book you want to be copied.

Edit a Message

E-mail can be created in any of three formats and has the additional option of using the powerful formatting capability of Microsoft Word for composing messages. Outlook handles all three formats quite easily, but sometimes you need to consider your recipients' computer resources and Internet connections:

- **HTML** (Hypertext Markup Language), the default format, lets you freely use design elements, such as colors, pictures, links, animations, sound, and movies (though good taste and the need to control the size of the message file might suggest a little discretion!).

- **Plain Text** format lies at the other extreme, eliminating embellishments so that any computer can manage the message.

- **Rich Text Format** (RTF) takes the middle ground, providing font choices—including color, boldface, italics, and underlining—basic paragraph layouts, and bullets.

With Outlook, you can edit messages you create as well as those you receive. Regardless which of the three formats you choose, some editing processes are always available, as shown in Table 3-1.

Using HTML or Rich Text Format provides a wide range of options for enhancing the appearance of a message. See the "Formatting Messages" QuickSteps for a rundown of additional formatting selections. Finally, you

NOTE

If your Message window is not maximized, you may not see all available formatting buttons. In some cases, the commands will be available in menus. You can click the group down arrow to see the menu of commands, or click the **Maximize** button on the title bar to increase the size of the window.

can also create the message in another program and copy and paste it into a message body. HTML will preserve the formatting exactly, and Rich Text Format will come close.

SELECT A MESSAGE FORMAT

The message format displays in the title bar of the new Message window. You can either set a format for an individual message, or you can set a default for all message formats.

Agenda for Board Meeting - Message (Plain Text)

To set a default format for all e-mail:

1. With Outlook open (not in a message), click the **Tools** menu, click **Options**, and click the **Mail Format** tab, shown in Figure 3-4.

2. Click the **Compose In This Message Format** down arrow, and select one of the choices.

3. Click **OK** to close the Options dialog box.

To set formatting for an individual message:

1. In the Message window, click the **Options** tab.

2. In the Format group, click the formatting button you want.

Use Stationery

It's easy to choose stationery for a message. You can pick a different type of stationery for every new message or set a default style for all messages (until you change it).

SET A DEFAULT STATIONERY THEME

You can set a default for your stationery that will be used each time you write a new e-mail. You can also select a theme for your stationery

TO		DO THIS	
Insert new text in message body		Click where new text belongs, and type new text.	
Indent the start of a paragraph		Click before the first letter of the paragraph, and press **TAB**.	
Replace a	Word	Double-click the word.	Type new text.
	Line	Click left of the line	
	Paragraph	Double-clicking to the left selects a paragraph. Triple-clicking to the left selects all the text in the message.	
Move a	Word	Double-click the word.	Drag to a new location in the message.
	Line	Click left of the line.	
	Paragraph	Double-click to the left of the paragraph.	
Delete a	Word	Double-click the word.	Press **DELETE**.
	Line	Click left of the line.	
	Paragraph	Double-click to left of the paragraph.	

Table 3-1: Standard Editing Operations

QUICKSTEPS

FORMATTING MESSAGES

To format text in the Message window, use the Format Text tab or the Message tab to access formatting commands. You can format text before you start typing, or you can select text and then format it after composing the message. See Table 3-1 for a list of selection methods.

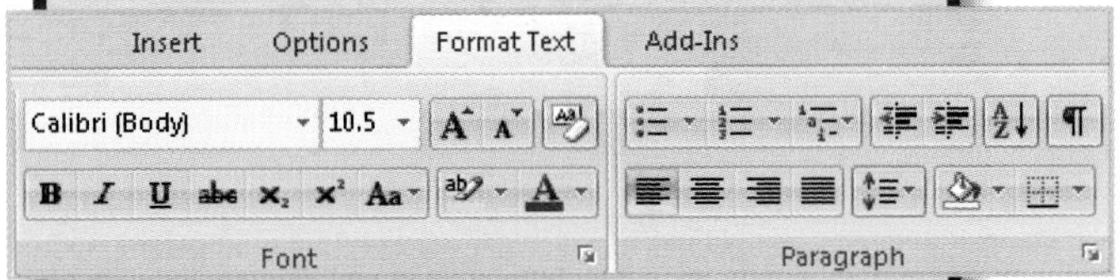

Insert   **Options**   **Format Text**   **Add-Ins**

Calibri (Body)   10.5   A A A^

B *I* <u>U</u> abe x₂ x² Aa   ab · A ·

Font   Paragraph

CHOOSE A FONT AND ITS SIZE

A typeface can immediately set the tone of your message.

1. Select your text or paragraph.

2. In either the Format Text tab Font group or the Message tab Basic Text group, click the **Font** down arrow in the Font group, and move the pointer over several fonts and see how they affect your selected text. Select a font you want to use.

3. Click the **Font Size** down arrow next to the font, and again move the pointer over several sizes and notice the effects. Select a type size you want.

Calibri   10.5   A A A^

Segoe Script
Segoe UI
SHOWCARD GOTHIC
Shruti
SimHei
Simplified Arabic   أبجد هوز
Simplified Arabic Fixe
SimSun
SimSun-ExtB
Snap ITC
STENCIL
Sylfaen
Symbol   ΑβΧδΕφΓηΙφ
Tahoma
Teletext 43
Teletext 83
Tempus Sans ITC
Times New Roman
Traditional Arabic   أبجد هوز
Trebuchet MS
Tunga

Continued . . .

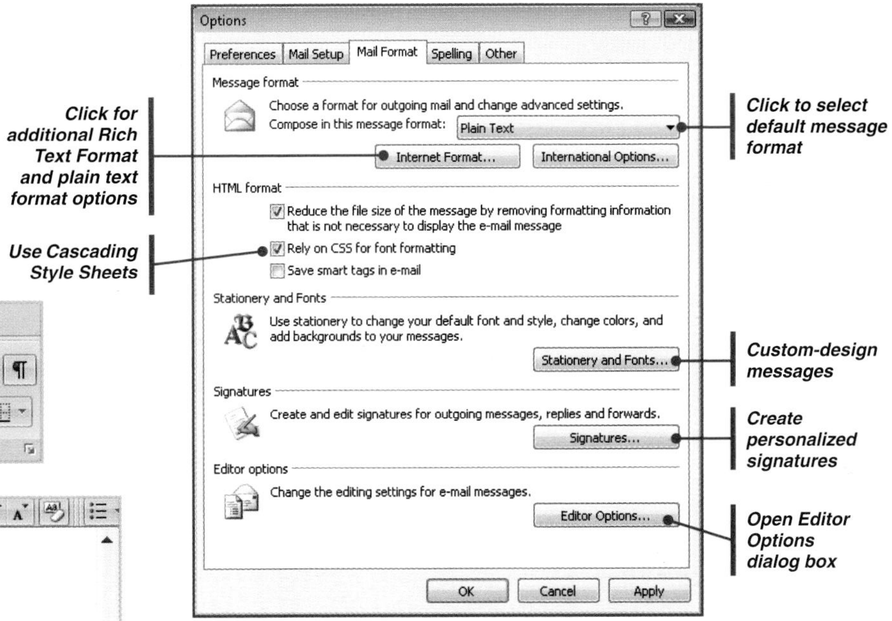

Click for additional Rich Text Format and plain text format options

Use Cascading Style Sheets

Options

Preferences | Mail Setup | Mail Format | Spelling | Other

Message format
Choose a format for outgoing mail and change advanced settings.
Compose in this message format: Plain Text

● Internet Format...   International Options...

HTML format
☑ Reduce the file size of the message by removing formatting information that is not necessary to display the e-mail message
☑ Rely on CSS for font formatting
☐ Save smart tags in e-mail

Stationery and Fonts
Use stationery to change your default font and style, change colors, and add backgrounds to your messages.
Stationery and Fonts...

Signatures
Create and edit signatures for outgoing messages, replies and forwards.
Signatures...

Editor options
Change the editing settings for e-mail messages.
Editor Options...

OK   Cancel   Apply

Click to select default message format

Custom-design messages

Create personalized signatures

Open Editor Options dialog box

Figure 3-4: You can create personal message designs that distinguish you as the sender.

and still have your own unique fonts. You can vary fonts as well, either for new e-mails or for those you reply or forward. To set a default stationery:

1. Click the **Tools** menu, click **Options**, and click the **Mail Format** tab.

2. Make sure that **HTML** has been selected as the message format.

3. Click the **Stationery And Fonts** button. Click the **Personal Stationery** tab to open the dialog box shown in Figure 3-5. Select from these choices:

   ● Click the **Theme** button, and under Choose A Theme, click the theme you want, and click **OK**. When you choose a theme, the fonts will be automatically defined for you, and those buttons will become unavailable or grayed.

QUICKSTEPS

FORMATTING MESSAGES *(Continued)*

CREATE BOLD, ITALIC, OR UNDERLINED FONTS

Select the text, and click the **Bold**, **Italic**, or **Underline** effect in the Font group.

B *I* <u>U</u>

COLOR THE FONT

Select the text, click the **Font Color** down arrow, and select a color.

ALIGN PARAGRAPHS

Click an alignment, which, from left to right, provides a left-aligned margin, centered text, a right-aligned margin, or justified margins (where both the left and right margins end evenly).

CREATE NUMBERED, BULLETED, OR MULTILEVEL LISTS

Select the text to be affected, and click the **Bullets**, **Numbering**, or **Multilevel List** button (the latter is only in the Format Text tab Paragraph group).

SHIFT THE PARAGRAPH

The Decrease Indent and Increase Indent buttons move the selected paragraph in fixed increments. You can alternate clicking them until you are satisfied with the location. However, because they will not move the paragraph beyond the message margins, they have no effect on centered paragraphs.

Click within a paragraph to be shifted, and click the appropriate button.

INSERT A HORIZONTAL LINE

Set off paragraphs with lines:

1. Click where the separation is desired (usually at the end of a paragraph).

2. In the Format Text tab Paragraph group, click the **Borders** down arrow, and click **Horizontal Line**.

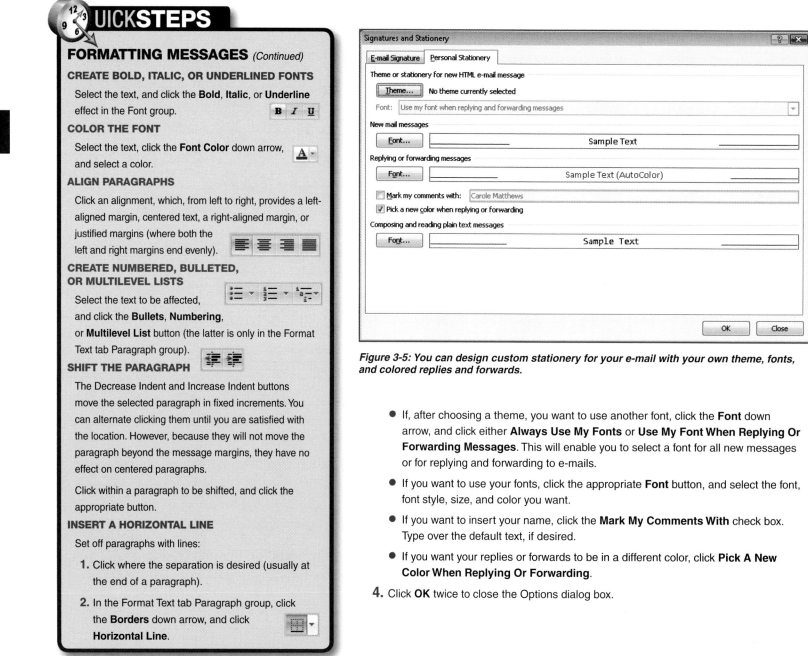

Figure 3-5: You can design custom stationery for your e-mail with your own theme, fonts, and colored replies and forwards.

- If, after choosing a theme, you want to use another font, click the **Font** down arrow, and click either **Always Use My Fonts** or **Use My Font When Replying Or Forwarding Messages**. This will enable you to select a font for all new messages or for replying and forwarding to e-mails.

- If you want to use your fonts, click the appropriate **Font** button, and select the font, font style, size, and color you want.

- If you want to insert your name, click the **Mark My Comments With** check box. Type over the default text, if desired.

- If you want your replies or forwards to be in a different color, click **Pick A New Color When Replying Or Forwarding**.

4. Click **OK** twice to close the Options dialog box.

APPLY STATIONERY TO A SINGLE MESSAGE

1. Click the **Insert** tab in the Outlook new Message window, and click the **Signature** button in the Include group. Click **Signatures** on the menu. The Signature And Stationery dialog box appears.

2. Click the **Personal Stationery** tab.

3. Change the theme and fonts, as described in "Set a Default Stationery Theme."

4. Click **OK**.

USE A STANDARD MICROSOFT OFFICE THEME

You can use a standard Microsoft Office theme in your e-mail that differs from the Outlook themes used for stationery. You might use these to coordinate your regular Word correspondence with your e-mail, thus creating a consistent and professional look. These themes are easy to use and available in your new Message window.

1. In the new Message window, click the **Options** tab if it is not already selected.

2. In the Themes group, if you can't see Colors, Fonts, and Effects, click **Themes**. Then, in any case, click the **Themes** down arrow, and click the standard theme you'd like to use for your e-mail, as shown in Figure 3-6:

   - Click **Colors** and click a combination of colors to change the color scheme.

   - Click **Fonts** and click a font style to change the fonts used.

   - Click **Effect** and click an effect to change the special effects of the graphics.

3. Type your new message and send it.

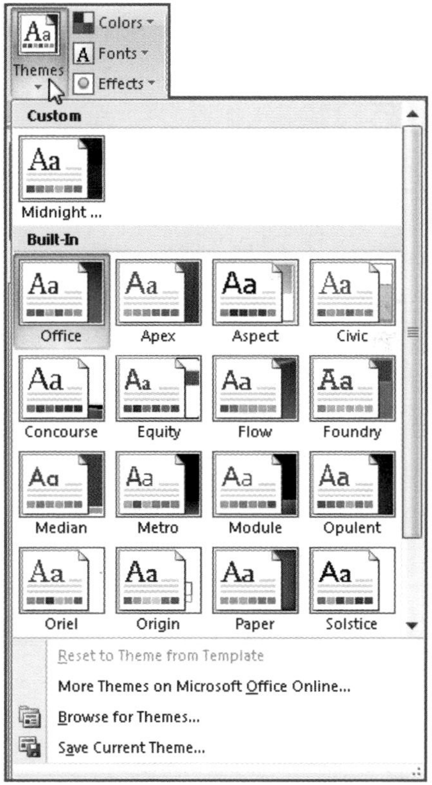

Figure 3-6: Using a standard Office theme allows you to coordinate your e-mail and regular Word correspondence.

NOTE

In the Message window, when you click the **Themes** button in the Themes group on the Options tab, you will see additional options at the bottom of the gallery of theme thumbnails. You can search for additional themes online by clicking **More Themes On Microsoft Office Online** or search for your own custom theme by clicking **Browse For Themes**. If you alter a standard theme with new colors, fonts, or effects, you can save these changes as a custom theme to use again later by clicking **Save Current Theme**.

INCLUDING HYPERLINKS

You can add hyperlinks (whether links to an Internet site, to other locations in the current document, or to other documents) to your e-mail by typing them into the message body or by copying and pasting them. Outlook creates a live link, which it turns to a blue, underlined font when you type or paste any kind of Internet protocol (http://, mailto:, www.*something.com*:), regardless what mail format you use. Only HTML, however, will make a live link out of an e-mail address: *something@something .com*. Also, only in HTML can you substitute different text for the actual Uniform Resource Locator (URL) or e-mail address and still retain the link—by dragging to select the hyperlink and typing something different. In addition to typing the hyperlink address, you can also click the **Insert** tab and click **Hyperlink** in the Links group. Then find the location of the link—in an existing file or Web page, a place in a document, a new document, or an e-mail address—and click **OK**.

REMOVE STATIONERY

To remove stationery from a single message:

In Outlook, click the **Actions** menu, click **New Mail Message Using**, and select **HTML (No Stationery)**.

Actions	Help
New Mail Message Ctrl+N	Send/Receive ▾ Se
New Mail Message Using ▸	More Stationery...
Junk E-mail ▸	Plain Text
Reply Ctrl+R	Rich Text
Reply to All Ctrl+Shift+R	HTML (No Stationery)

To stop having standard stationery as a default:

1. Click the **Tools** menu, click **Options**, and click the **Mail Format** tab.
2. Click the **Stationery And Fonts** button.
3. On the Personal Stationery tab, click **Theme** and click **(No Theme)** at the top of the theme list.
4. Click **OK** three times.

Theme or Stationery

Choose a Theme:
(No Theme)

Attach Files

Sometimes you will want to send or receive a message that is accompanied by other files: pictures, word-processed documents, sound, or movie files. Creating attachments is like clipping newspaper stories and baby pictures to a letter. If you are editing or otherwise working on the item you want to attach, make sure that you save the latest version before you proceed. After that, click **New** to open the new Message window, and use one of the following attachment procedures.

DRAG A FILE TO A MESSAGE

Find the file to be attached by using My Computer or Windows Explorer, and drag it to the message.

INSERT A FILE

When you attach a file to an e-mail message, it can either be attached as a file or entered as text into the body of the message. In some cases, it may be attached

Send	To...	Al Bar (al@aol.com)
	Cc...	Alice Bergdorf (aliceb@hotmail.com)
	Bcc...	
	Subject:	Strategy Recommendation

Hi Al,
Here is the presentation we discussed.

as a hyperlink. The attached file and its commands are identified with a paper clip icon.

1. To display the Insert File dialog box:

- Click the **Insert** tab, and then click **Attach File** in the Include group.

  –Or–

- In the Message tab, click the **Attach File** icon in the Include group.

2. The Insert File dialog box appears. Find and select the file to be attached. Then:

- Click **Insert** to insert the file as an attachment. If the e-mail format is HTML (Hypertext Markup Language) or plain text, it will be attached in a field labeled "Attached" beneath the Subject field. If the format is Rich Text Format, the file attachment will be in the body of the message.

- Click the **Insert** down arrow, and choose between inserting the file as an attachment and inserting it as text in the body of the message. If you choose **Insert As Text**, the file is entered as text in the message. The file content of certain file types, such as .txt, .doc, and .eml, and the source code of others, such as HTML or HTA (HTML Application) , will become part of the message. Everything else—pictures, sound, and movie—will generate nonsense characters in the message body.

- Click **Insert As Hyperlink** to insert the selected file as a hyperlink. (This option is not always available from the Attach File command.)

3. Complete and send the e-mail message.

EMBED A PICTURE INTO A MESSAGE

Though any kind of file you save on your computer or on a disk can be sent by following the previous steps, you have the added option of placing pictures (.gif, .jpg, .bmp, .tif, and so on) right into the message body.

1. Click in the message body to set the insertion point.

2. Click the **Insert** tab, and click **Picture** in the Illustrations group. The Insert Picture dialog box appears, as shown in Figure 3-7.

3. Find the picture file you want, and click Insert. From the submenu:

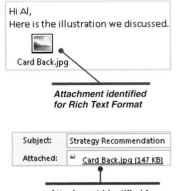

Attachment identified
for Rich Text Format

Attachment identified for
HTML or plain text format

- Click **Insert** to embed the picture in the message. You can then drag it to size it correctly for your message or right-click to display the Format Picture dialog box and edit the photo.

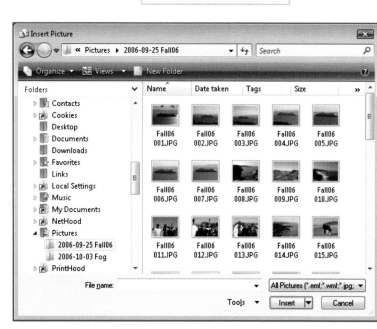

Figure 3-7: You can insert a picture or a link to it using the Insert Picture dialog box.

This message has not been sent.

To... Al Bar (al@aol.com)

Cc...

Bcc...

Send

Subject: New photo of Michael!

- Click **Link To File** to send a link to where the file is stored. This reduces the size of the message.
- Click **Insert And Link** to both embed the photo and send a link to its location.
- Click **Show Previous Versions** to list the previous versions of the files so that you can select the version you want to attach.

4. Complete and send the e-mail message.

Sign Messages

You can create closings, or signatures, for your e-mail messages. Outlook signatures can contain pictures and text along with your name. You can create

NOTE

If you link a picture to your message rather than embed it, you will need to either send the picture with the document or store the picture in a shared network folder available to the message recipient. Otherwise, your e-mail will be seen with a red X where the photo should be.

TIP

If you are on a Microsoft Exchange Server network, you can even insert voting options that the recipient has only to click for a response. To do this, create a message, click the **Options** tab, and click the **Use Voting Buttons** down arrow in the Tracking group. Select the kind of reply you need or click **Custom** to type new options separated by semicolons (;) in the Use Voting Buttons text box.

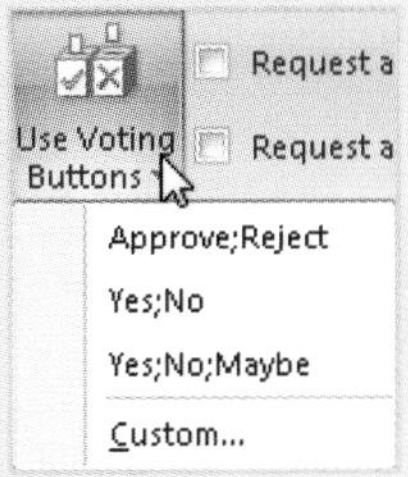

☐ Request a	
☐ Request a	
Approve;Reject	
Yes;No	
Yes;No;Maybe	
Custom...	

NOTE

See Chapter 10 on how to create and use electronic business cards and insert them within a signature.

QUICKSTEPS

USING SIGNATURES

You can use certain signatures for certain accounts, and you can still pick a different one for a particular message.

Click **Tools**, click **Options**, and on the Options dialog box, click the **Mail Format** tab.

ASSIGN SIGNATURES TO ACCOUNTS

1. Click the **Signatures** button, and then click the **E-mail Signature** tab.

2. Click the **E-mail Account** down arrow, and select an account.

Continued . . .

signatures in different styles for the different kinds of messages you write: friendly, formal, or business.

CREATE A SIGNATURE

With Outlook open:

1. Click **Tools** and click **Options**. The Options dialog box appears. Click the **Mail Format** tab.

2. Click **Signatures** in the Signatures panel, and then click **New**.

3. Type a name for your signature, and click **OK**. The Signatures And Stationery dialog box appears and the E-mail Signature tab is selected, as shown in Figure 3-8.

4. In the Edit Signature text box, type (or paste from another document) any text you want to include in your closing, including your name.

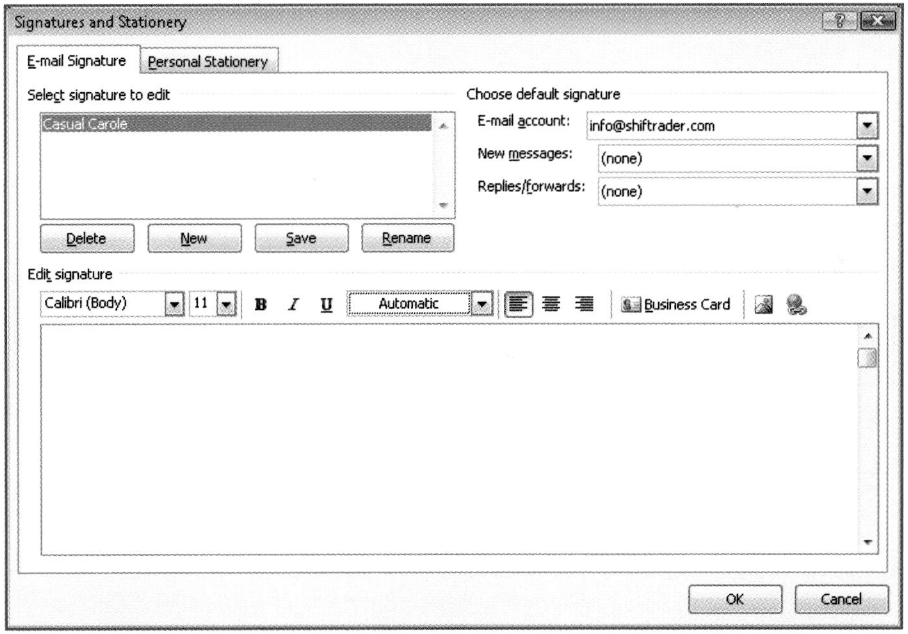

Figure 3-8: You can create one or more signatures with custom-designed characteristics that will be included in the bottom of your e-mail.

USING SIGNATURES *(Continued)*

3. Click the **New Messages** down arrow, and click the signature name to be used.

4. Click the **Replies/Forwards** down arrow, and click the signature name to be used.

5. Repeat steps 1–4 for each of your accounts, and then click **OK** twice.

INSERT A SIGNATURE IN A MESSAGE

Sometimes, you will want to replace a defined signature with another one or define a signature at the time of a message.

1. Create an e-mail message.

2. Click in the body of the message where you want the special closing. Click the **Insert** tab, and click **Signature** in the Include group. Choose one of the following options:

   > Signature
   >> Business Carole
   >> Casual Carole
   >> Signatures...

   • Click the name of an existing signature, and it will be inserted in the message. If you already have a message that was inserted automatically, it will be replaced by the one you select.

   • Click **Signatures**, and the Signatures And Stationery dialog box will appear. Create a new signature, as described in "Sign Messages."

5. To apply formatting, select the text and click any of the formatting buttons in the toolbar. You can even insert a business card, picture, or hyperlink. Use the tips found earlier in the "Formatting Messages" QuickSteps. Plain text messages, by definition, cannot be formatted.

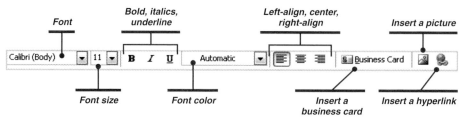

6. Click **OK** twice to close the dialog boxes.

Use Digital Signatures

A *digital signature* certifies that everything contained in the message—documents, forms, computer code, training modules, whatever—originated with the sender. Computer programmers and people engaged in e-commerce use them a lot. To embed a formal digital signature, you need to acquire a *digital certificate,* which is like a license, from a certificate authority, such as Wells Fargo or VeriSign, Inc.

Alternatively, you can create your own digital signature, although it is not administered by a certificate authority. A self-signed certificate is considered unauthenticated and will generate a security warning if the recipient has his or her security set at a high level.

ACQUIRE A DIGITAL CERTIFICATE

If you do not already have a digital certificate, Outlook can lead you to a Web site where you can find a commercial certification authority to issue one. Make sure you are online before you begin.

1. Click **Tools** and click **Trust Center**. The Trust Center dialog box appears. Click **E-mail Security**.

2. Under Digital IDs (Certificates), click **Get A Digital ID**.

3. Follow the instructions on the Digital ID Web page to obtain a certificate.

IMPORT OR EXPORT A DIGITAL ID

1. Click **Tools**, click **Options**, and click **Trust Center**. The Trust Center dialog box appears. Click **E-mail Security**.

2. Under Digital IDs (Certificates), click **Import/Export**. The Import/Export Digital ID dialog box appears.

3. Click **Import Existing Digital ID From A File** to import a digital ID, or click **Export Your Digital ID To A File** to export your own digital ID.

4. Fill in the requested information, and click **OK**.

ADD A DIGITAL SIGNATURE TO MESSAGES

1. In the initial Outlook window, click the **Tools** menu, and then click **Trust Center**. The Trust Center dialog box appears.

2. Click the **E-mail Security** option.

3. Under Encrypted E-mail, click the **Add Digital Signature To Outgoing Messages** check box.

4. To make sure that recipients can read the message if they don't have Secure/ Multipurpose Internet Mail Extensions (S/MIME) security, click the **Send Clear Text Signed Message When Sending Signed Messages** check box.

5. To receive a message confirming that your message got to the recipient, click the **Request S/MIME Receipt For All S/MIME Signed Messages** check box.

6. Click **OK**.

Check Spelling

For all the hip abbreviations that have emerged with e-mail and instant messaging, unintentional spelling errors still can be a problem. You can have Outlook check the spelling of your message when you finish, or you can have it automatically check messages before you send them.

CHECK A MESSAGE

Create a message and keep the cursor in the body when you are finished. Any spelling errors will be automatically flagged for you with a red wavy line. You will have these options:

- Right-click the flagged word, and if a correct spelling is suggested, click it.

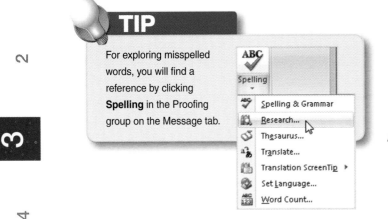

TIP

For exploring misspelled words, you will find a reference by clicking **Spelling** in the Proofing group on the Message tab.

ABC
Spelling

ABC Spelling & Grammar
🔍 Research...
📖 Thesaurus...
a̤ Translate...
📋 Translation ScreenTip ▶
🌐 Set Language...
ABC 123 Word Count...

- If you do not see the correct spelling, then the flagged word cannot be found in the dictionary. Either look it up in a reference and type it in, or type another spelling to see if it is correct.

- If you know the flagged word is correct and you want to add it to the dictionary, use the Spelling And Grammar dialog box. See "Add a Word to the Dictionary," next.

ADD A WORD TO THE DICTIONARY

To add a flagged word to the dictionary so that it will not continue to be flagged as a potential misspelling:

1. Highlight the flagged word, and click **Spelling** in the Proofing group of the Message tab. Click **Spelling & Grammar**. The Spelling And Grammar dialog box will appear, as seen in Figure 3-9.

2. Click **Add To Dictionary**.

3. Click **Close**.

CHECK MESSAGES BEFORE SENDING

To automatically check spelling in messages before sending them:

1. With Outlook open, click **Tools**, click **Options**, and click the **Spelling** tab.

2. Click **Always Check Spelling Before Sending**, and click **OK**.

Options

Preferences | Mail Setup | Mail Format | Spelling | Other

General options

ABC ✓ ☑ Always check spelling before sending
☑ Ignore original message text in reply or forward

Spelling and AutoCorrection...

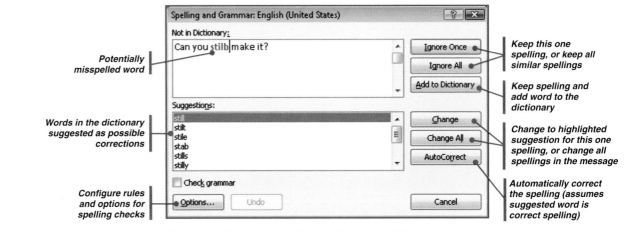

Spelling and Grammar: English (United States)

Not in Dictionary:

Can you stilb|make it?

Potentially misspelled word

Suggestions:

still
stilt
stile
stab
stills
stilly

Words in the dictionary suggested as possible corrections

☐ Check grammar

Configure rules and options for spelling checks

Options...   Undo

Ignore Once
Ignore All
Add to Dictionary

Keep this one spelling, or keep all similar spellings

Keep spelling and add word to the dictionary

Change
Change All
AutoCorrect

Change to highlighted suggestion for this one spelling, or change all spellings in the message

Cancel

Automatically correct the spelling (assumes suggested word is correct spelling)

Figure 3-9: The default spelling dictionary contains everyday words rather than technical or scientific terms. You can add special words to it.

Send Messages

No extra postage, no trip to the post office, no running out of envelopes. What could be better? Once a message is ready to go, you can just click a button. Outlook provides features that let you exercise more control over the process than you could ever get from the postal service, or "snail" mail.

Make sure that your message is complete and ready to send, and then click **Send** on the message toolbar.

When you have more than one account, your Message window contains an Account button that is not available otherwise. To send a message from a particular account:

Click **Accounts** beneath the Send button on the Message window, select an account, and click **Send**.

Reply to Messages

When you receive a message that you want to answer, you have three ways to initiate a reply:

- Open the message and click **Reply** in the Respond group on the Message tab.

  –Or–

- Right-click the message in the folder pane, and select **Reply** from the context menu.

  –Or–

- Click the message in the folder pane, and click **Reply** on the standard toolbar.

Whichever way you use, a reply Message window opens, as illustrated in Figure 3-10. The message will be formatted using the same format the sender used, the subject will be "Re:" plus the original subject in the Subject line. By default, the pointer blinks in the message body above the original message and sender's address (see also "Change the Reply Layout" later in this chapter). Treat it like a new Message window: type a message, add attachments or links, and click **Send**.

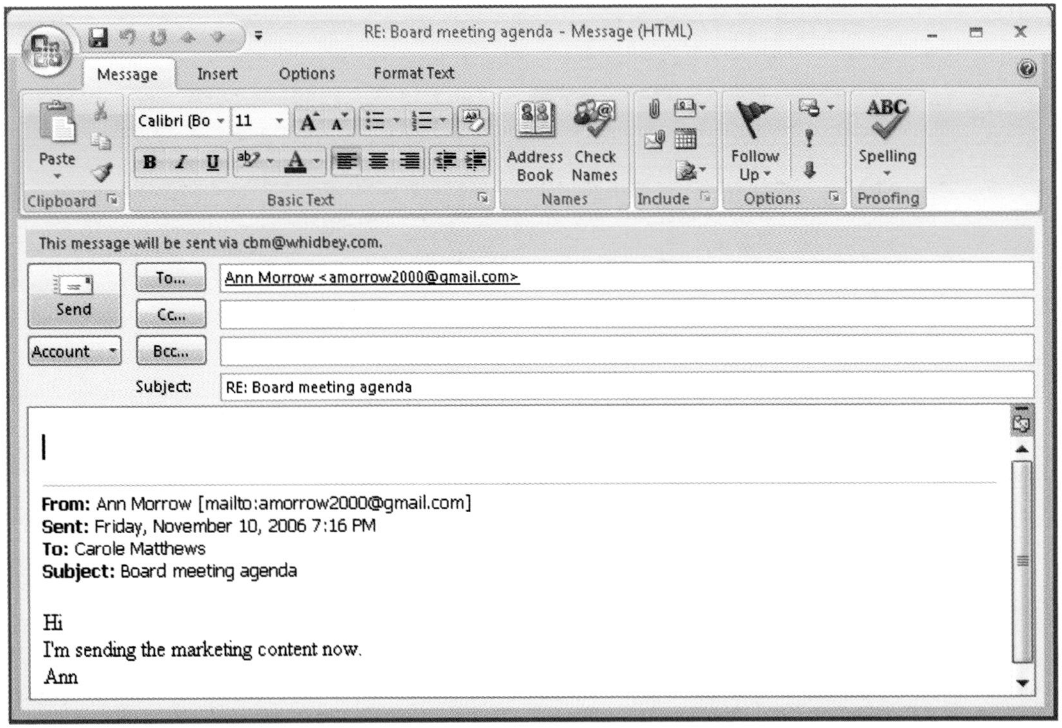

REPLY TO ALL RECIPIENTS

If the To field in the message contains several recipients, all of whom should read your reply, Outlook makes it simple. Using any of the three ways just listed, select **Reply To All**. The reply Message window will list all original recipients in the To and Cc fields. Send the message as usual.

CHANGE THE REPLY LAYOUT

You can select from five different ways to incorporate the original message. Also, if you'd rather just insert your responses into the original text, Outlook lets you decide how to identify your remarks.

Figure 3-10: The Reply window uses the sender's message format and subject to make the e-mail conversation easy to track and respond to.

1. With Outlook open, click **Tools**, click **Options**, and, at the top of the Preferences tab, click the **E-mail Options** button.

2. Click the **When Replying To A Message** down arrow, and select how you want the original message included.

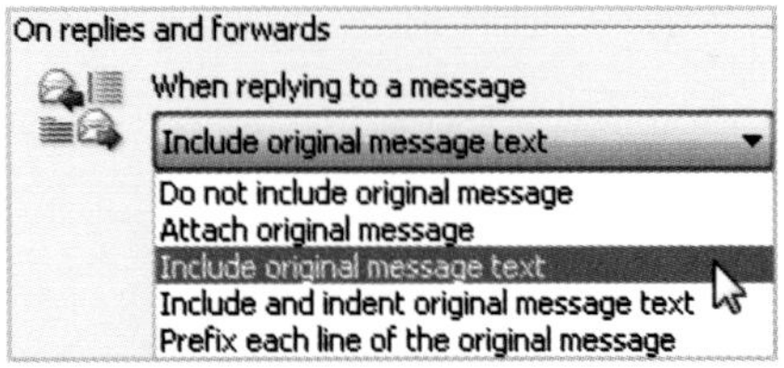

   On replies and forwards
   When replying to a message
   Include original message text
   - Do not include original message
   - Attach original message
   - Include original message text
   - Include and indent original message text
   - Prefix each line of the original message

3. Click the **Mark My Comments With** check box, and type the label you want.

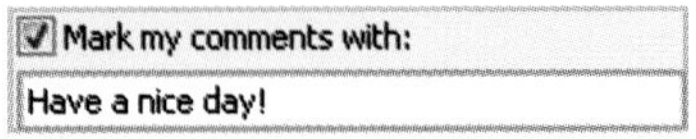

   ☑ Mark my comments with:
   Have a nice day!

4. Click **OK** twice.

SET AUTOMATIC REPLY

Organizations that use Microsoft Exchange Server for e-mail can create an automatic reply during times when you are not available to answer messages.

Each sender will receive only one notification, no matter how many messages he or she sends before you return. This procedure explains how to set up the Out Of Office Assistant with Exchange 2007. If you are using an earlier version of Exchange Server, there is a slightly different set of options.

1. With Outlook open, click **Tools** and click **Out Of Office Assistant**. (If this command is not on your Tools menu, you are not using an Exchange account.)

2. Click **Send Out Of Office Auto-Replies**.

3. If useful, click **Only Send During This Time Range**, and click the **Start Time** and **End Time** down arrows for the date and times you'll be gone.

4. In the Auto Reply Only Once panel, type the message you want in your reply, both for inside and outside your organization.

5. To turn it off, click **Tools**, click **Out Of Office Assistant**, and click **Do Not Send Out Of Office Auto-Replies**.

6. Click **OK** to close the assistant.

Forward Messages

When you forward a message, you send an incoming message to someone else. You can send messages to new recipients, using the same techniques as with the Reply feature.

When you receive a message that you want to forward to someone else, use one of these techniques:

- Open the message and click **Forward** in the Respond group on the Message tab.

  –Or–

- Right-click the message in the folder pane, and select **Forward** from the context menu.

  –Or–

- Click the message in the folder pane, and click **Forward** on the standard toolbar.

A Forward Message window opens, with the cursor blinking in the To field and a space above the original message for you to type your own. Once the forward Message window opens, the simplest action is to enter the recipient(s) address(es), insert attachments as needed, and send as usual.

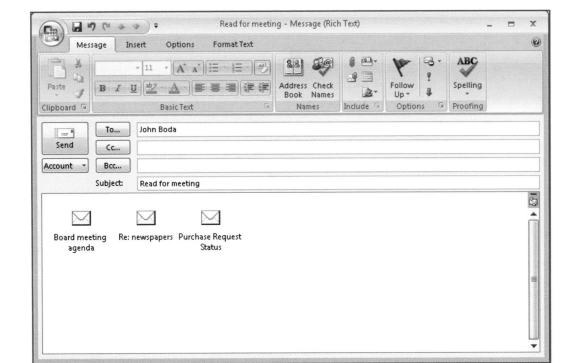

Figure 3-11: You can group and forward e-mails as attachments.

FORWARD MULTIPLE MESSAGES

Rather than forward a bunch of messages one by one, you can bundle them and forward them in one message.

1. Press **CTRL** while you click each message in the message list that you want to forward.

2. Right-click one of the messages in the group, and click **Forward Items**. A new mail message opens with the messages included as attachments, as seen in Figure 3-11. You may also see the attachments in the Attached box rather than in the message area.

3. Complete the message and send as usual.

Set Message Priority

If your recipient gets a lot of messages, you might want to identify your message as important so that it will stand out in his or her Inbox. Outlook includes a red exclamation point in the message list to call attention to messages set with high importance and a blue down arrow to indicate messages with low importance. In the Message window, you flag your e-mail messages with the appropriate flag.

1. Create a message. In the Options group on the Message tab, select one of these options:

   ● Click **High Importance** to insert a red exclamation point to indicate high importance.

   ● Click **Low Importance** to insert a blue down arrow to indicate low importance.

2. Send the message as usual.

Request Receipts

Anyone who has sent an important message and has not heard a peep from the recipient can appreciate receipts. When the addressee receives or reads the message, you are notified. You can request receipts for all your messages or on a message-by-message basis.

OBTAIN RECEIPTS FOR ALL MESSAGES

1. Click **Tools**, click **Options**, and click the **E-mail Options** button.

2. In the E-mail Options dialog box, click the **Tracking Options** button.

3. On the lower half of the dialog box, click **Read Receipt**, **Delivery Receipt**, or both.

4. If you like, choose an option for responding to other senders' requests for a receipt— **Always Send A Response**, **Never Send A Response**, or **Ask Me Before Sending A Response** (the default).

5. Click **OK** three times.

OBTAIN A SINGLE RECEIPT

1. Create a message and click the **Options** tab in the Message window.

2. In the Tracking group, click **Request A Delivery Receipt**, **Request A Read Receipt**, or both. (If you have set these options for all mail, this message will reflect those settings.)

3. Click **Close**.

Delay Delivery with a Rule

You can create a rule to control when messages leave your system after you click **Send**.

1. With Outlook open, click **Tools** and click **Rules And Alerts.**

2. If you are told that messages sent and received with HTTP (such as Hotmail, Gmail, and Yahoo) cannot be filtered using Rules And Alerts. Click **OK.**

3. In the Rules And Alerts dialog box, click **New Rule.**

4. In the Rules Wizard, under Start From A Blank Rule, click **Check Messages After Sending**, and click **Next**.

QUICKSTEPS

SENDING MESSAGES

You can fire off your messages now or later or on a schedule.

SEND MESSAGES MANUALLY

By default, as long as you are connected to the Internet, clicking **Send** in the Message window sends the completed message. You can turn this off so that clicking Send in the Message window only puts the message in the Outbox folder. You must then additionally click **Send/ Receive** in the Outlook standard toolbar to send all the messages in the Outbox folder.

TURN OFF AUTO-SEND

To prevent a message from being automatically sent unless you click Send in the Message window:

1. Click **Tools**, click **Options**, and click the **Mail Setup** tab.

2. Under Send/Receive, clear the **Send Immediately When Connected** check box.

3. Click **Send/Receive**. Under Settings For Group "All Accounts," clear the **Schedule An Automatic Send/Receive Every** check box. Also clear the **Perform An Automatic Send/Receive When Exiting** check box.

4. Click **Close** and then click **OK**.

SEND MESSAGES AT A CERTAIN TIME

1. Create the message and click the **Options** tab.

2. Click the Delay Delivery button in the More Options group. The Message Options dialog box appears.

3. Under Delivery Options, click **Do Not Deliver Before**.

Continued . . .

---

5. Click to select any desired conditions that limit which messages the rule applies to, and then click the link in the description panel (as you can see in Figure 3-12), which may display a dialog box to specify the exact criteria. Click **OK** and click **Next**.

6. Under Select Action(s), click **Defer Delivery By A *number* Of Minutes**.

7. In the description box, click the link for ***a number of*** minutes, and in the Deferred Delivery dialog box, type the total minutes (up to 120) that you want messages delayed, click **OK**, and click **Next**.

8. Click any exceptions, specify them in the description panel, click **OK** if necessary, and click **Next**.

9. Type a name for the rule, and click **Finish**. You are returned to the Rules And Alerts dialog box, which will now show your new rule, as shown in Figure 3-13.

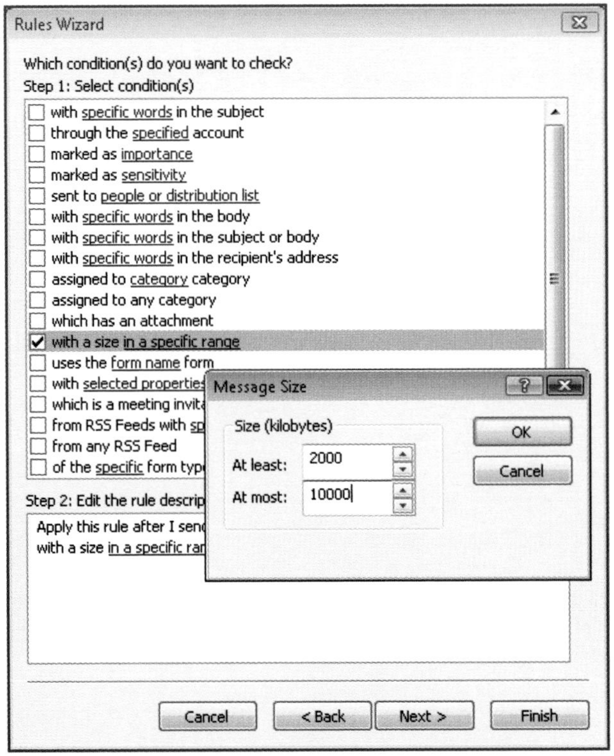

Figure 3-12: Outlook's rule-making feature has a large number of conditions that you can organize into rules.

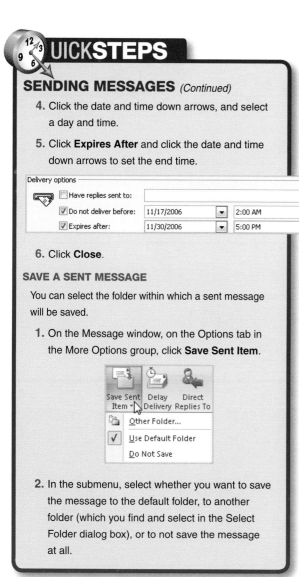

SENDING MESSAGES *(Continued)*

4. Click the date and time down arrows, and select a day and time.

5. Click **Expires After** and click the date and time down arrows to set the end time.

Delivery options			
☐ Have replies sent to:			
☑ Do not deliver before:	11/17/2006 ▼	2:00 AM ▼	
☑ Expires after:	11/30/2006 ▼	5:00 PM ▼	

6. Click **Close**.

SAVE A SENT MESSAGE

You can select the folder within which a sent message will be saved.

1. On the Message window, on the Options tab in the More Options group, click **Save Sent Item**.

Save Sent Item ▾   Delay Delivery   Direct Replies To

☐ <u>O</u>ther Folder...
✓ <u>U</u>se Default Folder
<u>D</u>o Not Save

2. In the submenu, select whether you want to save the message to the default folder, to another folder (which you find and select in the Select Folder dialog box), or to not save the message at all.

Rules and Alerts   [?] [□] [✕]

E-mail Rules | Manage Alerts

✉ <u>N</u>ew Rule...   C<u>h</u>ange Rule ▾   🗐 <u>C</u>opy...   ✕ <u>D</u>elete   ⬆ ⬇   <u>R</u>un Rules Now...   Op<u>t</u>ions

Rule (applied in the order shown)	Actions
☑ at least 2000 and at most 10000 kilobytes	🛠
☑ MBA	
☑ Clear categories on mail (recommended)	🛠

Rule description (click an underlined value to edit):

Apply this rule after I send the message
with a size <u>at least 2000 and at most 10000 kilobytes</u>
defer delivery by <u>10</u> minutes

☐ Enable rules on all RSS Feeds

[OK]   [Cancel]   [Apply]

*Figure 3-13: **The Rules And Alerts dialog box, opened from the Tools menu, provides for the creation and management of rules.***

Chapter 4

Managing Contacts

Taking a moment to create contacts can save you from typing—and later correcting—the whole e-mail address every time you send a message. Once you've entered a name as a contact, you can add business or personal information—like phone numbers, addresses, or an important anniversary—at your convenience. In this chapter you will learn how to create and maintain your contacts, as well as different ways to use contact information, including the new electronic business cards. If you are using Microsoft Office Outlook 2007 with Business Contact Manager, you'll find out how to set up Business Contact Manager to manage accounts and individual contacts.

Create Contacts

The kind of address books that fit in your pocket have spaces so tiny that phone numbers can trail down the margins. Lots of entries get scratched out and replaced because people move. Other listings are almost unreadable because family members now have multiple phone numbers.

Outlook Contacts provides a satisfying alternative, helping you keep everything straight and up-to-date, even information for acquaintances who don't have e-mail. You can create a new contact from within Outlook, from an e-mail message, from an electronic business card, and even from a public folder. After you open Outlook, click **Contacts** in the Navigation pane; your contacts will appear in the Folder pane of the Contacts window, as shown in Figure 4-1.

A name is all you need to save a contact. The Contact window, shown in Figure 4-2 and opened by clicking **New**, however, also provides a flexible layout that can store an immense amount of information, which you can use later for professional and social purposes. The ribbon provides for data entry and control in five different groups:

- **Actions** provide file management commands, including Save & Close, Delete, and Save & New. Click the **Save & New** down arrow, and click **New Contact From Same Company** to quickly add a new contact from the same company as the last entry you made.
- **Show** commands include all information about your new contact:
  - **General** contains basic information for identifying and getting in touch with the person (shown in Figure 4-2).
  - **Details** provides business and personal data.
  - **Activities**, a search tool, lists Outlook items (e-mail messages, notes, tasks, and so on) associated with the person.
  - **Certificates** imports and maintains a contact's digital ID. (See Chapter 3 for an explanation of digital certificates.)
  - **All Fields** lets you quickly look up the contents of a variety of fields completed for that contact.

NOTE

There is a significant distinction between the "Contacts window" (plural) that lists the people in a Contacts list (shown in Figure 4-1) and the "Contact window" (singular) where you enter and edit a contact (shown in Figure 4-2).

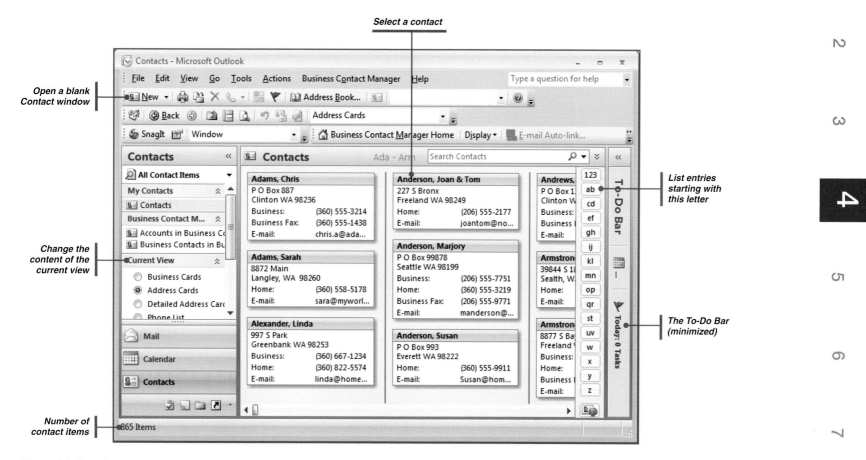

Select a contact

Open a blank Contact window

Change the content of the current view

Number of contact items

List entries starting with this letter

The To-Do Bar (minimized)

Figure 4-1: Creating contacts, which begins in the Contacts window, can save you a lot of time looking up birthdays and postal addresses.

- **Communicate** commands give you tools to telephone your new contact, be connected to the contact's Web site, and, with an Internet connection, see a map based on the contact's address.

- **Options** commands allow you to modify the contact's electronic business card, add a picture to your Contact dialog box, choose one of six categories that you can customize, create follow-up flags and reminders for this contact, mark an item as private, access the Address Book, and check names and e-mail addresses to ensure you have typed the information correctly.

- **Proofing** commands include tools for checking spelling, looking up synonyms, doing research, and translating.

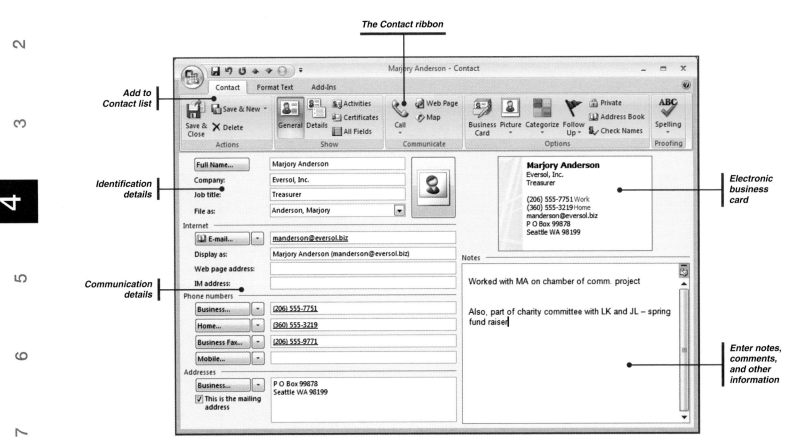

The Contact ribbon

Add to Contact list

Identification details

Communication details

Electronic business card

Enter notes, comments, and other information

Figure 4-2: The Contact window displays fields into which you can enter information for reaching a contact in a variety of ways.

Add a New Contact

To add a new contact to Outlook 2007 from the Contacts window:

1. Click **New** on the standard toolbar.

   –Or–

   Click **CTRL+N**.

   –Or–

   From anywhere in Outlook, click **CTRL+SHIFT+C**.

   In any case, the Contact window opens.

2. If you don't see the Contact window shown in Figure 4-2, in the Contact tab Show group, click **General**. This opens a number of fields that allow you to enter basic contact information. Use the **TAB** key to move through the fields, or click in the desired fields:

  a. Full Name   Click the button to enter separate fields for title, first, middle, and last name; or type a full name in the text box. This is all that is required to create a contact.

  b. Company   Type the name of the company or organization the person is affiliated with.

  c. Job Title   Type any title that you need to remember.

  d. File As   Click the down arrow beside the text box to select the combination of name and company that will dictate its place in the Contacts window. You need to enter the name and company first before you can access this information.

  e. Internet fields allow you to enter:

   I. E-mail   Click the down arrow to select up to three e-mail addresses to be associated with the person. For each one, type an address in the text box.

   II. Display As   Press **TAB** or drag to select the default display, and, if desired, type a new name. This is the field that determines how the person's name will appear in the To field in an e-mail message.

   III. Web Page Address   Type the person's URL.

   IV. IM Address   Type the Internet mail address that the person uses for instant messaging.

  f. Phone Numbers   Click the down arrow beside each button to select among 19 number types, and then click the label button to enter detailed information about it, or type the number in the text box.

  g. Addresses   Click the down arrow beside the button to select among three types of addresses, and then click the button to enter detailed information; or type the address in the text box. If you have more than one address for a contact, click **This Is The Mailing Address** to specify the address to be used for mail.

  h. Notes   Type any comments or notes in the large text box.

3. In the Contact tab Show group, click **Details** to display the Detail fields:

  a. Specific Office Information   Complete the text fields as needed.

  b. Personal Information   Type information, selecting from drop-down date boxes, as appropriate.

  c. Internet Free-Busy   Type an Internet address (URL) that has information about the person's schedule availability.

Birthday: Mon 11/13/2006

Anniversar

November 2006

Su Mo Tu We Th Fr Sa
29 30 31 1 2 3 4
5 6 7 8 9 10 11
12 **13** 14 15 16 17 18
19 20 21 22 23 24 25
26 27 28 29 30 1 2
3 4 5 6 7 8 9

Today   None

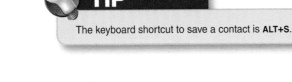
4. In the Contact tab Show group, click **Activities**, click the **Show** down arrow, and select an area from which to list items related to the person. The search can take quite a while before producing a list.

Show:	All Items ▼
	All Items
	Contacts
	E-mail
	Journal
	Notes
	Upcoming Tasks/Appointments

5. In the Contact tab Show group, click **Certificates**, and click **Import** to browse for the person's digital certificate (see Chapter 3). Click a certificate in the list, and click **Properties** to review details. Click **Set As Default** to use the selected certificate by default.

6. In the Contact tab Show group, click **All Fields**, select a type of field from the drop-down list, and review the contents of the associated fields.

7. In the Contact tab Actions group, click **Save & Close** when finished. If you need to enter another contact, click **Save & New** to open a new Contact window.

ADD A CONTACT FROM THE SAME COMPANY

If you already have a contact for someone in a company and you want to add another, Outlook helps you out by filling in the company information.

1. Open an existing contact from the company.

2. In the Contact tab Actions group, click the **Save & New** down arrow. Click **New Contact From Same Company**. A new Contact window opens with the company data displayed.

3. Fill in any other information, save the contact, and close the window.

Add Multiple Contacts

Outlook is designed to save steps when you are repeating the same task. When you are entering many contacts at once, you can tell Outlook to save the one you just created and start a new one, all at the same time.

dress books

Show Buttons on One Row

Add or Remove Buttons ▾   Standard   ▶

Customize...

Customize

Toolbars   Commands   Options

To add a command to a toolbar: select a category and drag the command out of this dialog box to a toolbar.

Categories:

File
Edit
View
Favorites
Go
Tools
Actions
Help
Macros
Menu Bar

Commands:

New Contact
New Contact from Same Company
New Distribution List
Send as Business Card
Send Full Contact   ▶
In Internet Format (vCard)

Modify Selection ▾   Rearrange Commands...

Close

ADD MULTIPLE COMPANY CONTACTS

You can add to the toolbar a command that, with one click, saves business contact information and opens another business contact form with the previous contact's corporate information included.

1. In the main Contacts window, click a contact, and then double-click a blank area to the right of the toolbars and outside of a toolbar.

–Or–

Click the right end of a toolbar, choose **Add Or Remove Buttons**, and click **Customize**. The Customize dialog box appears.

2. Click the **Commands** tab, and click **Actions** in the Categories list.

3. Scroll to locate **New Contact From Same Company**, and drag it to a toolbar.

4. Right-click **New Contact From Same Company**, click **Begin A Group** to insert a separation bar in the toolbar, and click **Close** in the Customize dialog box.

5. Complete the form for the new contact. Then, in the Contact tab Actions group, click the **Save & New** down arrow, and then click **New Contact From Same Company**. The contact is saved, and a new Contact window opens with the company information already completed.

6. Create the remaining contacts.

7. Click **Save & Close** when finished.

Copy Contacts from E-mail

When you copy an address in the From or Cc e-mail message fields, the Contact window opens with the name and e-mail address fields filled in.

1. Open an e-mail message you have received.

2. Right-click the name in the message window, and click **Add To Outlook Contacts**. Fill in any additional information you want.

3. Click **Save & Close**. The name and e-mail address are added to your contacts.

Schedule a Meeting...
Send Mail
Additional Actions
Send Options...
Add to Outlook Contacts
Look up Outlook Contact...
Outlook Properties
Copy

QUICKSTEPS

EDITING CONTACTS

Once you have created a contact, you can change the information as much as you want. Just open the contact and change or enter new information. The following tasks all begin with an open Contact window and end with clicking **Save & Close**.

ADD A PICTURE

To insert an image in your electronic business card:

1. In the Contact tab Options group, click **Business Card** to open the Edit Business Card dialog box.

2. Click **Change** in the Image field.

3. Locate the photo file on your computer, and double-click the image to select it.

4. Click **OK**.

Edit Business Card

Linda Bakerman
Badson Company
Treasurer

(360) 555-2297 Work
(360) 555-3322 Home
lbakerman@badson.biz
P O Box 09877
Greenbank WA 98253-0987

Card Design
Layout: Image Left
Background:
Image: Change...
Image Area: 16%
Image Align: Fit to Edge

Fields
Full Name
Company
Job Title
Blank Line
Business Phone

Edit
A⁺ A⁻ **B** *I* U
Linda Bakerman
Label: No Label

Continued . . .

CREATE CONTACTS BY DRAGGING

Any Outlook item, like an e-mail message, turns into a contact if you drag it onto the Contacts view bar in the Navigation pane. This is especially useful with important e-mail messages whose senders you need in your contacts. The name and e-mail address go into their respective fields, and the important message displays in the Contact window comments text box. You'll need to save and close the Contact window in order to save the contact.

CREATE A CONTACT FROM AN ELECTRONIC BUSINESS CARD

Electronic business cards pack contact information into a small, easy-to-share package. If another Outlook user sends you an electronic business card attached to an e-mail message, you can automatically create a new contact when you save the message.

1. Open the e-mail message.

2. Double-click the electronic business card attachment. The Contact window opens.

3. Click **Save & Close**.

4. If you already have a contact with the same name, Outlook will display the Duplicate Contact Detected dialog box:

    - Click **Add New Contact** if you want a duplicate contact, which will include the electronic business card.

    - Click **Update Information Of Selected Contact**, and then double-click the contact you want to update. The Contact window will open. Make the necessary changes, and save the contact information.

Create a Distribution List

Avoid entering the address for each member of a group to which you send messages. Instead, create and name a distribution list for the group, as shown in Figure 4-4. It will appear as an entry of its own in your Contacts list, so sending a message to the group will send a message to each member. Review Chapter 3 to see how to send e-mail messages using a distribution list.

QUICKSTEPS

EDITING CONTACTS *(Continued)*

ADD A FILE

To place a copy of a photo, document, spreadsheet, or any other kind of file in the contact:

1. Click inside the **Notes** section of the Contact window.

2. In the Insert tab Include group, click **Attach File**. The Insert File dialog box will appear.

3. Select the file you want to attach by double-clicking the file name. A link to the file is displayed in the Notes section, as shown in Figure 4-3.

4. Double-click the file to open it.

ADD AN ITEM

You can place a copy of an Outlook item (e-mail message, task, appointment, and so on) in the contact.

1. Open the contact and in the Insert tab Include group, click **Attach Item**. The Insert Item dialog box appears.

2. Select the item you want to include with your contact. You may insert:

   - Text only
   - An attachment
   - A shortcut to the item

3. When you are done, click **OK**.

1. In the main Contacts window, on the standard toolbar, click the **New** down arrow, and select **Distribution List**. The Distribution List window opens.

2. Type a name for the list in the Name text box. In the Distribution List tab Members group, click **Select Members** to display your current Contacts list.

3. Double-click each name to include it in your distribution list.

4. Click **OK** at the bottom of the Select Members window when you have chosen all the names you want in your list.

5. If you need to add a name that is not in your Contacts list, in the Distribution List tab Members group, click **Add New** to display the Add New Member dialog box.

6. Click in the **Display Name** text box, and type the name you want displayed in your distribution list.

7. Click in the **E-mail Address** text box, and type the e-mail address for this list member.

8. Click **Add To Contacts** if you want to add this person to your Contacts list.

Figure 4-3: You can attach any type of file in your Contact window.

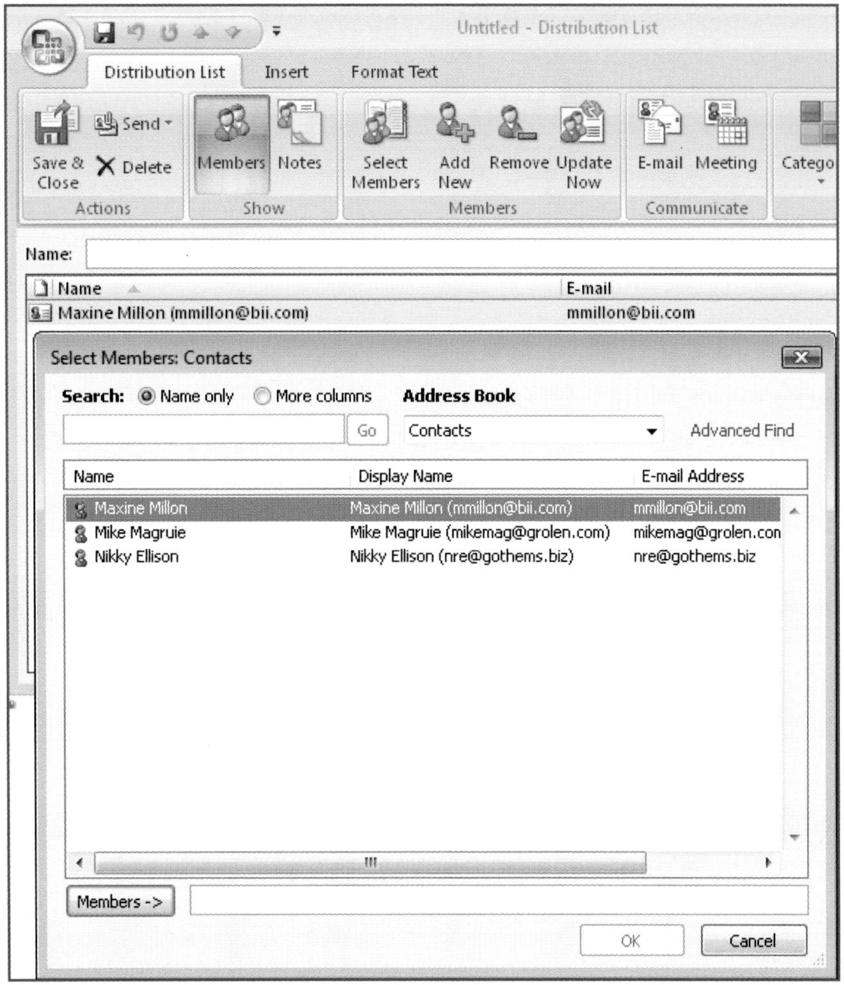

Figure 4-4: Distribution lists ensure that your e-mail message goes to every member of the group.

9. Click **OK** to close the dialog box.

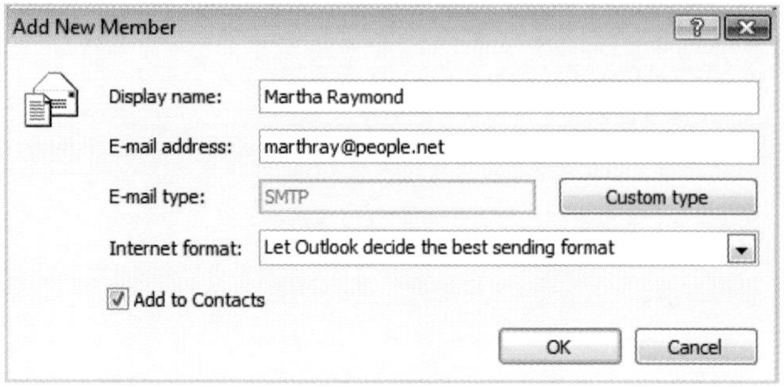

10. You may add notes to your distribution list. In the Distribution List tab Show group, click **Notes** to display the Notes window. Type any notes that pertain to this distribution list.

11. In the Distribution List tab Actions group, click **Save & Close** to save your new list.

Remove a Name from a Distribution List

You can count on change affecting the people in your list. To keep your messages going to the right places, you can add or remove members and update current information directly from your Address Book.

1. To remove a name, open the Contacts window, and locate the distribution list. Double-click the list to open it.

2. In the Distribution List tab Show group, click **Members** to display the list of members, if it isn't already displayed.

3. Click the member name you want to remove. In the Members group, click **Remove**. The name is removed from your distribution list. This does not remove the name from your Contacts list, only from the distribution list.

4. In the **Actions** group, click **Save & Close** to save your changes.

TIP

When you send e-mail to a distribution list, you don't have to let the members see who's on it—enter the name of the list into the Bcc field. To display the Bcc field from the e-mail message window, in the Options tab Fields group, select **Show Bcc**.

NOTE

You can create a new distribution list from anywhere in Outlook 2007. Press **CTRL+SHIFT+L** to open a new Distribution List window.

CATEGORIZE YOUR DISTRIBUTION LIST

If you use color categories to organize Outlook 2007, you can easily assign one or more to your distribution list.

1. To assign one color category to your distribution list, open the Contacts window, and locate the distribution list. Double-click the list to open it.

2. In the Distribution List tab Options group, click **Categorize** to display the Categorize menu.

3. Click the category you want. The category is displayed above the name of your distribution list. The menu closes automatically.

4. To assign more than one color category, follow steps 1–3, except click **All Categories** at the bottom of the Categorize menu. The Color Categories dialog box appears.

5. Click the check boxes for the categories you want.

6. Click **OK** to close the dialog box and return to your distribution list. All of the color categories you chose appear above the name of your distribution list.

7. In the Distribution List tab Actions group, click **Save & Close** to close the Distribution List window.

Use Contacts

Once you enter a contact, you can do a lot with it besides fill in e-mail addresses quickly and accurately—though that alone makes it worth far more than any effort involved. You can share contact information, sort contacts, flag them for future action, use an automated telephone dialer built into the contact, and even create a postal service letter using the contact.

Add Contacts to E-mail

The information you have for a contact may be useful to someone else. Whether it's a business associate or a relative, sharing the information by way of e-mail prevents typos, copying errors, and tedium. You can send the contact as an item—both in text and as an attachment—or as an electronic business card, which you can send to other Outlook users, or you can send a vCard (.vcf file) to those who don't use Outlook. No matter how you send it, the recipient treats the contact like any other attached file.

ADD A CONTACT TO E-MAIL

You can include an Outlook contact as an attachment to an e-mail message, as plain text, or as an electronic business card.

Include

To include a contact with your e-mail as an attachment or as plain text:

1. In the e-mail message window, in the Insert tab Include group, click **Attach Item**.
2. The Insert Item dialog box will appear. Click **Contacts** and select the contact you want to include.
3. Click **Attachment** to send the information as an attachment.

    –Or–

    Click **Text Only** to send the information as plain text. All of the contact's information will appear in the body of the e-mail message.
4. Click **OK** to close the Insert Item dialog box.

To include a contact as an electronic business card:

1. In the e-mail message window, in the Insert tab Include group, click **Business Card**.
2. Click **Other Business Cards** to display the Insert Business Card dialog box.
3. Click the contact name you want to include. The electronic business card will appear in the body of the e-mail message.
4. Click **OK** to close the dialog box.

If you choose to send your contact as an electronic business card, the way your e-mail recipient sees it depends on his or her computer system:

- If your recipient uses Outlook 2007, she will see the card exactly as you see it, with all of its graphics and color. She may save the information on the card by right-clicking it and saving it to her Contacts list.

- If the recipient uses an e-mail application that views e-mail as HTML (Hypertext Markup Language), he will see the electronic business card as an image. The same recipient receives the information in the form of a .vcf file that is attached to the e-mail. He can save the contact information to his Address Book from that .vcf file.

Insert Business Card ? ✕

Look in: Contacts ▼

🗋	🖉	Filed As /	Job Title	Company
	📇	Anderson, Marjory	Treasurer	Eversol, Inc.
	📇	Anderson, Susan		Boeing
	📇	Andrews, Gerry	Purchasing Man...	Middleton Mfg. ...
	📇	Armstrong, Jennifer		
	📇	Armstrong-Cavern, Carolee	Administrative A...	Mitchell, Smith ...
	📇	Baker, Matthew	President	Baker Incorporat...
	📇	Bakerman, Linda	Treasurer	Badson Company

Business Card Preview

Sarah Adams

(360) 558-5178 Home
sara@myworld.com

8872 Main
Langley, WA 98260

OK   Cancel

• If the recipient uses a plain-text e-mail viewer, she will not see the graphic electronic business card. Instead, the recipient will receive an attached .vcf file from which the information can be saved.

SEND A DISTRIBUTION LIST

You can send a distribution list through e-mail.

Attached: Mike Magruie.vcf (3 KB)

1. Open the Contacts window, and locate and select the distribution list you want to send.

2. Press **CTRL+F**. This opens an e-mail message window. The distribution list appears as an attachment.

3. Create and send the message as usual.

Arrange Contacts

You probably create contacts for different reasons, to serve various purposes, with some more important than others. Therefore, Outlook provides different ways for you to organize and look at them.

CATEGORIZE A CONTACT

Like e-mail messages and all other Outlook items, contacts can be sorted into categories. When you create a new contact, you might want to assign the person to a category right away.

1. With the new Contact window open, in the Contact tab Options group, click **Categorize**.

2. Click the category you want. The menu will close and the Rename Category dialog box will appear. Type a new category name, if you want one, select a color, and click **Yes**. The chosen category displays at the top of the Contact window.

Rename Category

This is the first time you have used "Purple Category." Do you want to rename it?

Name: Purple Category

Color: ▾ Shortcut Key: (None) ▾

Yes   No

3. Click **Save & Close** to close the Contact window.

1 2 3 4 5 6 7 8 9 10

QUICKSTEPS

WORKING WITH COLOR CATEGORIES

Outlook 2007 color categories give you a way to organize your contacts and other items. You can assign a color category not just to a contact, but also to e-mail messages, calendar items, and so forth. There are 25 colors you can use to designate a category, including the six standard colors that are displayed. Only the 10 most recently viewed color categories are displayed on the Categorize menu, but you can see the rest by clicking **All Categories** from the Categorize menu.

CREATE A NEW COLOR CATEGORY

To create a new color category:

1. In the Contacts window, click **Actions** on the menu bar.

2. Click **Categories** and then click **All Categories** to display the Color Categories dialog box.

3. Click **New**. The Add New Category dialog box appears:

   a. Enter the name you want for this category.

   b. Click the **Color** down arrow, and click a color from the palette. You can use any of the 25 colors.

   c. Click the **Shortcut Key** down arrow, and click a keyboard shortcut. You have 11 choices of keyboard shortcut keys.

   d. Choose one of the keyboard shortcuts displayed, or leave the default selection (None).

Continued . . .

CATEGORIZE MULTIPLE CONTACTS

After you have created a lot of contacts, you might want to group them into their respective categories.

1. In the Contacts window, select the contacts you wish to place in a specific category.

2. Right-click any of the selected contacts to open a menu.

3. Click **Categorize** and select the color category into which you want them grouped.

4. The menu closes automatically and the color category is added to your contact grouping.

CHANGE THE VIEW OF CONTACTS

Just as you can select and customize the view of other parts of Outlook, you can choose from eight standard views of the Contacts window, and you can change the view to suit your needs. If you do not see the eight views, click the two downward arrows to the right of Current View on the Navigation pane:

- **Business Cards** shows the electronic business cards for each contact.

- **Address Cards** shows names, e-mail addresses, phone numbers, and mailing addresses.

- **Detailed Address Cards**, in addition to showing the information in Address Cards view, presents a condensed version of all the information for the contact.

- **Phone List** gives each contact one line in a table, with headings you can click to use for sorting the table.

- **By Category** clusters contacts that have been assigned to categories.

- **By Company** groups contacts for which companies have been entered.

- **By Location** clusters contacts for which a country or region has been entered.

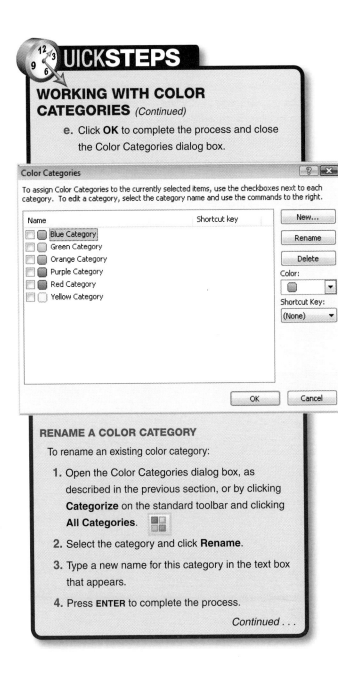

WORKING WITH COLOR CATEGORIES *(Continued)*

e. Click **OK** to complete the process and close the Color Categories dialog box.

Color Categories

To assign Color Categories to the currently selected items, use the checkboxes next to each category. To edit a category, select the category name and use the commands to the right.

Name	Shortcut key
☐ ⬤ Blue Category	
☐ ⬤ Green Category	
☐ ⬤ Orange Category	
☐ ⬤ Purple Category	
☐ ⬤ Red Category	
☐ ◯ Yellow Category	

New...
Rename
Delete

Color:
⬛ ▼

Shortcut Key:
(None) ▼

OK   Cancel

RENAME A COLOR CATEGORY

To rename an existing color category:

1. Open the Color Categories dialog box, as described in the previous section, or by clicking **Categorize** on the standard toolbar and clicking **All Categories**.

2. Select the category and click **Rename**.

3. Type a new name for this category in the text box that appears.

4. Press **ENTER** to complete the process.

Continued . . .

- **Outlook Data Files** are the storage files that Outlook 2007 creates from items you've saved. There are two types of data files:

    - **Personal Folders (.pst)** files are the default type of data that is used for standard e-mail. This is the standard format for most home users of Microsoft Outlook.

    - **Offline Folders (.ost)** files are used only with Microsoft Exchange. Microsoft Exchange is used primarily by larger organizations.

It's easy to try the various views to find which one works best for you and then to customize that view.

1. Click a current view option in the Navigation pane.

    –Or–

2. Click the **View** menu, click **Current View**, and click a current view.

3. Open the Customize View dialog box by clicking the **View** menu, clicking **Current View**, and clicking **Customize Current View**.

Customize View: Phone List

Description

Fields...	Icon, Attachment, Full Name, Company, File As, Business P...
Group By...	None
Sort...	File As (ascending)
Filter...	Off
Other Settings...	Fonts and other Table View settings
Automatic Formatting...	User defined fonts on each message
Format Columns...	Specify the display formats for each field

Reset Current View   OK   Cancel

4. Each view has its own dialog box, in which you can click a button to edit an element of the view. The availability of each element depends on the view with which you

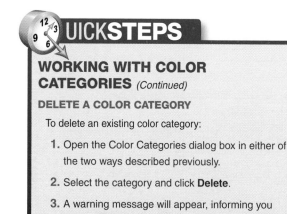

QUICKSTEPS

WORKING WITH COLOR CATEGORIES (Continued)

DELETE A COLOR CATEGORY

To delete an existing color category:

1. Open the Color Categories dialog box in either of the two ways described previously.

2. Select the category and click **Delete**.

3. A warning message will appear, informing you that deleting the category removes it from your list but does not affect previously categorized items.

4. Click **Yes** to delete the category or click **No** to leave it on the list.

are working. In each element, click OK to close the element's dialog box and save any changes. The possible elements are:

- **Fields** displays available fields on the left side of the Show Fields dialog box and fields that are actually used on the right. The fields displayed on the right are in the order in which they appear in the view you selected.

- **Group By** allows you to choose how your items are grouped.

- **Sort** alphabetically orders the contents. If Group By is also used Sort will provide a secondary ordering within the groups.

- **Filter** lets you filter by words, categories, and other advanced options.

- **Other Settings** control how the data looks, such as the font style and size.

- **Automatic Formatting** lets you set rules for the selected view.

- **Format Columns** lets you change the format and labels of columns within a view.

SORT CONTACTS BY FIELDS OR COLUMNS

You can change how your contacts are displayed when working with one of the list views.

1. From your Outlook window, click **Contacts** in the Navigation pane. Your Contacts list is displayed on the right side of the Contacts window.

2. In the Navigation pane, choose which current view you want from the five choices that display as a list. These are:
   - Phone List
   - By Category
   - By Company
   - By Location
   - Outlook Data Files

3. In the Contacts window, click the column name by which you want to sort.

4. The default is to sort by lowest number to highest number and then by A to Z. Click the column name a second time to reverse the sort order from highest number to lowest number and then by Z to A.

REMOVE A SORT ORDER

To remove a sort order from a selected view:

1. Click the **View** menu, click **Arrange By**, and click **Custom** to display the Customize View dialog box.

2. Click **Reset Current View** to return to the original settings, and click **OK** to close the dialog box.

3. Click **Sort** to open the Sort dialog box:
   a. Click the **Sort Items By** down arrow to display a list of sort choices.
   b. Choose **File As** in the first box and **(none)** in each of the other three boxes.
   c. Click **OK** to close the Sort dialog box.

4. Click **OK** to close the Customize View dialog box.

Find a Contact

While you may use the Address Book that appears in the new message window for e-mail messages, you need to know how to find a contact for the other information it contains. The method you use will probably depend on how

5 Items

many contacts you have and the views you use. As with your e-mail items, the number of contacts you have in your Contacts folder is displayed on the lower-left corner of the Contacts window.

USE THE SCROLL BAR

If you have fewer than 50 contacts, scrolling will probably work just fine. With the Address Cards view selected in the Navigation pane, the contacts move vertically when you drag the scroll button or click the scroll bar or scroll arrows. Other views may have a horizontal scroll bar, which works in the same way as the vertical scroll bar.

USE THE FIND TOOL

With the Find tool, you don't have to be sure what the contact's whole name is to start sifting through your contacts. This can be comforting when you are talking about hundreds of contacts.

Click in the **Find A Contact** text box in the standard toolbar. This field has "Search Address Books" in it. Type as much of the name as needed to get the contact you want, and press ENTER. If there are several contacts with that name, the Choose Contact dialog box will appear. Double-click the contact you want to open that person's Contact window.

TIP

If you have searched for this contact before, click the down arrow in the Search Address Books field. All previously searched names will appear, and you can click the name you want.

USE THE ALPHABETIC INDEX TO FIND A CONTACT

If you have a hundred or so contacts and the current view is one of the cards views, you'll find the alphabet bar handy. The alphabet bar searches by the File As name. To use the alphabet bar:

1. In the Contacts window, click a letter button on the alphabet bar to display the first name in your list beginning with that letter.

2. Use either the horizontal or vertical scroll bar (depending on the view you are in) to scroll to the name you want to use.

NOTE

By default, the Instant Search feature can display up to 10 of your recent searches. Click the down arrow by the Instant Search box, and click **Recent Searches**. Click the search you want to perform again.

UNDERSTANDING INSTANT SEARCH

Outlook 2007 provides Instant Search to help you find any information, whether it is in your mail folder, your contacts, or any other folder. This utility uses the same technology as the Windows Desktop Search utility. The Instant Search box appears in the same location in all parts of Outlook—in the title bar of the list pane, as you saw in the Contacts window—and it works the same.

If you are using Windows XP and have not already installed the Windows Desktop Search utility, you will be prompted to download and install it the first time you open Outlook 2007. Once you install the program, you must restart your computer. If you are using Windows Vista, the feature is already installed and you will see no prompts—Instant Search is automatically enabled.

If you are using Windows XP, you can change your settings so that the prompt does not appear.

1. In the Outlook window, click the **Tools** menu, and click **Options**.

2. Click the **Other** tab, and then click **Advanced Options**.

3. Under General Settings, clear the **Show Prompts To Enable Instant Search** check box. This check box does not appear if you are running Windows Vista or if you have already installed the Windows Desktop Search utility in Windows XP.

4. Click **OK** to close the dialog box.

TIP

When you are finished using the results of a search and want to redisplay all of your contacts, click **Contacts** in the Navigation pane.

USE SEARCH CONTACTS

You can use the Search Contacts box to search for any information that is included in your Contacts list. For example, to find all of your contacts in a certain city:

1. In the Contacts window, click in the **Search Contacts** box at the top of the Contacts list.

2. Type the name of the city.

3. All of the contacts that meet the criteria you typed will immediately display without you needing to press **ENTER**.

4. To clear the search, click **X**.

REFINE YOUR SEARCH

You can also add more criteria to your search.

1. Click the two down arrows to the right of the Instant Search box to display commonly used fields.

2. Click **Add Criteria** to display even more fields.

3. Enter the information for which you want to search in one or more of the field boxes. Your information appears. Again, by default, you do not need to press **ENTER**.

Print Contact Information

Outlook lets you print contacts to fit a variety of standard organizers, as well as a standard list.

1. Sort your contacts, as described in "Arrange Contacts" elsewhere in this chapter, so that you print only the group you want in the order you want.

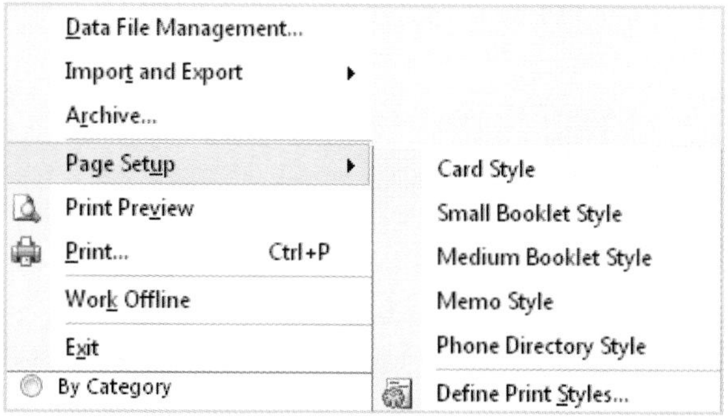

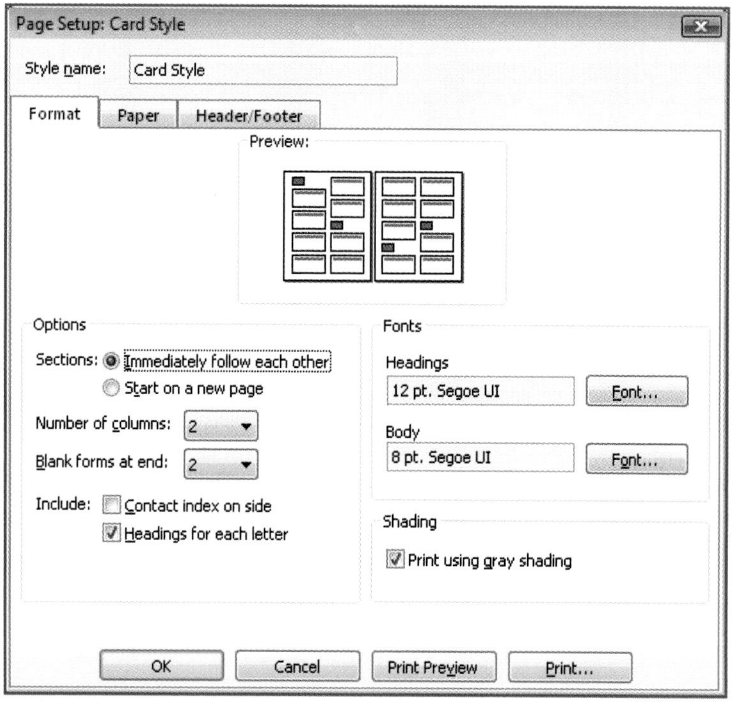

Data File Management...
Import and Export ▸
Archive...
Page Setup ▸   Card Style
Print Preview   Small Booklet Style
Print...   Ctrl+P   Medium Booklet Style
Work Offline   Memo Style
Exit   Phone Directory Style
By Category   Define Print Styles...

Page Setup: Card Style

Style name: Card Style

| Format | Paper | Header/Footer |

Preview:

Options

Sections: ● Immediately follow each other
      ○ Start on a new page

Number of columns: 2 ▾

Blank forms at end: 2 ▾

Include: ☐ Contact index on side
       ☑ Headings for each letter

Fonts

Headings
12 pt. Segoe UI   [Font...]

Body
8 pt. Segoe UI   [Font...]

Shading

☑ Print using gray shading

[OK]   [Cancel]   [Print Preview]   [Print...]

Figure 4-5: Page Setup allows you to determine exactly how your finished product will look.

2. On the menu bar, click **File** and then click **Page Setup** to determine how your list will print.

3. Choose the view option you want to use. Not all options are available in every view. The options are:

   a. **Card Style** prints your selected items on the selected paper size, grouped with each contact immediately following the one before it.

   b. **Small Booklet Style** prints your list in a ⅛-sheet booklet format.

   c. **Medium Booklet Style** prints in a ¼-sheet booklet form.

   d. **Memo Style** prints only one contact.

   e. **Phone Directory Style** prints on a 8½ x 11-inch sheet of paper

   f. **Table Style** prints each chosen record in a columnar style.

4. Click **Format** to choose your options and font style, as shown in Figure 4-5.

5. Click **Paper** to:

   ● Choose the paper size. The default is letter-size paper, 8½ x 11 inches.

   ● Select the page size. The default depends on the style you have selected.

   ● Set the margins for your printed list.

   ● Define the orientation: Portrait or Landscape.

6. Click **Header/Footer** to:

   a. Create a header and set its font.

   b. Click in the left, center, or right boxes under Header.

   c. Type your header.

   d. Use the TAB key to move from box to box.

   e. Create a footer in the same way.

   f. To delete the page number that appears on each page of your list by default, click the center Footer box, highlight **[Page #]**, and press DELETE. See Figure 4-6 for an example.

7. Click **Print Preview** to see how your list will appear when printed.

8. When you are satisfied with all of the settings, click **Print** and then click **OK** to print.

Figure 4-6: A header and footer make the pages look like they were professionally printed, and they can help you track the age of the data.

PRINT A SINGLE CONTACT

1. From the Contacts window, double-click a contact to open the Contact window.

2. At the top of the Contact window, click the **Office Button**. The Office menu appears.

3. Click **Print** to open the Print dialog box.

4. Review the settings, make any changes you want, and click **OK** to print the information.

   –Or–

   Click **Preview** if you want to see how the information will print.

5. From the Print Preview window, click **Print** and then click **OK** to print the information.

Phone a Contact

If your computer is sharing a line with a telephone, you can have Outlook dial your contacts. This means that the modem is connected to a regular voice line. If you use e-mail, then the modem is probably set up for automatic phone dialing. Give it a try and find out.

1. Make sure you are not online if you have a dial-up connection.

2. In the Contacts window, double-click a contact for whom you have entered a phone number. From the Contact tab Communicate group, click the **Call** down arrow.

3. Click a phone number. The New Call dialog box appears with the selected phone number in the Number field.

4. Click **Start Call** to dial the number. The Call Status dialog box appears. You are directed to lift the receiver and click **Talk**.

Dialing Options

Settings for speed dialing

Name | Phone number

[ ] [▼]   Add

Name	Number
Jessica Baldwin	(605) 555-1234
Bernie Round	(605) 555-8732

Delete

Settings for phone number formatting and dialing

[ ] Automatically add country/region code to local phone numbers

Dialing Properties...

Connect using line

Actiontec MD56ORD V92 MDC Modem [▼]   Line Properties...

OK   Cancel

5. A message appears if Outlook cannot locate a dial tone. Click **OK** to close the message box.

6. When you are finished with your call, hang up, click **End Call**, and click **Close**.

USE SPEED DIALING

For impatient people, there's speed dialing. Of course, you first need to enter the numbers.

1. From your Contacts window, double-click any contact to open the Contact window.

2. In the Contact tab Communicate group, click the **Call** button.

3. In the New Call dialog box, click **Dialing Options** to open the Dialing Options dialog box.

4. Type a name and phone number in the text boxes.

5. Click **Add** to add this number to the speed dialing settings.

6. Enter any additional information required.

7. Click **OK** and click **Close**.

8. To place a speed dial call, click the **Call** down arrow to display the Call menu.

9. Click **Speed Dial** and choose a number. The New Call dialog box appears.

Call ▼

Business: (605) 555-1234
Home: (605) 555-9876
Redial ▶
Speed Dial ▶   Jessica Baldwin: (605) 555-1234
New Call...   Bernie Round: (605) 555-8732

10. Proceed as described earlier in "Phone a Contact."

See a Map for a Contact's Address

If you have an Internet connection, you can use Outlook 2007 to obtain a map and get directions to an address you have recorded in your list of contacts. To see a map:

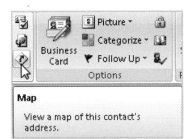

1. Open the Contact window for your selected contact.

2. Click the **Addresses** down arrow, and select the address you want from the menu that appears.

3. In the Contact tab Communicate group, click **Map**.

4. A map will display, as seen in Figure 4-7.

5. Click **See This Location In Bird's Eye View** to see the selected address as if you were in a helicopter flying over it.

6. Click **Close** to close the map and return to your Contact window.

GET DRIVING DIRECTIONS TO A CONTACT'S LOCATION

On the map of the location:

1. Type the address from which you want to start into the **Start** field.

2. Use the TAB key to move to the **End** field.

Figure 4-7: Using the Internet, Outlook 2007 gives you a utility to get directions to any address in your Contacts list.

Driving directions

Clear   Reverse   E-mail   Print ▼

Start

Mukilteo-Clinton Ferry (ferry terminal), Washington, United States

End

33rd Ave S, Seattle, WA 98188, United States

◉ Shortest time
○ Shortest distance

    Get directions

Route summary

Start: Mukilteo-Clinton Ferry (ferry terminal), Washington, United States

End: 33rd Ave S, Seattle, WA 98188, United States

Total distance: 40.2 mi
Estimated time: 1 Hour, 16 Minutes

Driving directions

Depart on SR-525 (East) (0.1 mi)

❶ *Check timetable* Take Mukilteo-Clinton Ferry (South-East)

❷ Take SR-525 [Mukilteo Speedway] (South) (5.6 mi)

❸ Keep STRAIGHT onto SR-525 (2.9 mi)

Miles | Kilometers

Welcome   ×

© 2006 Microsoft Corporation   Privacy

Figure 4-8: Driving directions to and from any point are parts of the Map utility in Outlook 2007.

3. Type the address where you want the directions to end.

4. Click either **Shortest Time** or **Shortest Distance**, depending on which option you want.

5. Click **Get Directions**. A driving map appears with the driving directions in text on the left side of the map, as shown in Figure 4-8.

6. Click **Print** to print the information:

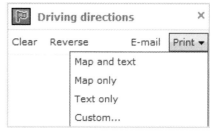

- Click **Map And Text** to print both.
- Click **Map Only** to print just the map.
- Click **Text Only** to print just the driving directions.
- Click **Custom** to open the Custom Print Options window, where you can choose the map size and style.
- Click **Print** from the Custom Print Options dialog box.

7. Click **Close** to close the map and return to Outlook.

Use Business Contact Manager

Several versions of Microsoft Office 2007 include a program called Business Contact Manager, which contains a number of tools to help you make your business a success. With this program you can:

- Create account records for companies with whom you do business.

- Create separate business contacts for people with whom you do business and link these business contacts with your account records.

- Track new opportunities that may turn into customers or vendors.

- Create business projects, which are made up of one or more project tasks. You can link a business project with accounts, business contacts, and its related project tasks. Project tasks are any undertakings that you want to track from start to finish, and are discussed in Chapter 6.

- Create marketing campaigns to build more profits.

- Link historical items, such as e-mail messages, appointments, or tasks, with business contacts.

To save time in Outlook 2007, you can use keyboard shortcuts. A keyboard shortcut usually requires that you hold down one or two keys and then press another. Some of the most popular contact related shortcuts in Outlook are shown in the following table.

SHORTCUT	ACTION PERFORMED
CTRL+N	Creates a new contact from anywhere in Contacts
CTRL+SHIFT+C	Creates a new contact from anywhere else in Outlook 2007
ALT+S	Saves and closes a contact
CTRL+D	Deletes a contact
CTRL+1	Switches to your Mail folder
CTRL+SHIFT+L	Creates a new distribution list (Inside a mail message, this shortcut produces a bullet)

Set Up Business Contact Manager

Business Contact Manager is not installed by default. To install it:

1. Insert the CD with Business Contact Manager on it. The Startup window will open. (If it does not, click **Start**, click **Computer**, and double-click the drive letter for your CD.)

2. When you next start Outlook 2007, the Business Contacts Manager Startup wizard appears. Click one of the Startup options, and click **Next**.

3. Follow the directions given by the Startup wizard, clicking **Next** as needed. This will create a new database and provide an introduction to Business Contacts Manager. Click **Finish**.

A new Business Contact Manager toolbar appears. Also, there is a Business Contact Manager menu item on the menu bar between Actions and Help.

Create Contact Records

You can generate contact records for both the account and representatives of the organization. The *account* is the company or organization you do—or plan to do—business with, regardless if they are your customer or you are their customer (like a supplier). Within the account, you maintain individual contacts.

ADD AN ACCOUNT

1. From the Outlook window, click **Contacts** in the Navigation pane. Click **Accounts In Business Contact Manager** in the Navigation pane under Business Contact Manager.

2. On the standard toolbar, click **New** or simply double-click in the Accounts window. A blank account window opens. If you don't see the Account window, as shown in Figure 4-9, in the Account tab Show group, click **General**.

3. Click in the **Account Name** text box, and type the name you want to enter.

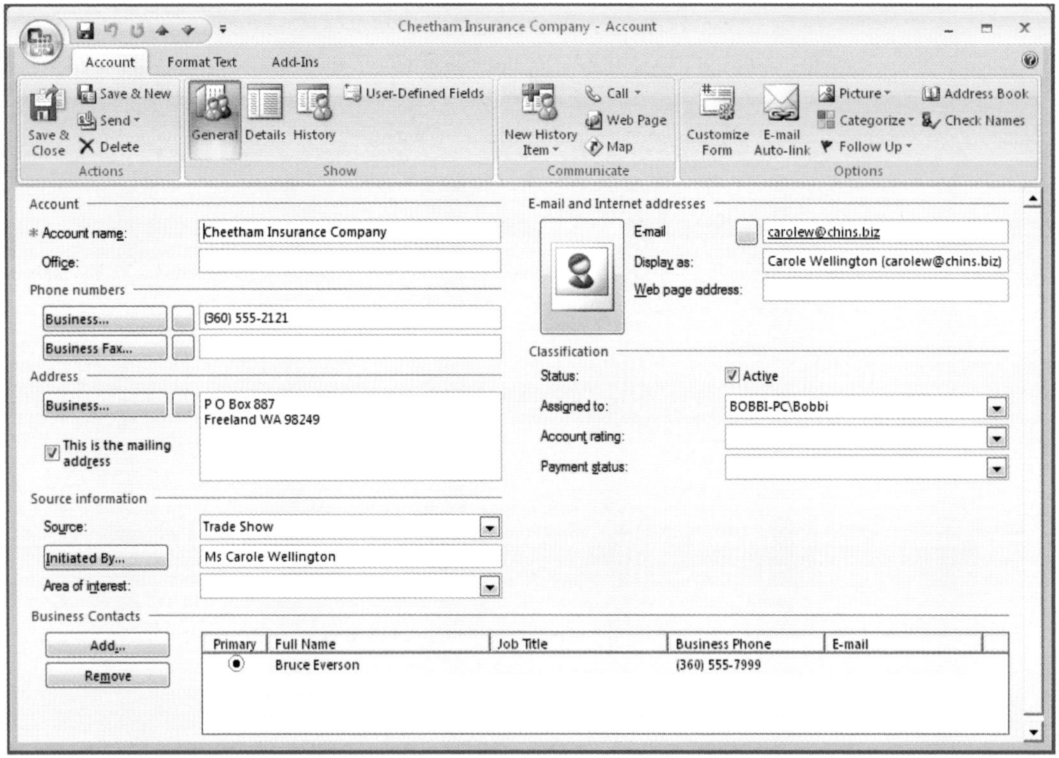

Figure 4-9: A new account in Business Contact Manager can be linked to other business contacts in your list.

4. Continue through the window, pressing **TAB** to enter any additional information you currently possess, as shown in Figure 4-9.

5. In the Account tab Show group, click **Details** to enter information such as an account number, the type of business, or preferred method of communication.

6. In the Account tab Show group, click **History** to enter any communication history items you want attached to this account, like telephone logs and meeting notes.

7. In the Actions group, click **Save & Close** to save your record.

CREATE INDIVIDUAL BUSINESS CONTACTS

Business contact records have similar information to other contact records. To create one:

1. Click **Business Contacts In Business Contact Manager** in the Navigation pane under Business Contact Manager.

2. On the standard toolbar, click **New** to open a new Business Contact window.

   –Or–

   Double-click within the Business Contact window to open a new Business Contact window.

3. Type the name in the **Full Name** field. This is the only information needed to save the new business contact.

4. Continue through the window, entering any information you have about this business contact.

5. To link this business contact with an account, click **Account** to open the Select An Account To Link To This Business Contact dialog box.

6. If the name appears in the Account Name list, double-click the name you want linked to this business contact. This name will appear in the Link To field.

7. If you do not see the account name with which you want this business contact linked, click **New** in the dialog box to open a new Account window and add the new account name.

8. Click **OK** to close the Select An Account dialog box.

9. To save the record, in the Actions group, click **Save & Close**.

CHANGE OR REMOVE ACCOUNT RECORDS

You can change or delete any records in Business Contact Manager in the same way you do in any Outlook Contact window.

To change a record:

1. Click either **Accounts** or **Business Contacts** in the Navigation pane.

2. Double-click the account or contact you want to change to open its window.

3. Make any necessary changes.

4. In the Actions group, click **Save & Close**.

To remove a record:

1. Click either **Accounts** or **Business Contacts** in the Navigation pane.

2. Right-click the record you want to delete.

3. In the context menu that appears, click **Delete**.

Prepare Business Contact Manager Reports

The Business Contact Manager reports that you can generate with two clicks of the mouse look like you put a lot more into them. To generate a report:

1. Click the **Business Contact Manager** menu, and click **Business Contact Manager Home**.

   –Or–

   Click **ALT+M**

   The Business Contact Manager – Home window will open.

2. Click the **Select A Report Type** down arrow in the Reports section.

3. Click a report type from the drop-down list.

4. Click the **Select A Report** down arrow to display a list of reports. Click one.

Reports ⊗ | ✕

Select a report type: Business Contacts ▼ [Display...] [Print...]

Select a report: Report: Business Contacts by Account ▼

NOTE

Depending on the number of contacts in your database and the speed of your computer, it may take a few moments for your system to generate the report.

Report: Business Contacts by Account

File   Edit   View   Actions   Help

Save Report | 🖨 🔍 | 📧 📋 🔄 ⏷= Filter Report | ⚙ Modify Report

NOTE

To see the fields included with each main group of columns, press the plus sign (+) that appears to the left of the column name. When all of the information is displayed, a minus sign (−) appears to the left of the column name.

5. Click **Display** to have the report appear.

6. Click **Print** to open the Print dialog box.

7. Click **OK** to print the report.

CHANGE A REPORT

1. In any Business Contact Manager report window, click **Modify Report**. The Modify Report dialog box appears.

2. Click **Filters** to open the Filter Business Contacts dialog box, where you select the type of records you want to include in your report.

3. Click the **Advanced Filter** tab to add conditional rules that will refine the record and data selection.

4. Click **Review Results** and look at what is selected with the filter you have created.

5. After you have made your selections or changes, click **OK**.

6. Click **Columns** and choose which columns you want displayed on the report. You may choose from:

   - **Basic Columns** shows the account name, full name of the contact, and so forth.
   - **Address Columns** include city, state, and ZIP code information.
   - **Contact Columns** include e-mail, fax, and telephone data.
   - **Other Columns** have personal information about the account.
   - **Tracking Columns** show such information as when and by whom the account was created or modified.

7. Click **Fonts And Numbers** to change the font and number styles on your report.

8. Click **Header And Footer** to enter information that will appear on each page of the report.

9. Click **Save Report** to open the Save As dialog box. Type a name for your modified report, and click **OK**.

Chapter 5

Scheduling and the Calendar

5

The Calendar is second only to mail in its importance in Outlook. The Calendar works closely with contacts and tasks to coordinate the use of your time and your interactions with others. The Calendar lets you schedule appointments and meetings, establish recurring activities, and tailor your calendar to your area, region, and workdays.

In this chapter you will see how to use and customize the Calendar, schedule and manage appointments, and schedule and track meetings and resources.

Use the Calendar

The Calendar has a number of unique items in its Outlook window, as seen in Figure 5-1:

- Buttons allow you to quickly switch the view of your Calendar between daily, weekly, and monthly views, as well as to show or hide details of your activities.

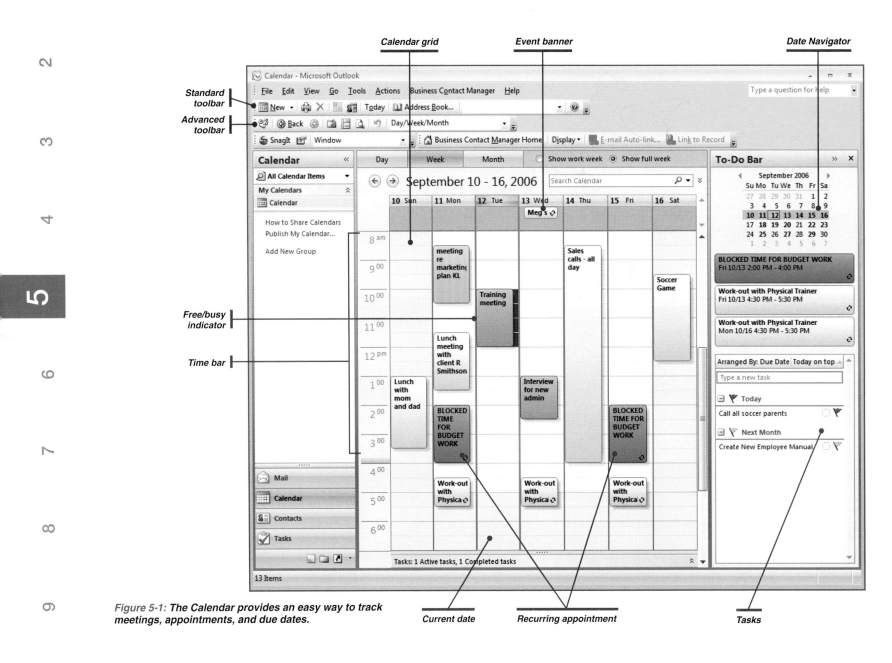

Calendar grid   Event banner   Date Navigator

Standard toolbar

Advanced toolbar

Free/busy indicator

Time bar

Figure 5-1: **The Calendar provides an easy way to track meetings, appointments, and due dates.**

Current date   Recurring appointment   Tasks

- Forward and back buttons let you move quickly to the next month, week, or day.
- The To-Do Bar displays the Date Navigator, an Appointments section, your Task list, and the Task Input panel. In Outlook 2007, your Daily Task list displays in the Day and Week views of the Calendar as well.

Explore the Calendar

The Calendar is designed for you to easily keep track of appointments, meetings, events, due dates, anniversaries, birthdays, and any other date-related happening. You can schedule several different types of activities, as shown on Table 5-1.

To open your Calendar, start Outlook in one of the ways described in Chapter 1. Then:

1. Click **Calendar** in the Navigation pane.

   –Or–

   Press **CTRL+2** on the keyboard.

Appointments	Appointments only involve you.	
Meetings	Meetings happen at a scheduled time, just like an appointment. The difference is that other people are involved. You invite others via e-mail, and the Meeting displays in your Calendar with the location and meeting organizer's name.	
Events	Events last all day long. Events that you put on your Calendar do not block out time like a meeting or an appointment, so you can have other entries for that day display on your Calendar.	
Tasks	Tasks are activities that do not need time scheduled for them and involve only you. Your tasks will display in the Day and Week views of your Calendar, as well as on your To-Do Bar.	

Table 5-1: Common Calendar Activities

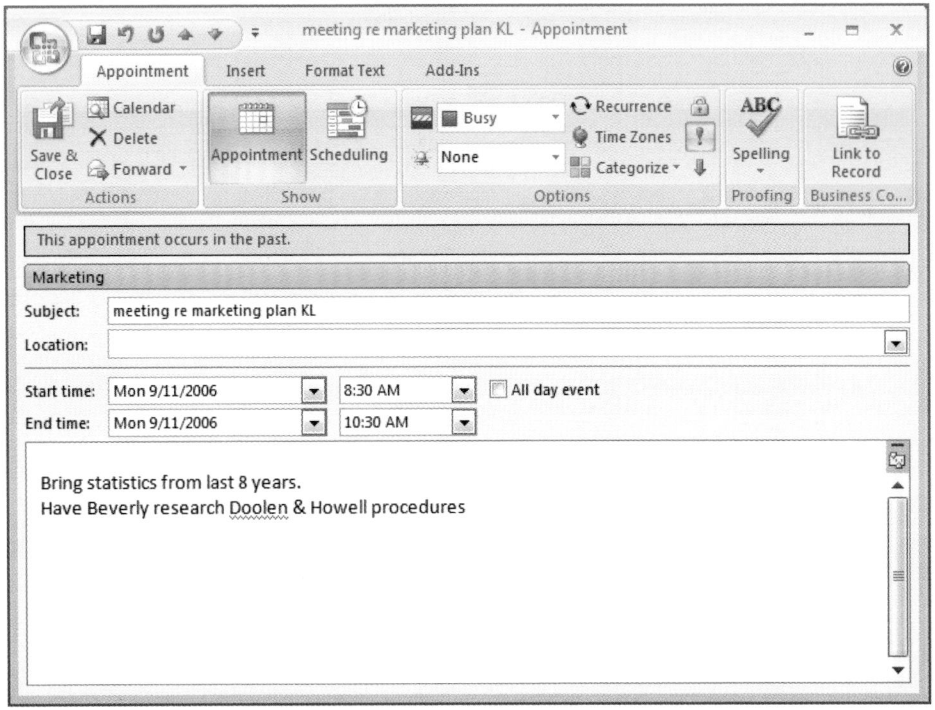

meeting re marketing plan KL - Appointment

Appointment   Insert   Format Text   Add-Ins

Save & Close   Calendar   Delete   Forward
Actions

Appointment   Scheduling
Show

Busy   Recurrence   Time Zones   None   Categorize
Options

ABC Spelling
Proofing

Link to Record
Business Co...

This appointment occurs in the past.

Marketing

Subject: meeting re marketing plan KL

Location:

Start time: Mon 9/11/2006   8:30 AM   ☐ All day event

End time: Mon 9/11/2006   10:30 AM

Bring statistics from last 8 years.
Have Beverly research Doolen & Howell procedures

Figure 5-2: **An appointment or an all-day event can be any date-related activity, such as due dates or birthdays.**

2. Once the Calendar is open, you can start entering your activities. Double-click on any date in the Calendar. A new Appointment window will open, as shown in Figure 5-2. See "Create Appointments" elsewhere in this chapter for more information.

3. Click **Close** to close the Appointment window.

4. Double-click in the Tasks area below the To-Do Bar to open a Task window. In Outlook, a task involves only you, but it does not have a set block of time.

5. Click **Close** to close the Task window.

6. Double-click a date in the Date Navigator section of the To-Do Bar. If the Calendar is in either Day or Month view, the date you click will be displayed by itself in your center Calendar section and the view is changed from Month view to Day view. If the Calendar is in Week view, the week in which you've chosen the date displays in the center Calendar section.

Customize the Calendar

As you have seen with the rest of Outlook, there are many ways you can customize the Calendar to meet your needs. You can change the way the Calendar displays time intervals, as well as the font and font size, the background color, and any additional options as you require.

CHANGE THE TIME SCALES

The default display of time intervals, or *scales*, on your Calendar grid is 30 minutes. If you want to change these scales to reflect another time interval:

1. In the Calendar grid, right-click any blank area.

2. Click **Other Settings**.

3. Click the **Time Scale** down arrow to display a list of choices.

NOTE

When your Calendar is in Day or Week view, the Tasks area appears both under the To-Do Bar and underneath the Calendar.

NAVIGATING THE CALENDAR

The Date Navigator, which by default is in the upper-right corner of the Calendar window in the To-Do Bar, allows you to pick any date from April 1, 1601, to August 31, 4500. To cover this almost 2,900-year span, Outlook provides several efficient tools:

To-Do Bar ◄ ► ×

◄ September 2006 ►
Su Mo Tu We Th Fr Sa
27 28 29 30 31 1 2
3 4 5 6 7 8 9
10 11 12 13 14 15 16
17 18 19 20 21 22 23
24 25 26 27 28 29 30
1 2 3 4 5 6 7

- **Display a day** by clicking it in the Date Navigator, and then clicking the **Day** or **Month** button. Or, from anywhere in Outlook, click **Calendar** on the Navigation pane.

- **Display a day with appointments** by clicking a boldface day in the Date Navigator.

- **Display several days** by holding down CTRL while clicking the days.

- **Display a week** by clicking to the left of the first day of the week.

- **Display several weeks** by holding down CTRL while clicking to the left of the weeks.

- **Display a month** by dragging across the weeks of the month.

- **Change the month from one to the next** by clicking the left or right arrow in the month bar.

- **Scroll through a list of months** by dragging the heading up or down for an individual month.

- **Directly display any date** by clicking the **Go** menu and clicking **Go To Date** or pressing CTRL+G.

4. Click the scale you want to show in the Calendar.

5. Click **OK** to close the dialog box.

Format Day/Week/Month View ? ×

Day and Week

Time Font... | 16 pt. Segoe UI   Time scale: | 30 minutes ▼   OK

Font... | 8 pt. Segoe UI
5 minutes
6 minutes
10 minutes   Cancel
15 minutes

Month
30 minutes
Font... | 8 pt. Segoe UI   ☑ Show end | 60 minutes

General settings
☑ Bolded dates in Date Navigator represent days containing items
☑ Bold Subjects in the Calendar

5

CHANGE THE FONT FACE AND SIZE

You can change the font in both your Calendar and your Daily Task list.

1. Right-click any blank area in the Calendar grid.

2. Click **Other Settings**.

3. Click **Time Font** to change the font in your Daily Task list in the Day and Week views.

   –Or–

   Click **Font** under Day and Week to change the font as it displays in the Day and Week views.

4. Choose **Font** to change the font face.

5. Choose **Font Style** to have the font appear as bold, italic, or bold italic, depending on the font you have chosen in step 4.

6. Click **Size** to choose a size from the drop-down box, or type another font size in the Size field.

7. Click **OK** to close the Font dialog box and save your choices.

8. Click **Font** under Month, and follow steps 4–7.

9. Click **OK** to close the Format Day/Week/Month dialog box.

TIP

To change your Calendar display from Day view to Week to Month view, click the buttons above the Calendar grid.

NOTE

In Week view, click **Show Full Week** next to the Day, Week, or Month button to display Saturday and Sunday on your Calendar grid. Click **Show Work Week** to display only Monday through Friday.

SET ADDITIONAL SETTINGS

From the Other Settings dialog box, you can tell the Calendar how to display items in your Calendar and Date Navigators.

1. Under General Settings, click **Bolded Dates In Date Navigator** to have dates with activities display in bold type on the Date Navigator.

2. Click **Bold Subjects In The Calendar** to have the headings or subjects of your activities appear in bold type in your Calendar grid.

3. Click **OK** to close the dialog box.

CUSTOMIZE WITH THE VIEW MENU

The View menu includes several options that are available on the standard or advanced toolbars, and those options will be discussed with their respective sections. Some of the options are also available when you display a menu by right-clicking in a blank area of the Calendar grid, as discussed previously.

| View | Go | Tools | Actions | Business Contact Manager | Help |

Current View	▶	✓	Day/Week/Month
Navigation Pane	▶		Day/Week/Month View With AutoPreview
To-Do Bar	▶		All Appointments
Reading Pane	▶		Active Appointments
Daily Task List	▶		Events
[1] Day	Ctrl+Alt+1		Annual Events
[5] Work Week	Ctrl+Alt+2		Recurring Appointments
[7] Week	Ctrl+Alt+3		By Category
[31] Month	Ctrl+Alt+4		Outlook Data Files
Reminders Window			Customize Current View...
Toolbars	▶		Define Views...
✓ Status Bar			

1. Click the **View** menu.

2. Click **Current View** to display the options available:

- **Day/Week/Month** is the default view. Each view has its own button on the Calendar grid.

- **Day/Week/Month View With AutoPreview** displays detailed information about each appointment in Day view.

- **All Appointments** displays all the appointments you have set on this Calendar, both past and present.

- **Active Appointments** lists all current and future appointments.

- **Events** lists all events you have scheduled.

- **Annual Events** and **Recurring Appointments** list only those events that happen either annually or recur more than one time.

- **Category** lists all of your events and appointments by the category you have assigned. Those activities without a category are listed first.

- **Outlook Data Files** lists all of the data files you have created in Outlook if you use a Microsoft Exchange Server account. Exchange Server accounts are used primarily in a business, rather than in a home or personal setting.

USE THE STANDARD AND ADVANCED TOOLBARS

Both the standard and advanced toolbars have several buttons that are unique to the Outlook Calendar. In the standard toolbar, only one button, the View Group Schedules button, is available all the time. This button allows you to view the combined schedules of several people, as well as other resources from a public folder. Group scheduling requires a Microsoft Exchange 2000 or later account. See the "Creating a Group Schedule" QuickSteps later in this chapter.

The two buttons that are available all the time on the advanced toolbar are the Reading pane and the Current View buttons.

- Click **Reading Pane** and an activity in any view to display information about that activity in the Reading pane at the bottom of the Calendar grid.

- Click the **Current View** button to change the Calendar view.

Buttons on the standard and advanced toolbars that are used by the Calendar in various views are shown in Table 5-2.

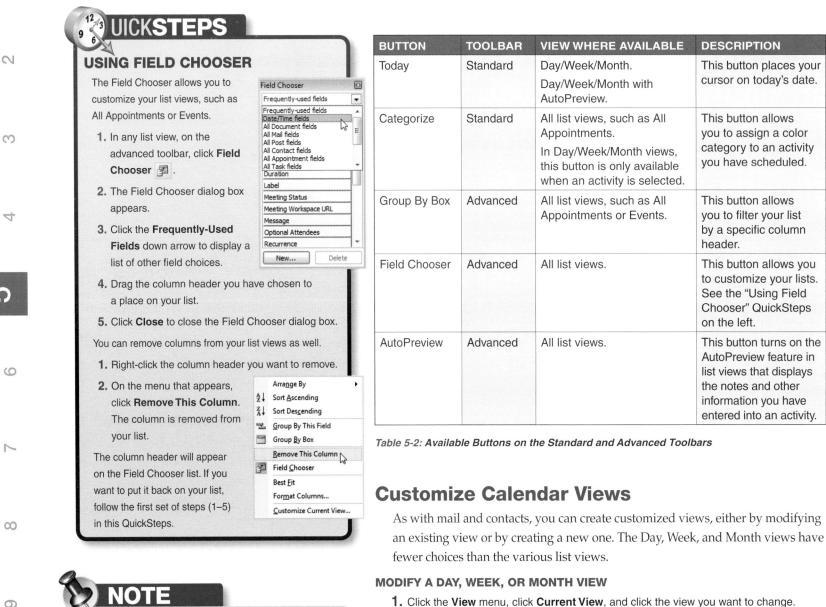

USING FIELD CHOOSER

The Field Chooser allows you to customize your list views, such as All Appointments or Events.

1. In any list view, on the advanced toolbar, click **Field Chooser** 🗒 .

2. The Field Chooser dialog box appears.

3. Click the **Frequently-Used Fields** down arrow to display a list of other field choices.

4. Drag the column header you have chosen to a place on your list.

5. Click **Close** to close the Field Chooser dialog box.

You can remove columns from your list views as well.

1. Right-click the column header you want to remove.

2. On the menu that appears, click **Remove This Column**. The column is removed from your list.

The column header will appear on the Field Chooser list. If you want to put it back on your list, follow the first set of steps (1–5) in this QuickSteps.

NOTE

Columns in Calendar views are also called *fields*.

BUTTON	TOOLBAR	VIEW WHERE AVAILABLE	DESCRIPTION
Today	Standard	Day/Week/Month. Day/Week/Month with AutoPreview.	This button places your cursor on today's date.
Categorize	Standard	All list views, such as All Appointments. In Day/Week/Month views, this button is only available when an activity is selected.	This button allows you to assign a color category to an activity you have scheduled.
Group By Box	Advanced	All list views, such as All Appointments or Events.	This button allows you to filter your list by a specific column header.
Field Chooser	Advanced	All list views.	This button allows you to customize your lists. See the "Using Field Chooser" QuickSteps on the left.
AutoPreview	Advanced	All list views.	This button turns on the AutoPreview feature in list views that displays the notes and other information you have entered into an activity.

Table 5-2: Available Buttons on the Standard and Advanced Toolbars

Customize Calendar Views

As with mail and contacts, you can create customized views, either by modifying an existing view or by creating a new one. The Day, Week, and Month views have fewer choices than the various list views.

MODIFY A DAY, WEEK, OR MONTH VIEW

1. Click the **View** menu, click **Current View**, and click the view you want to change.

2. Click the **View** menu, click **Current View**, and click **Customize Current View** to open the Customize View: Day/Week/Month dialog box, as seen in Figure 5-3.

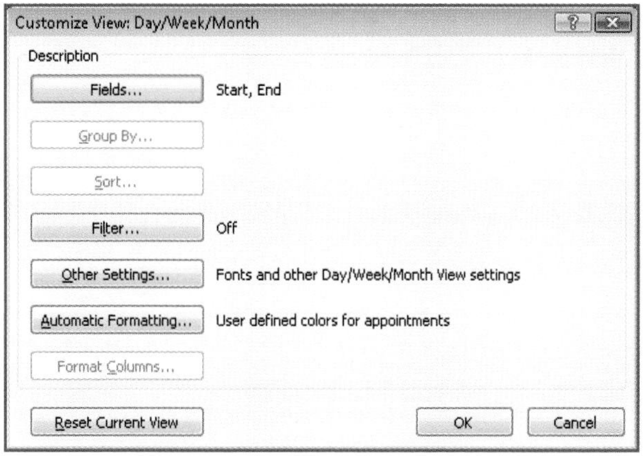

Customize View: Day/Week/Month

Description

Fields...	Start, End
Group By...	
Sort...	
Filter...	Off
Other Settings...	Fonts and other Day/Week/Month View settings
Automatic Formatting...	User defined colors for appointments
Format Columns...	

Reset Current View   OK   Cancel

Figure 5-3: Outlook provides a comprehensive set of tools to modify what you see on the screen so that it can fit almost any need.

NOTE

You can also open the Customize View dialog box from a Day, Week, or Month view by right-clicking an empty part of your Calendar grid and clicking **Customize Current View**.

3. Click **Fields** to open the Date/Time Fields dialog box:

   a. Click the field you want to add or change.

   b. Click **Start** if the new field is to replace the Start field.

   c. Click **End** if the new field is to replace the End field.

   d. Click **OK** to close the dialog box.

4. Click **Filter** to open the Filter dialog box:

   a. In the Appointments And Meetings tab, enter any words by which you want to filter your Calendar entries.

   b. Make additional choices, if necessary, in each of the other three tabs.

   c. Click **OK** to close the dialog box.

5. Click **Other Settings** to open the Format Day/Week/Month View dialog box:

   a. Click **Time Font** or **Font** to open the Font dialog box.

   b. Click the **Font**, **Font Style**, and **Size** options you want.

   c. Click **OK** twice to save your changes and return to the Customize View dialog box.

6. Click **Automatic Formatting** to open the Automatic Formatting dialog box:

   a. Click **Add** to create a new rule.

   b. Click in the **Name** text box, and type a name for this rule.

   c. Click the **Color** down arrow to choose a color for this rule.

   d. Click **Condition** to open the Filter dialog box. Type the word or words to create this filter.

   e. Click **In** to choose where Outlook is to find the words you are searching for.

   f. Enter any additional filter information you require.

   g. Click **OK** to close the Filter dialog box.

   h. Click **OK** to close the Customize View dialog box.

7. Click **OK** to save your changes.

8. If you want to undo a change you made to the current view, click **Reset Current View** in the Customize View dialog box.

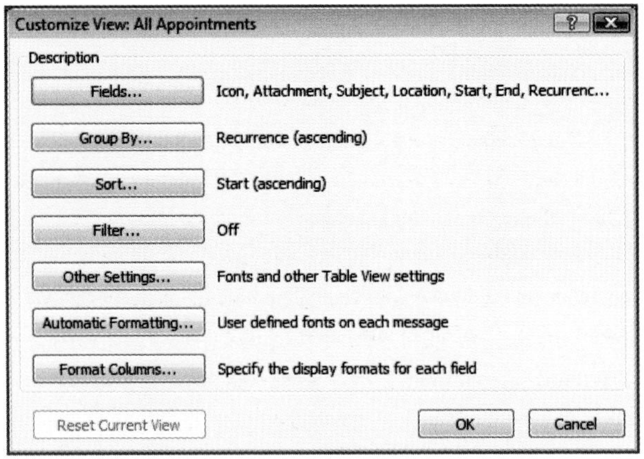

Figure 5-4: *The Customize View dialog box in list views offers more choices than the Day, Week, and Month views.*

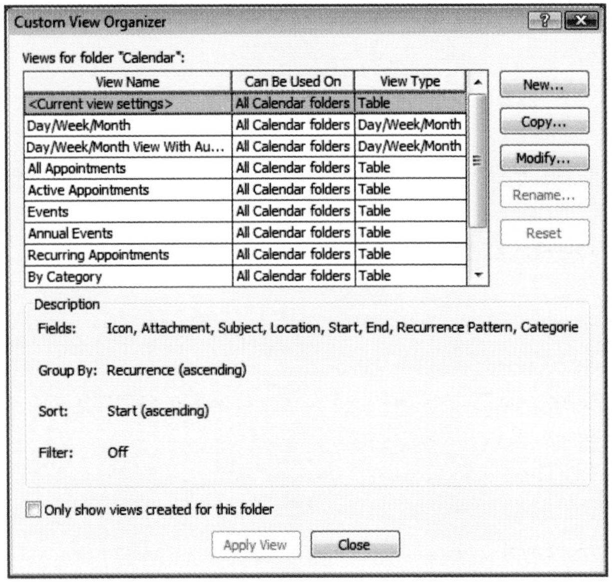

Figure 5-5: *The Custom View Organizer gives you a list and summary of the current view, as well as the ability to modify the current view and create new ones.*

MODIFY A LIST VIEW

1. Click the **View** menu, click **Current View**, and click the list view you want to change.

2. Click the **View** menu, click **Current View**, and click **Customize Current View** to open the Customize View dialog box.

3. The Customize View dialog box will appear for the selected list view. For example, Figure 5-4 shows the dialog box for the All Appointments view.

4. Follow the same steps as described in "Modify a Day, Week, or Month View" earlier in this chapter.

5. Click **OK** to close the Customize View dialog box.

CREATE A NEW VIEW

1. Click the **View** menu, click **Current View**, and click **Define Views**. The Custom View Organizer will open, as shown in Figure 5-5.

2. Click **New** to open the Create A New View dialog box:

   a. Type a name for this new view.

   b. Click the type of view this will be from the six options displayed.

   c. Click **This Folder, Visible To Everyone** if you want to make your new view available in this folder to everyone. Choose one of the other two options, if required.

   d. Click **OK** to open the Customize View dialog box.

   e. Follow the steps outlined in "Modify a Day, Week, or Month View" elsewhere in this chapter.

   f. Click **OK** to save the new view and close the dialog box.

3. Your new view will appear on the Custom View Organizer.

4. Click **Apply View** to immediately see the new view, or click **Close** to close the dialog box and stay in the current view.

Set Up the Calendar

The Calendar allows you to define your normal work week in terms of the days it contains and when it starts, the normal start and end of your working day, the holidays you observe, and what you consider the first week of the year. To set up your Calendar:

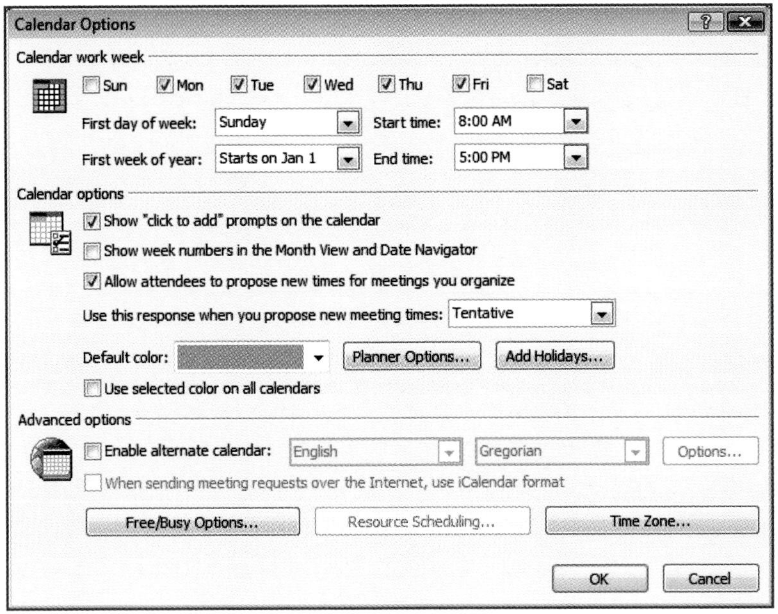

Calendar Options

Calendar work week

☐ Sun ☑ Mon ☑ Tue ☑ Wed ☑ Thu ☑ Fri ☐ Sat

First day of week: Sunday ▼   Start time: 8:00 AM ▼

First week of year: Starts on Jan 1 ▼   End time: 5:00 PM ▼

Calendar options

☑ Show "click to add" prompts on the calendar

☐ Show week numbers in the Month View and Date Navigator

☑ Allow attendees to propose new times for meetings you organize

Use this response when you propose new meeting times: Tentative ▼

Default color: [   ] ▼   [Planner Options...] [Add Holidays...]

☐ Use selected color on all calendars

Advanced options

☐ Enable alternate calendar: English ▼ Gregorian ▼ [Options...]

☐ When sending meeting requests over the Internet, use iCalendar format

[Free/Busy Options...] [Resource Scheduling...] [Time Zone...]

[OK] [Cancel]

Figure 5-6: You can set Calendar options, such as defining your work week and displaying week numbers, the time zone, and holidays.

1. In Outlook 2007, click **Calendar** in the Navigation pane, click the **Tools** menu, and click **Options**.

2. In the Options dialog box that appears, click **Calendar Options** to display the Calendar Options dialog box, as shown in Figure 5-6.

3. Click the days of the week you consider work days if they are different from the default of Monday through Friday.

4. Click the **First Day Of Week** down arrow to select the day of the week you want considered the first day of the week if it is a day other than Sunday. The weeks in the Date Navigator will begin with this day.

5. Click the **First Week Of Year** down arrow to choose a definition for the first week of the year if it does not begin January 1. If you turn on week numbering, week number 1 is defined in this manner.

6. Click the **Start Time** down arrow to choose the normal start time for your working day if it is other than 8:00 A.M. Click the **End Time** down arrow to change the end of your working day if it is other than 5:00 P.M. In the Day and Week views, non-working hours are blue, while working hours are pale blue by default.

7. Clear **Show "Click To Add" Prompts On The Calendar** if you do not want this default prompt to display.

8. Click **Show Week Numbers In The Month View And Date Navigator** to display week numbers.

9. Click **Allow Attendees To Propose New Times For Meetings You Organize** if you choose to allow this.

10. Click the **Use This Response When You Propose New Meeting Times** down arrow to change the automatic response to new meetings.

11. Click the **Default Color** down arrow to choose from a list of colors other than the default blue for the background on your Calendar grid.

12. Click **Use Selected Color On All Calendars** if you want this new color to be used on all Calendars you create.

13. Click **Planner Options** to display the Planner Options dialog box:

    a. Make your choices in both the Meeting Planner and the Group Schedule as they pertain to your use.

    b. Click **OK** to close the Planner Options dialog box.

14. Click **Add Holidays** to open the Add Holidays To Calendar dialog box:

    a. Click the check box for the country and/or religious holidays you want added.

    b. Click **OK** to close the dialog box.

15. Click **Enable Alternate Calendar**, if desired, and use the drop-down lists to choose them.

16. Under most circumstances, leave the **When Sending Meeting Requests** check box selected.

SETTING FREE/BUSY OPTIONS

If you and your coworkers are part of a Microsoft Exchange network, are willing to share your schedules over the Internet, or can all access a common server, you can store your free/busy times and make them available to each other to schedule meetings and other times together. In this case, requests for meetings will be handled automatically. The request will be matched against the group's free/busy schedule and meetings will be scheduled at available times. For an individual to set up his or her free/busy options:

1. From the Calendar Options dialog box, click **Free/Busy Options**. The Free/Busy Options dialog box appears.

2. Click in the **Publish** box to type the number of months of free/busy information you want to store on the server.

3. Click the **Update Free/Busy Information** text box to enter how often you want the server to update your information.

4. Click **Publish At My Location**, and enter the URL (Web address) of your Internet Calendar if that applies to your situation. See "Understand Internet Calendars" elsewhere in this chapter.

5. Click **Search Location** and type the URL of servers you want Outlook to search for the free/busy information of others.

6. Click **OK** to return to the Calendar Options dialog box.

SETTING TIME ZONES

You can choose up to two time zones to display. You can define and name your current time zone, as well as an additional one, if you choose.

NOTE

Setting up a group schedule is discussed in the QuickSteps "Creating a Group Schedule" later in this chapter.

Free/Busy Options

Options

Free/busy information is used by people sending meeting requests, to determine when you are available for meetings.

Publish [2] month(s) of Calendar free/busy information on the server

Update free/busy information on the server every [15] minutes

Internet Free/Busy

☐ Publish at my location:

Search location:

OK | Cancel

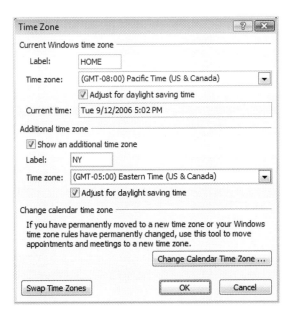

1. From the Calendar Options dialog box, click **Time Zone**. The Time Zone dialog box appears.

2. If you are going to use two time zones, click in the **Label** text box, and type a name that will identify the current time zone appearing in the Time Zone drop-down list.

3. Click **Show An Additional Time Zone** to add a second time zone.

4. Click in the **Label** text box, and type a name identifying this second time zone.

5. Click the **Time Zone** down arrow to display a list of time zones from which you can choose.

6. Click **Adjust For Daylight Saving Time** if it applies to either time zone you've selected.

7. Click **Change Calendar Time Zone** if you've permanently moved to a new time zone.

8. Click **Swap Time Zones** to swap which time zone is on the left.

9. Click **OK** to close the Time Zone dialog box.

10. Click **OK** to close the Calendar Options dialog box, and click **OK** a second time to close the Outlook Options dialog box. Both time zones appear on your Calendar grid.

Maintain Multiple Calendars

If your Calendar is becoming cluttered and hard to use, you might try separating it into two side-by-side Calendars. For example, create one for business appointments and one for family appointments.

1. In Outlook 2007, click **Calendar** in the Navigation pane, and click the **New** down arrow on the standard toolbar.

2. Click **Calendar** to open the Create New Folder dialog box.

3. Click **Name** and type a name for your new calendar.

4. Click **Calendar** and select where to place the new folder.

5. Click **OK** to close the Create New Folder dialog box. Your new Calendar is displayed in the Navigation pane.

6. Click the check box to the left of your new Calendar to display it side-by-side with your original Calendar, as seen in Figure 5-7.

CAUTION

At least one Calendar must always be displayed, but you can create up to 30 Calendars if you choose.

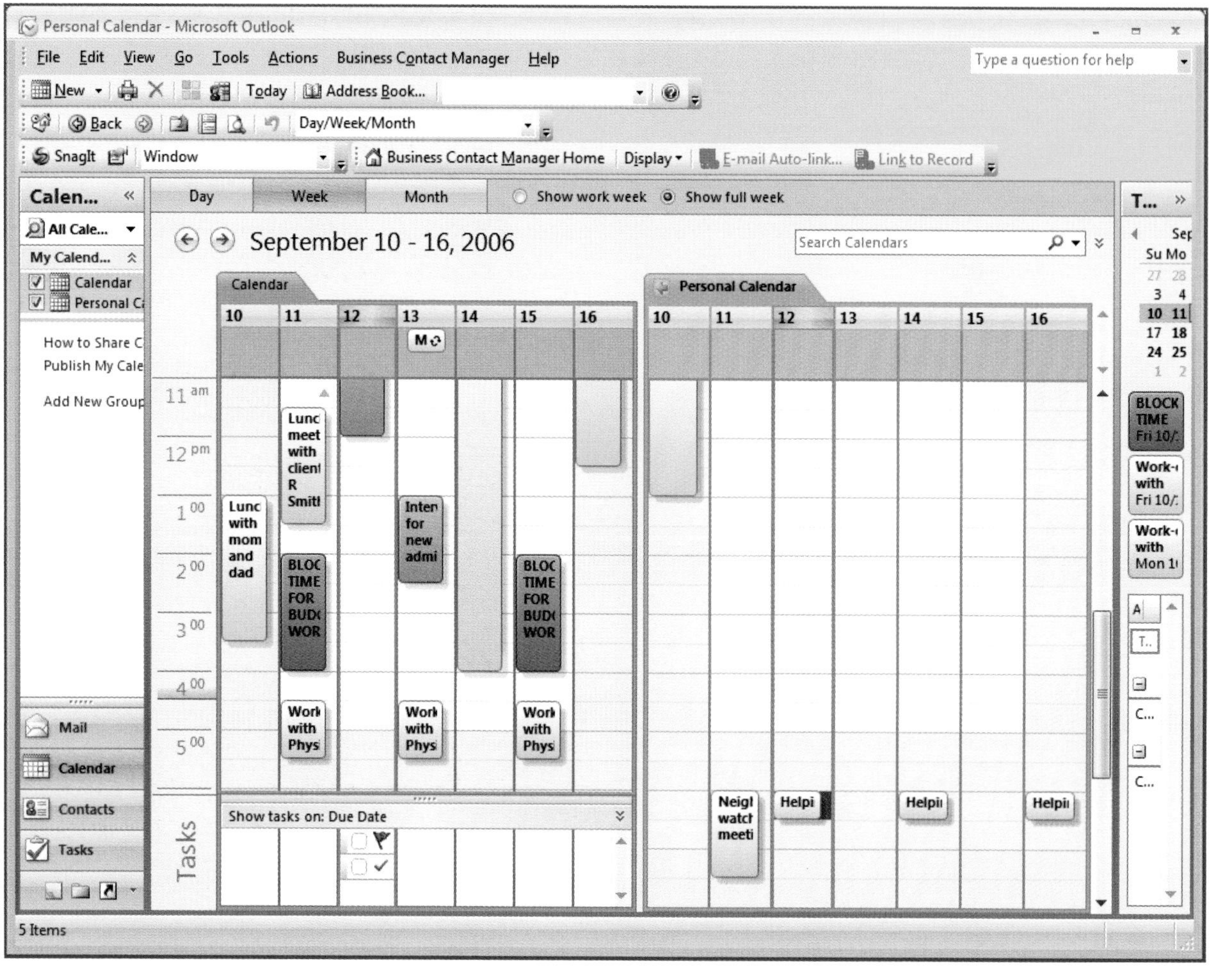

Figure 5-7: *By displaying two Calendars side-by-side, you can, for example, show personal appointments that have no effect on your work Calendar.*

VIEW MULTIPLE CALENDARS

You can view a Calendar in a new window, side-by-side, or stack transparent Calendars over each other to find a common free time slot on several different Calendars.

To view a second Calendar in a new window:

1. From Outlook 2007, with the Calendar open, right-click the name of the second Calendar in the Navigation pane under My Calendars.

2. In the resulting menu, click **Open In New Window**.

To open several Calendars side-by-side:

1. In the Calendar Navigation pane, click the check box for each Calendar you want to view.

2. All the Calendars will be displayed next to each other in your Calendar grid.

To overlay your Calendars:

1. In the Calendar, from the Navigation pane, click the check box for each Calendar you want to stack. The Calendars display next to each other in your Calendar grid.

2. On the tab of each Calendar you want to stack, click the arrow that points to the left.

3. All of the Calendars are stacked atop each other, and you can see any dates that may be free on all Calendars.

4. To undo the stack, click the right-pointing arrow on the tab of each Calendar. The Calendars are once again displayed side-by-side.

Share a Calendar

There are several ways to share your Outlook 2007 Calendar with others. You can send a Calendar via e-mail, publish your Calendar to Microsoft Office Online, or share your default Microsoft Exchange Calendar with others on the same server.

SEND A CALENDAR IN E-MAIL

You can send any Calendar you own to another in the body of an e-mail message. The person receiving the Calendar will see a snapshot of your Calendar at a given moment in time. If the recipient uses Outlook 2007, he or she can open the Calendar snapshot as an Outlook Calendar and display it either side-by-side or as an overlay with any other Calendars. The downside of using a Calendar snapshot is that the Calendar you send is not automatically updated when you make changes. If the e-mail recipient needs a regularly

Send a Calendar via E-mail

Specify the calendar information you want to include.

Calendar: `Calendar`

Date Range: `Today`

Tue 9/12/2006

Detail:
Availability only
Time will be shown as "Free," "Busy," "Tentative,"
or "Out of Office"

☐ Show time within my working hours only   Set working hours

Advanced: [Hide <<]

☐ Include details of items marked private

☐ Include attachments within calendar items

E-mail Layout: `Daily schedule`

[OK]   [Cancel]

updated Calendar, consider publishing your Calendar to Microsoft Office Online, using a calendar-publishing Web service, or, if your work has it, sharing your Calendars via an Exchange server.

To share a Calendar:

1. In the Calendar's Navigation pane, click **Send A Calendar Via E-mail**.

   –Or–

   In a minimized Navigation pane, right-click the Calendar you want to share. From the context menu, click **Send Via E-mail**.

   In either case, an e-mail message box opens with the Send A Calendar Via E-Mail dialog box in the message portion of the e-mail window.

2. Click the **Calendar** down arrow, and click the Calendar you want to e-mail.

3. Click the **Date Range** down arrow, and click the time period for which you want to send the Calendar.

4. Click the **Detail** down arrow, and click the type of Calendar information you want to send.

5. If you chose Availability Only, click **Show Time Within My Working Hours Only** if that is what you want.

6. Click **Set Working Hours** to display the Calendar Options dialog box and change your working hours. Close the Calendar Options dialog box if you opened it.

7. Click **Show** (located opposite Advanced), and, if desired, click **Include Details Of Items Marked Private** and/or click **Include Attachments**.

8. Click **E-mail Layout** and click either the **Daily Schedule** or **List Of Events** format.

9. Click **OK** to close the dialog box.

10. Click **To** and type the recipient's e-mail address.

11. Click **Send** to send the e-mail.

PUBLISH A CALENDAR TO MICROSOFT OFFICE ONLINE

Microsoft offers a publishing service for your Calendars. This method does not require Microsoft Exchange for either the user or the owner of the Calendar. The first time you use the service, you must register using your Microsoft Windows

CAUTION

Be careful when you set the date range of a Calendar snapshot. If you set it for a long period of time, the e-mail file might be too big for the recipient's e-mail box.

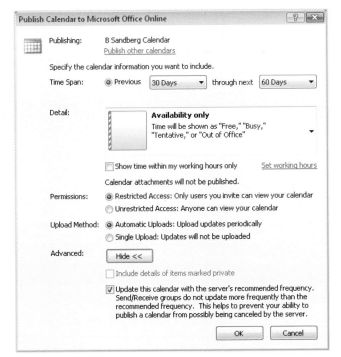

Live ID account. If you don't yet have an account, you may follow the instructions on the screen to obtain one for free.

1. In the Calendar's Navigation pane, click **Publish My Calendar**. Go through the registration procedure, if needed. The Publish Calendar To Microsoft Office Online dialog box appears.

2. Follow steps 4–6 in "Send a Calendar in E-mail."

3. Click **Restricted Access** if you want to allow only invited users to see your Calendar.

4. Click **Unrestricted Access** if you want to share your Calendar with anyone.

5. Click **Automatic Uploads** if you want Outlook 2007 to periodically update your published Calendar automatically.

6. Click **Single Upload** if you do not want to have your Calendar updated.

7. Click **Show** (located opposite Advanced), and, if desired, click **Include Details Of Items Marked Private**, and/or click **Update This Calendar** to use the server's recommended frequency for updates.

8. Click **OK** to publish your Calendar.

9. After your Calendar has been successfully published, you are prompted to create an e-mail announcing this fact. Click **Yes** to create the e-mail or click **No** to close the dialog box.

SHARE AN EXCHANGE CALENDAR

If you are connected to a Microsoft Exchange server, you can share your Calendars with others and they can share theirs with you.

1. In the Calendar, from the Navigation pane, click **Share My Calendar**.

2. In the e-mail message box that opens, click **To** and type the name of the person to whom you are granting access to your Calendar.

3. Click **Subject** and type a subject for your e-mail.

4. Click **Allow Recipient To View Your Calendar**.

5. Click **Request Permission To View Recipient's Calendar** if you want access to their Calendar as well.

6. Click in the body of the e-mail, and type any additional information.

7. Click **Send**.

8. A confirmation dialog box will appear. If all appears correct, click **OK** to close the dialog box.

NOTE

If Share My Calendar is not available in the Navigation pane, you are not connected to a Microsoft Exchange network.

TIP

Try using text dates, as described in the "Entering Dates and Times" QuickSteps, and you'll be amazed at how Outlook can interpret what you enter.

TIP

Combine direct entry and window entry to get the benefits of both.

Use the Calendar

Within the Calendar, you can enter several types of activities:

- **Appointments** take time on your calendar, are less than 24 hours long, and do not require inviting others within Outlook to attend. Examples include a sales call, lunch with a buyer, or time you want to set aside to write a report.

- **Meetings** are appointments that require that others be invited and/or that resources be reserved. Meetings are set up using e-mail.

- **Events** are 24 hours or longer, do not occupy time on your Calendar, and appear as a banner on each day's calendar. Examples are conferences, birthdays, or your vacation.

- **Tasks** are activities that do not need time scheduled for them and involve only you. Your tasks display in the Day and Week views of your Calendar as well as your To-Do Bar.

All types of activities can be entered in several ways and with a number of options.

Create Appointments

Appointments can be entered in any view and in several different ways. Independent of the view, the different ways can be grouped into direct entry and window entry. *Direct entry* means simply typing directly on the Calendar, while *window entry* uses a window to gather the information, which is then displayed on the Calendar. Direct entry is fast if you want to make a quick notation. Window entry allows you to select and set a number of options.

ENTER APPOINTMENTS DIRECTLY

You can directly enter an appointment on the Calendar in Day, Week, or Month view by clicking a time and typing the description. If you want the entry longer or shorter than the default half hour (or whatever standard duration you have selected), just drag the top or bottom border up or down to change the time. If you want to move the appointment, simply drag it to where you want it in the current day or to another day in the Date Navigator. To change the properties

QUICKSTEPS

ENTERING DATES AND TIMES

The Outlook Calendar allows you to enter dates and times as text and convert that text to numeric dates and times. For example, you can type next tue and be given next Tuesday's date, or you can type sep ninth and see that date. You can type this way in any date or time field in Outlook, such as the Go To Date dialog box, reached by pressing **CTRL+G** or right-clicking any empty spot on the Calendar grid while in Day, Week, or Month view. Likewise, you can type in the Start and End date and time fields in the appointment and event views or the Meeting dialog box. Some of the things you can do include:

- Abbreviate months and days (for example, *Dec* or *Fri*).

- Ignore capitalization and other punctuation (for example, *wednesday, april,* and *lincolns birthday*).

- Use words that indicate dates and times (for example, *noon, midnight, tomorrow, yesterday, today, now, next week, last month, five days ago, in three months, this Saturday,* and *two weeks from now*). Words you can use include: *after, ago, before, beforehand, beginning, end, ending, following, for, from, last, next, now, previous, start, that, this, through, till, tomorrow, yesterday, today,* and *until.*

- Spell out specific dates and times (for example, *August ninth, first of December, April 19th, midnight, noon, two twenty pm,* and *five o'clock a.m.*).

- Indicate holidays that fall on the same date every year (for example, *New Year's Eve, New Year's Day, Lincoln's Birthday, Valentine's Day, Washington's Birthday, St. Patrick's Day, Cinco de Mayo, Independence Day, Halloween, Veterans' Day, Christmas Eve, Christmas Day,* and *Boxing Day*).

of an appointment, right-click the appointment, which opens the context menu, where a number of properties can be set.

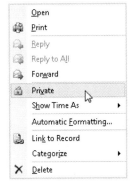

To directly enter appointments:

1. In Outlook 2007, click any date and time in the Calendar grid in the Day, Week, or Month view. Type a short description of the appointment, and press **ENTER**.

2. Place the mouse pointer on the sizing handle at the bottom border of the appointment. Drag the border down until the end of the appointment time.

3. If you need to change the beginning time of your appointment, drag the top border up or down until the proper time is reflected in the Calendar.

ENTER EVENTS DIRECTLY

An event is an activity that normally lasts at least 24 hours (although you can designate something as an event that lasts less than 24 hours but takes most of your time that day, such as a company picnic). Examples of events are conferences, seminars, and holidays. If events are tied to specific dates, they are considered annual events, such as a birthday or holiday. When you enter an event, it is considered free time, not busy. You create events differently than appointments. All events appear in the banner at the top of the daily schedule, while all appointments are on the Calendar itself. To directly enter an event:

1. With the Outlook Calendar open in Day, Week, or Month view, select a day in the Calendar grid when the event will take place.

You can move an appointment without changing the duration by dragging it in any direction. This will change your start and end times but leave the duration constant.

2. Click in the dark blue area at the top of the daily schedule, just under the date header, type the event name, and press **ENTER**.

September 13, 2006 | Search Calendar

13	Wednesday
	Meg's b'day
	Click to add event

ENTER APPOINTMENTS IN A WINDOW

As an alternative to directly entering appointments and events, you can use a New Appointment window, as seen in Figure 5-8, to accomplish the same objective and immediately be able to enter a lot more information. To open a New Appointment window:

1. In the Outlook Calendar, click the **New** down arrow on the standard toolbar, and click **Appointment** to open the New Appointment window.

2. In the Appointment tab Show group, click **Appointment** if it is not already selected.

3. Click **Subject** and type the subject of the appointment. This text becomes the description in the Calendar, with the location added parenthetically and the date and time determining where the appointment goes on the Calendar.

4. Press **TAB**. Type the location, if relevant, in the Location text box.

5. Click the **Start Time** down arrow on the left to display a small calendar in which you can choose a date.

6. Click the down arrow on the right, and select a start time.

7. Click the **End Time** down arrows and select the end date and time. By default, the end date for an appointment is the same date as the start date.

8. Press **TAB** twice and type any notes or other information necessary.

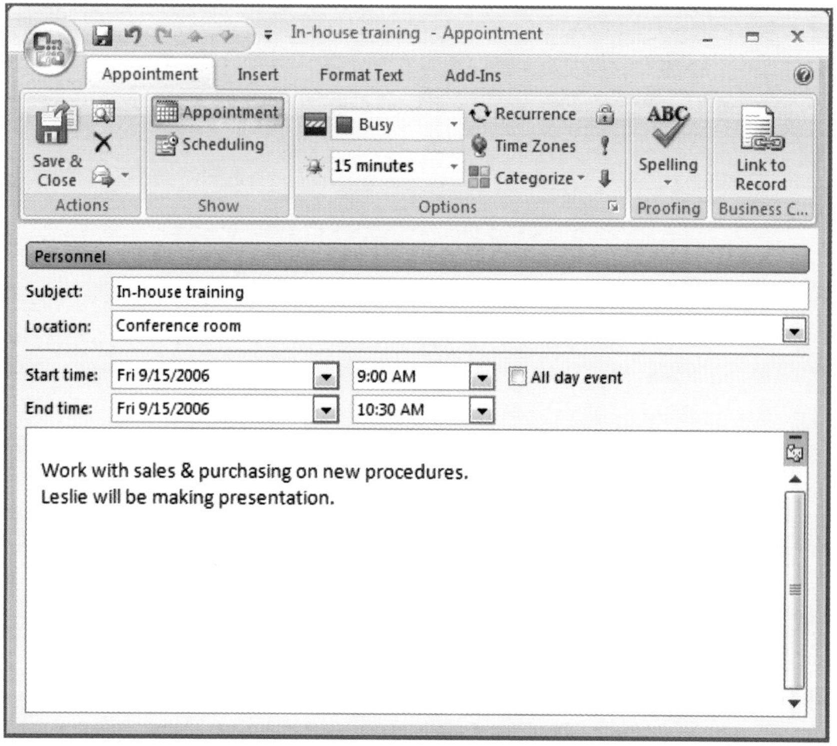

Figure 5-8: *The Appointment window is used to set up or change an appointment.*

Depending on what is selected on the Calendar grid, the window that opens when you click New may be either an Appointment window or an Event window. The only difference, other than the title, is that All Day Event is selected and the free/busy indicator is set to Free for an event. If you get an Event window when you want an Appointment window, simply clear the All Day Event check box.

9. In the Appointment tab Options group, click the **Show As** down arrow, and tell Outlook how to display this time slot on your Calendar:

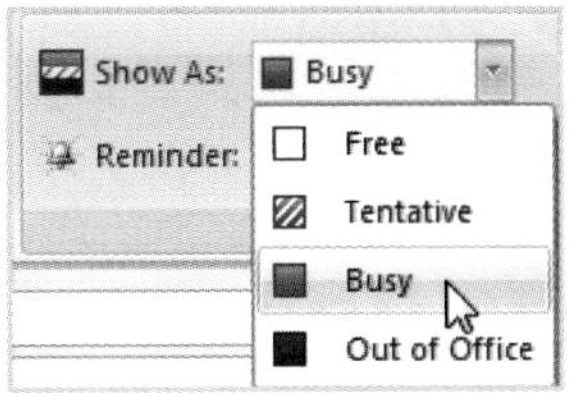

a. Free

b. Tentative

c. Busy

d. Out Of Office

10. In the Appointment tab Options group, click the **Reminder** down arrow, and set the reminder time. See "Use Reminders" later in this chapter for more information.

11. In the Appointment tab Actions group, click **Save & Close** to save your appointment.

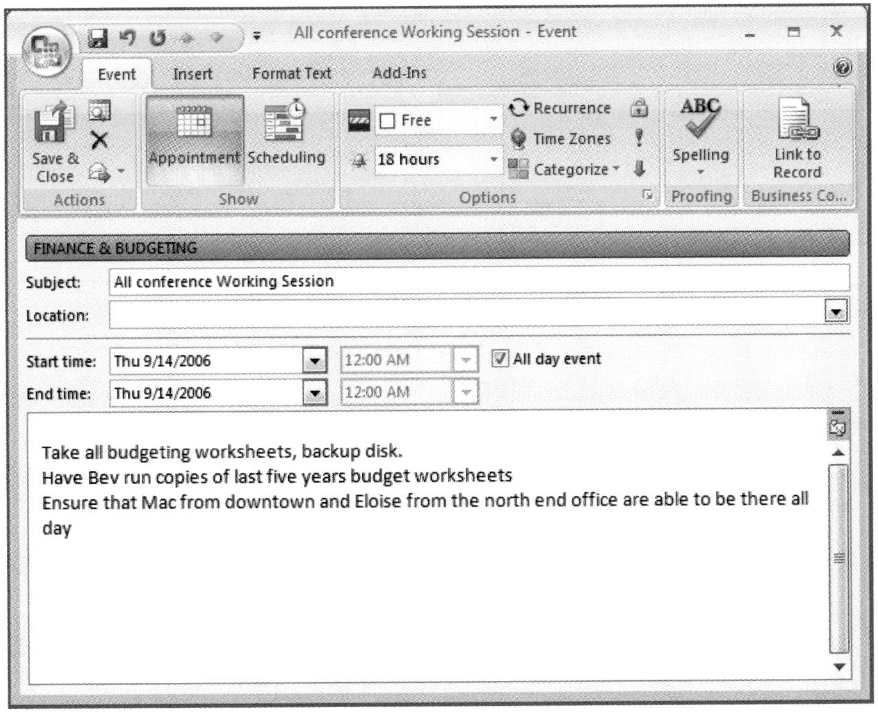

ENTER AN EVENT IN A WINDOW

To enter an all-day event:

1. In the Outlook Calendar, right-click any blank date in any Calendar view.

2. Click **New All Day Event**. The New Event window opens.

3. Click **Subject** to enter text describing the event as it will appear on your Calendar.

4. Click **Location** to type information about the location. By default, All Day Event is selected.

5. Repeat steps 8–11 from "Enter Appointments in a Window." The start and end times disappear; the reminder, by default, goes to 18 hours, and Show Time As changes to Free, as seen in Figure 5-9.

Enter Recurring Appointments

Often you'll have appointments and events that recur predictably, for example, a weekly staff meeting, a monthly planning meeting, a monthly lunch with a friend, and birthdays. You obviously do not want to re-enter these every week, month, or year. Outlook has a feature that allows you to enter these activities once and have them reappear on a given frequency for as long as you want.

Figure 5-9: A New Event window looks much like the New Appointment window, except All Day Event is selected.

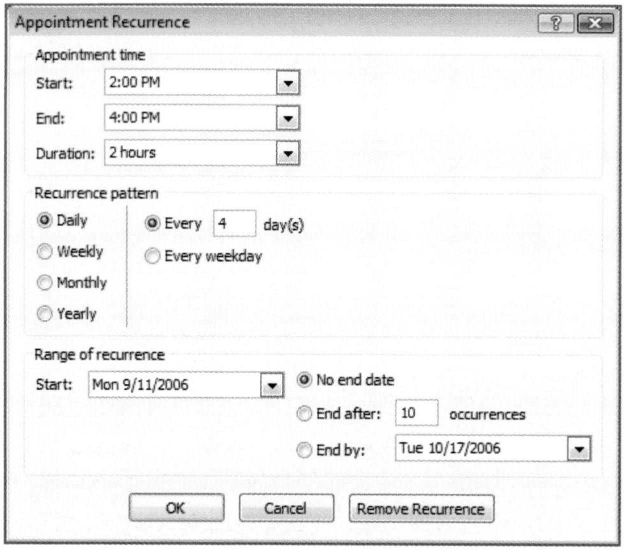

Appointment Recurrence

Appointment time

Start: 2:00 PM

End: 4:00 PM

Duration: 2 hours

Recurrence pattern

- ⦿ Daily   ⦿ Every 4 day(s)
- ○ Weekly   ○ Every weekday
- ○ Monthly
- ○ Yearly

Range of recurrence

Start: Mon 9/11/2006   ⦿ No end date

○ End after: 10 occurrences

○ End by: Tue 10/17/2006

OK   Cancel   Remove Recurrence

Figure 5-10: Use the Appointment Recurrence dialog box to schedule recurring appointments automatically.

Open Recurring Item

⚠ "BLOCKED TIME FOR BUDGET WORK" is a recurring appointment. Do you want to open only this occurrence or the series?

⦿ Open this occurrence.

○ Open the series.

OK   Cancel

NOTE

Recurring appointments and events can save you a lot of time re-entering activities, but they can also generate a lot of entries, which may unnecessarily fill your Calendar. Enter only the recurring appointments that you want to remember.

1. Create a new appointment as described in "Enter Appointments in a Window."

2. In the Appointments tab Options group, click **Recurrence**. The Appointment Recurrence dialog box appears, as shown in Figure 5-10.

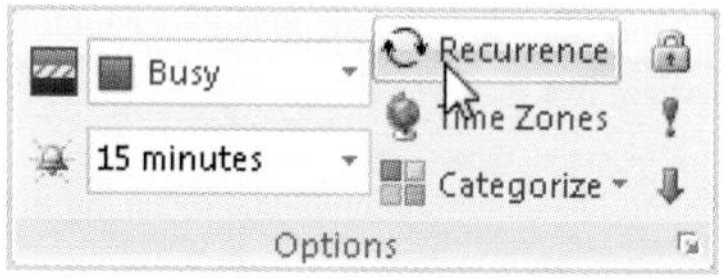

■ Busy   🔄 Recurrence
15 minutes   ⏱ Time Zones
Categorize ▾

Options

3. Click the **Start** down arrow, and select the start time of this recurring appointment.

4. Click the **End** down arrow, and select the end time.

5. Click the **Duration** down arrow, and select the length of time this appointment lasts.

6. Click **Recurrence Pattern** and choose how often this appointment occurs.

7. Under Range of Recurrence, click the down arrow, select the date this appointment starts, the number of times it occurs, and its ending date.

8. Click **OK** to close the Appointment Recurrence dialog box.

EDIT RECURRING APPOINTMENTS

To change one instance of a recurring appointment:

1. In the Outlook Calendar, locate and double-click a recurring appointment in any Calendar view. The Open Recurring Item dialog box appears.

2. Click **Open This Occurrence** if you want to make a change to only this instance of the appointment.

3. Click **OK** to open the Appointment window and make the necessary changes to this occurrence of the appointment.

4. In the Recurring Appointment tab Actions group, click **Save & Close**.

To change all instances of a recurring appointment:

1. In the Calendar, locate and double-click the recurring appointment in any Calendar view. The Open Recurring Item dialog box appears.

2. Click **Open The Series** if you want to make a change to the recurring appointment itself.

3. Click **OK** to open the Appointment window.

TIP

You can delete a single instance of a recurring activity without affecting the rest of the series. If you choose to delete a recurring activity, the dialog box asks if you want to delete the current instance of the activity or the entire series.

TIP

You can copy an activity by right-dragging it (use the right mouse button) to where you want the copy and selecting **Copy** from the context menu that appears when you release the right mouse button.

4. In the Recurring Appointment tab Options group, click **Recurrence** (if you forgot to click Open The Series in step 2, you will see "Edit Series" in place of "Recurrence). The Appointment Recurrence dialog box appears.

5. Make the necessary changes to this appointment, and click **OK**.

6. In the Recurring Appointment tab Actions group, click **Save & Close**.

Move Appointments

If an appointment changes times within a day, you can move it to its new time by simply dragging it to that new time, as you saw earlier. If you entered an event on the wrong day, or if an appointment changes days, you can drag it to the correct or new day in the Week or Month view or in the Date Navigator. You cannot drag a recurring appointment to a date that skips over another occurrence of the same appointment. You can, however, change a recurring appointment to another date before the next one occurs. The different ways to move appointments or events are:

- Drag the appointment to the day you want in a Week or Month view Calendar or the Date Navigator.

- You can drag an appointment anywhere in the Calendar grid by dragging from anywhere in the appointment, except at the expansion points on the middle of the sides.

- When you drag an appointment to a new day, it will be placed in the same time slot. You can change the time by dragging it to the new time, either before or after you move it to the new day.

Use Reminders

When you have set a reminder for an appointment, the Reminder dialog box appears at the time you have set before the appointment. You have several choices in the dialog box.

- Click **Dismiss All** to close the reminder and tell it not to appear again.

- Click **Snooze** to tell the dialog box when to remind you again but close the reminder for now.

- Click **Open Item** to open the Appointment window so that you can make changes to the appointment, the reminder, or both.

- Click **Dismiss** to close only the highlighted reminder.

5 Reminders

All conference Working Session

Start time: Thursday, September 14, 2006 12:00 AM

Subject	Due in
neighborhood watch meeting!!	13 minutes
Lunch with Mom	1 day overdue
BLOCKED TIME FOR BUDGET WORK	4 hours overdue
In-house training	4 days overdue
All conference Working Session	5 days overdue

Dismiss All   Open Item   Dismiss

Click Snooze to be reminded again in:

5 minutes   Snooze

Page Setup: Weekly Style

Style name: Weekly Style

Format | Paper | Header/Footer

Preview:

Options

Arrange days: ○ Top to bottom ● Left to right

Layout: 1 page/week

Tasks: No Tasks

Include: ☐ Notes area (blank) ☐ Notes area (lined)

Print from: 7:00 AM

Print to: 7:00 PM

☐ Only Print Workdays

Fonts

Date headings
24 pt. Segoe UI   Font...

Appointments
8 pt. Segoe UI   Font...

Shading
☑ Print using gray shading

OK   Cancel   Print Preview   Print...

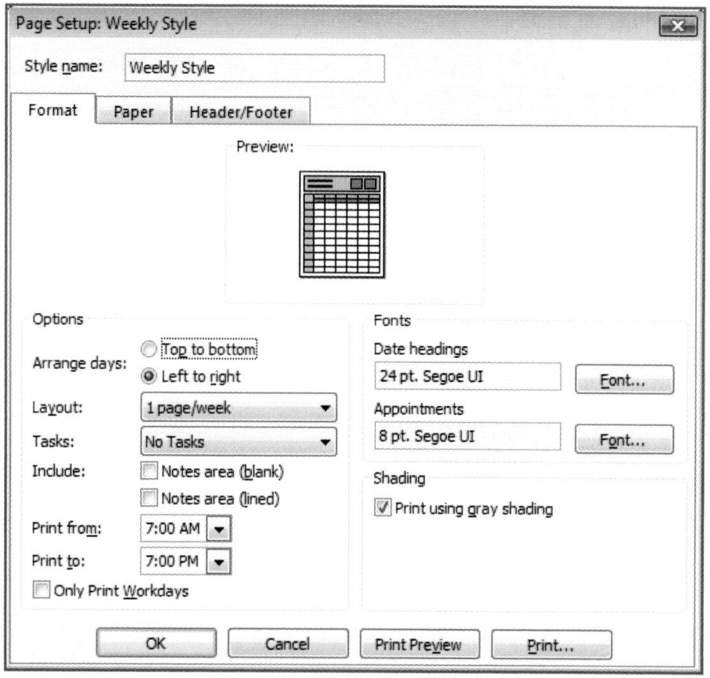

Figure 5-11: The Page Setup dialog box gives you considerable flexibility with regards to the print style, the format, paper specifications, and header/footer information.

Print Calendars

When you have completed making entries on your Calendar, you may want to take it with you, away from your computer, for reference and to jot new appointments on. For this reason, Outlook includes a number of printed formats to fit your needs.

To print your calendar:

1. In any view in Outlook Calendar, choose the day, week, or month you want to print.

2. Click the **File** menu.

3. Click **Page Setup** and click the **Style** you want to print. Your choices are determined by the Calendar view you have chosen. Figure 5-11 shows an example of the weekly style and the related options from which you can choose.

4. Click the **Format** tab, and make any changes in the Options and Fonts sections.

5. Click the **Shading** check box if you want gray shading to be used in your printed Calendar.

6. Click **Paper** to choose the paper specifications.

7. Click **Header/Footer** to add the professional touch of a header and/or a footer.

8. When you are ready, click **Print Preview** to see how your printed Calendar will look.

9. Click **Print** to print your Calendar.

Plan Meetings and Request Attendance

In addition to using Outlook 2007 for scheduling appointments and events, you can use Outlook to plan and schedule meetings. In Outlook, a meeting is an appointment to which others are invited.

Schedule a Meeting

You create a meeting by identifying the people you want to invite and picking a meeting time. You e-mail a meeting request to people in your Outlook Contacts who you want to attend.

QUICKSTEPS

CREATING A GROUP SCHEDULE

A group schedule tracks the free/busy status of several people in one place. It is like the in/out board at a reception desk. To use group schedules, all the members of the group must be on a Microsoft Exchange network.

1. In the Calendar, click the **Actions** menu.

2. Click **View Group Schedules**. The Group Schedules dialog box will appear.

3. Click **New**.

4. In the Create New Group Schedule dialog box, type a name for this group schedule, and click **OK**.

5. Click **Add Others** and click **Add From Address Book** to open the Select Members dialog box.

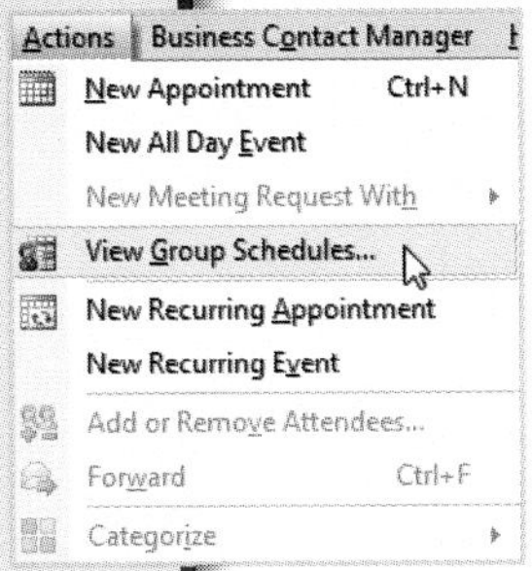

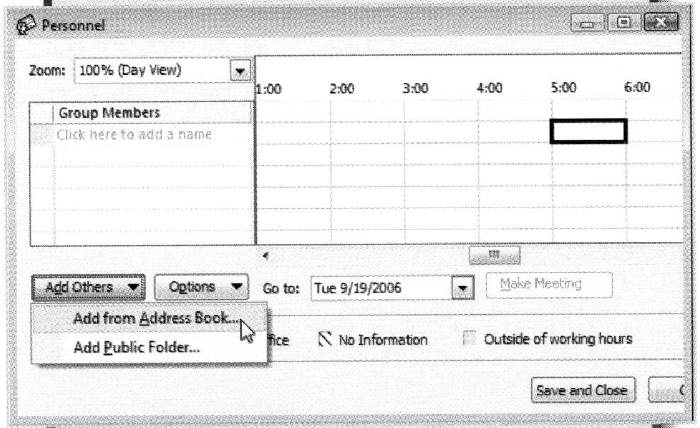

6. Double-click the names you want in the group schedule.

7. Click **OK** when you have chosen all the names you want.

8. Click **Save And Close** to close the Group Schedule dialog box.

1. In Outlook 2007, click the **File** menu, click New, and click **Meeting Request**.

   –Or–

   Press **CTRL+SHIFT+Q**.

   In either event, the New Meeting window opens, as seen in Figure 5-12.

2. Click **To**, double-click your attendees from your Contacts list, and click **OK**.

3. Click in the **Subject** text box, and type a description for your meeting. This description will appear on all Calendars.

4. Click in the **Location** text box, and type the location information, if necessary.

5. Click the **Start Time** down arrow, and select the date and time the meeting is to start.

6. Click the **End Time** down arrow, and select the date and time the meeting is scheduled to end.

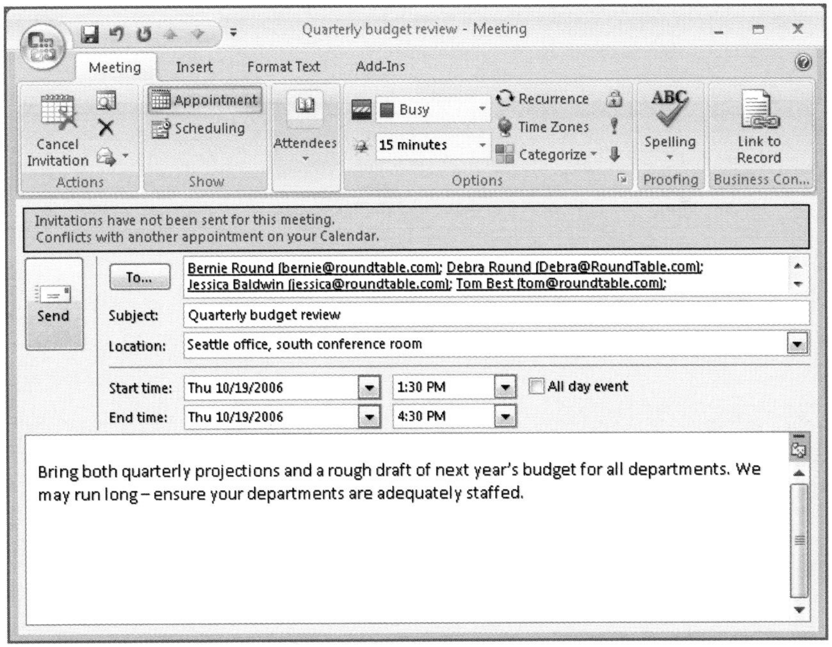

Figure 5-12: The Meeting window allows you to send out invitations, track who can attend, and schedule resources for the meeting.

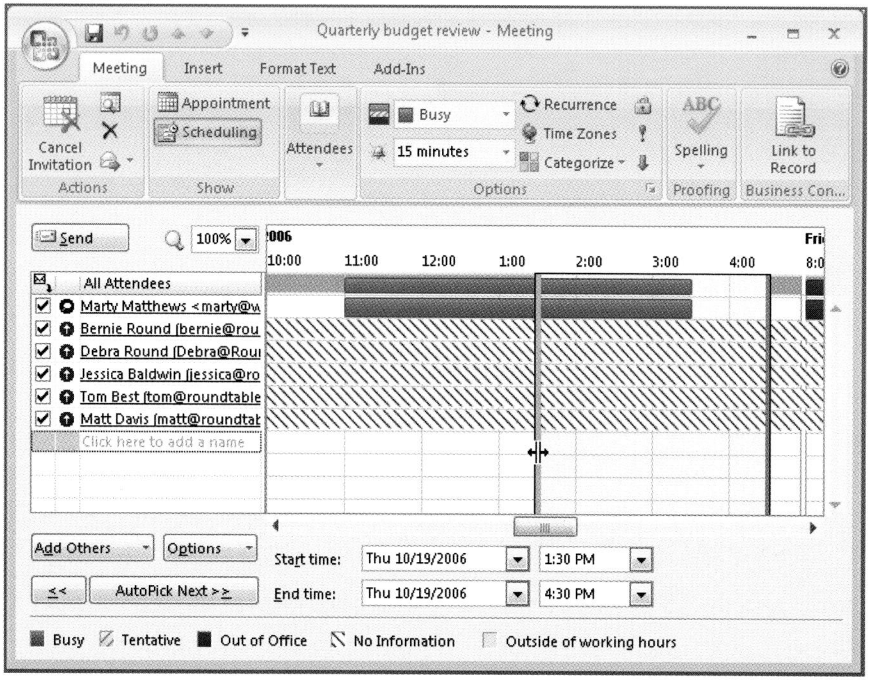

Figure 5-13: *The Scheduling Assistant determines when a meeting will be held and helps you select attendees.*

7. Click **All Day Event**, if necessary.

8. Enter any additional information in the Notes section of the Meeting window that may be needed by the attendees.

9. In the Meeting tab Show group, click **Scheduling Assistant**. If you use Outlook 2007 with Business Contact Manager, in the Meeting tab Show group, click **Scheduling**.

10. If necessary, click **Add Others** to include others in the meeting.

11. If you want to change the meeting times, you can enter the start and ending times, or you can drag the edges of the vertical meeting line, as shown in Figure 5-13.

12. After you have entered all of your information, click **Send**.

Respond to an Invitation

When you receive a meeting request, a message appears in your Inbox with an icon that is different from the normal e-mail icon.

1. In Outlook, open the meeting notification or request.

2. On the Message tab the Respond group, click one of the following:
   - Accept
   - Tentative
   - Decline

3. To send your response with no comments, click **Send The Response Now**. Click **OK**.

4. To include comments with your response, click **Edit The Response Before Sending**.

5. Type your comments and click **Send**.

6. To send no response, click **Don't Send A Response**, and click **OK**. The meeting is added to your Calendar.

Chapter 6

Using Tasks

Keeping organized and meeting appointments and deadlines is important to us all. Outlook can help you stay organized and can even alert you to events and appointments. Outlook defines a task as something you create and track until the item is complete. Any incomplete tasks appear on the new To-Do Bar, along with any other Outlook items you have marked for follow-up. The To-Do Bar appears in every Outlook 2007 area, so you can see what you need to accomplish at a glance. An Outlook item can be an e-mail you need to answer, a contact you have marked to call back next week, or some other uncompleted task. In this chapter you will learn how to create and manage tasks, mark items for follow-up by both you and e-mail recipients, modify and delete tasks, and even share task information with others.

Use the Task Window

Tasks are Outlook items, just like e-mail and calendar entries, and when you create tasks, they are stored in a specific Outlook window. The Tasks window keeps all of your tasks in one place and automatically keeps them organized for you. In this section, you'll see how to use the Tasks window and how to view tasks.

Explore the Tasks Window

You can easily access the Tasks window and view your tasks.

1. Open Outlook as described in Chapter 1 if it is not already open.

2. Click the **Go** menu, and click **Tasks**.

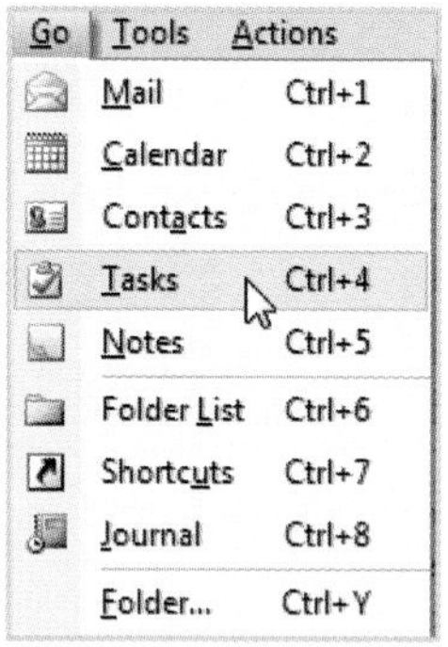

–Or–

Click the **Tasks** button in the View bar of the Navigation pane, as shown in Figure 6-1.

Either way, the Tasks window opens with your tasks listed in the center of the window, as shown in Figure 6-2. The window contains a listing of any existing tasks, which also appear in the Tasks section of the To-Do Bar on the right side of the window.

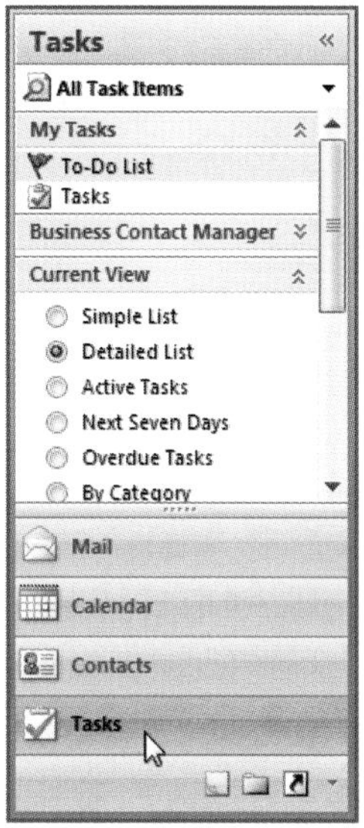

Figure 6-1: **The Navigation pane provides the fastest way to open the Tasks window.**

View Tasks

By default, Outlook gives you a simple list view of your tasks in the Tasks window. You see the name of the task, the due date, and any flags you have assigned to the task. However, you can re-sort these tasks in various ways using several different views, depending on the information you need, which can make your work easier.

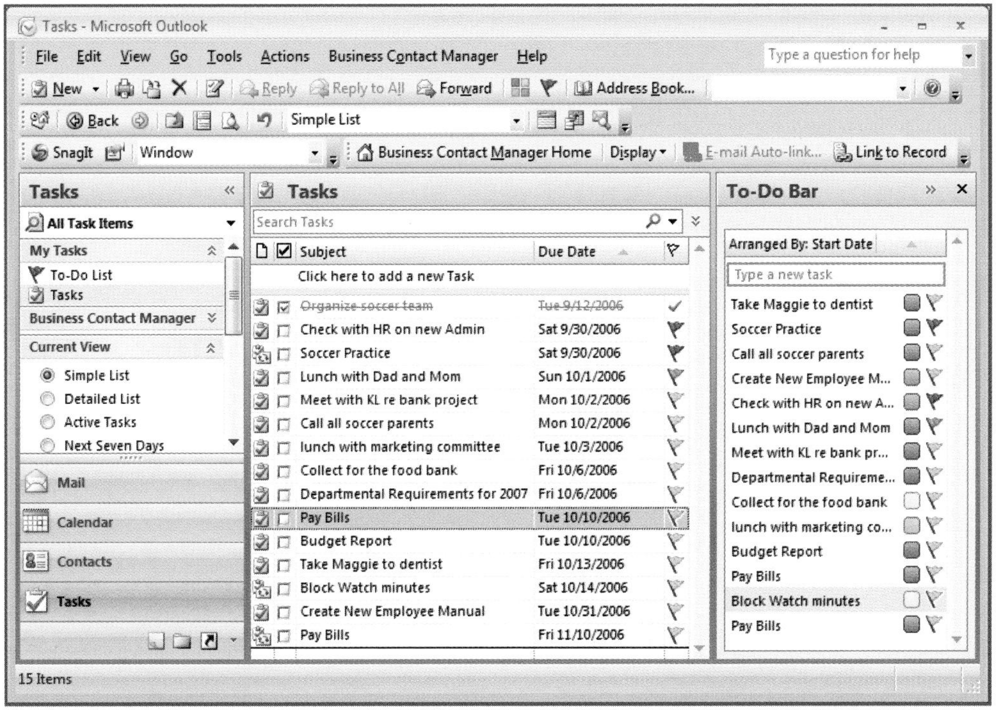

*Figure 6-2: **The Tasks window displays a listing of your tasks in both the center pane and in the To-Do Bar.***

1. Click **Tasks** in the Navigation pane to open the Tasks window.

2. In the Navigation pane, under Current View, notice that Simple List is selected by default. However, you can change your view of the tasks by clicking the different options:

   - **Simple List** displays a listing of your tasks with the subject, due date, folder, and flags shown.

   - **Detailed List** displays the subject, status, due date, percent completed, categories, and flags, as shown in Figure 6-3.

   - **Active Tasks** is the same as the Detailed List, but only shows tasks that are currently active—that is, tasks that have not been deferred or completed.

   - **Next Seven Days** is the same as the Detailed List, but only shows tasks for the next seven days.

   - **Overdue Tasks** is the same as the Detailed List, but only shows tasks that are overdue.

- **By Category** is the same as the Detailed List, but the tasks are organized by the categories that have been assigned to tasks.

- **Assignment** shows your tasks that have been assigned to others. This view shows you the task, the owner, the due date, and the status of each task.

- **By Person Responsible** organizes your tasks into collections according to the person responsible for each task. You see the subject, who requested the task, the owner, the due date, and the status.

- **Completed Tasks** shows you all tasks that have been completed.

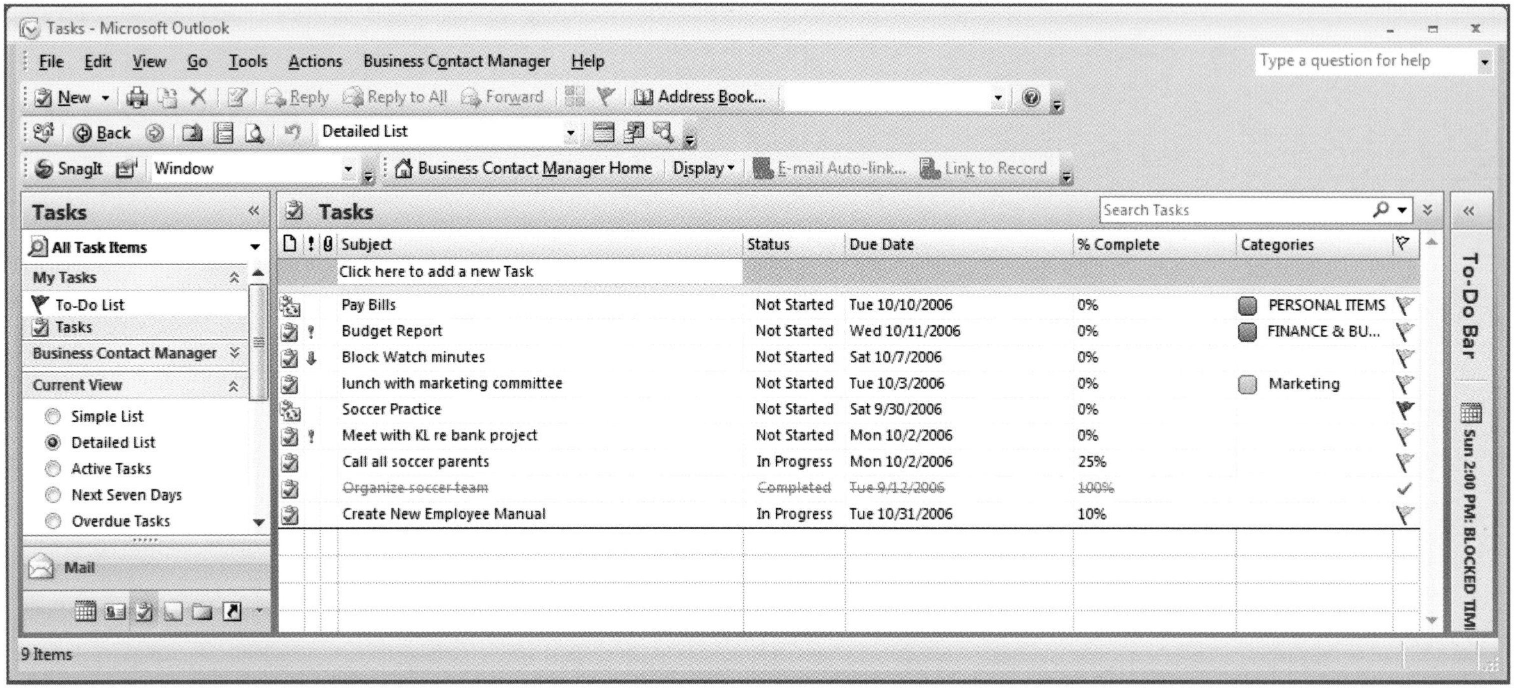

Figure 6-3: *The Detailed List gives you additional information about a given task.*

TIP

You can change views at any time by simply clicking a different view option button on the Navigation pane in the Tasks window.

- **Task Timeline** turns the Tasks window into a timeline view, where you can see the tasks that are due according to calendar dates, as shown in Figure 6-4.

- **Server Tasks** are used with Microsoft Exchange accounts. This view includes the name of the person to whom the task has been assigned.

- **Outlook Data Files** are the data files you have created in Outlook 2007. For most users, this list is the same as the Simple List view, except it displays the file in which your task resides.

CUSTOMIZE YOUR VIEWS

You can modify any task view to fit your needs.

1. In the Tasks Navigation pane, at the bottom of the Current View list, click **Customize Current View** to open the Customize View dialog box. Each description button provides options from which you can choose, for example Sort, shown on the next page:

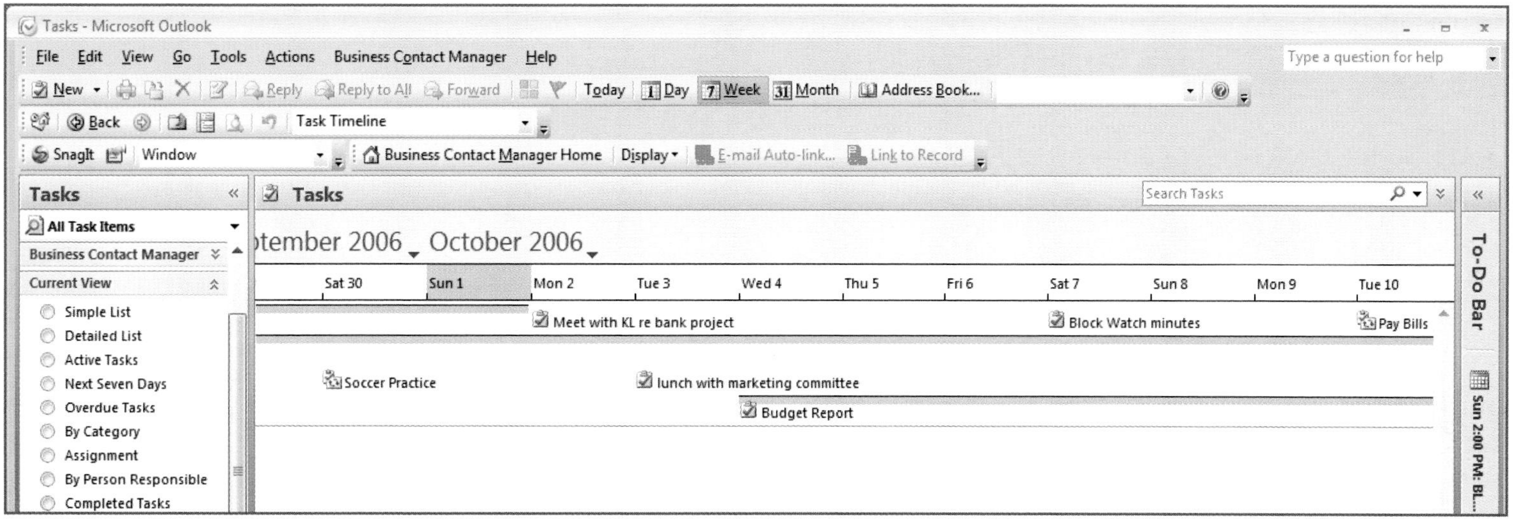

Tasks - Microsoft Outlook

File   Edit   View   Go   Tools   Actions   Business Contact Manager   Help   Type a question for help

New ▾ | 🖶 🛅 ✕ | 📝 | 🗐 Reply 🗐 Reply to All 🗐 Forward | 🔡 ▼ | Today | 🔢 Day | 7 Week | 31 Month | 🛄 Address Book...   ▾ | ⊘ ▾

📷 | ⊙ Back ⊙ | 🗐 🗐 🗐 | 🔟 | Task Timeline   ▾ ▾

Snaglt 📕 | Window   ▾ ▾ | 🏠 Business Contact Manager Home | Display ▾ | 📩 E-mail Auto-link... 📩 Link to Record ▾

| Tasks « | 📝 Tasks   Search Tasks   🔎 ▾ ✕ « |

Tasks

🔎 All Task Items   ▾

Business Contact Manager ▾ ≫

Current View   ≫

◯ Simple List
◯ Detailed List
◯ Active Tasks
◯ Next Seven Days
◯ Overdue Tasks
◯ By Category
◯ Assignment
◯ By Person Responsible
◯ Completed Tasks

otember 2006 ▾ October 2006 ▾

| | Sat 30 | Sun 1 | Mon 2 | Tue 3 | Wed 4 | Thu 5 | Fri 6 | Sat 7 | Sun 8 | Mon 9 | Tue 10 |

☑ Meet with KL re bank project   ☑ Block Watch minutes   ☑ Pay Bills

📅 Soccer Practice   ☑ lunch with marketing committee

☑ Budget Report

To-Do Bar

Sun 2:00 PM: BL...

Figure 6-4: **The timeline view gives you a quick look at the upcoming tasks.**

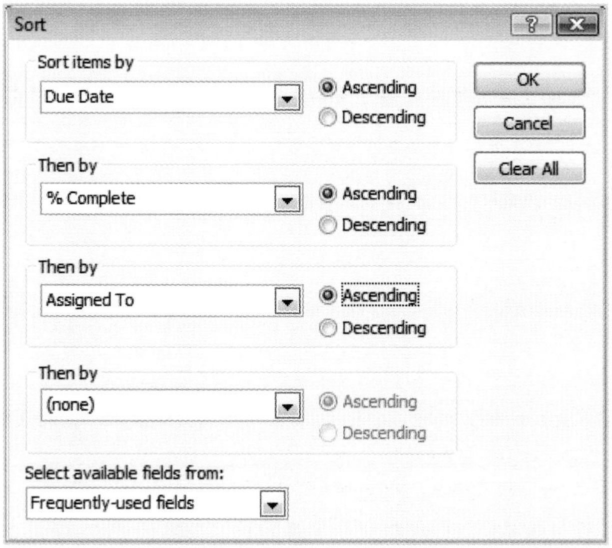

Sort   ? ✕

Sort items by

| Due Date   ▾ | ⦿ Ascending | OK |
| | ◯ Descending | Cancel |

Then by

| % Complete   ▾ | ⦿ Ascending | Clear All |
| | ◯ Descending | |

Then by

| Assigned To   ▾ | ⦿ Ascending |
| | ◯ Descending |

Then by

| (none)   ▾ | ◯ Ascending |
| | ◯ Descending |

Select available fields from:

| Frequently-used fields   ▾ |

2. Click **Fields** and double-click the fields you want displayed in your Tasks window. Click **OK** when you are finished.

3. Click **Group By**, click the **Group Items By** down arrow, click the item on which to group, click **Ascending** or **Descending**, and choose whether to show the field. Repeat this process for up to three more sub-groupings, and then click **OK**.

4. Click **Sort**, click the **Sort Items By** down arrow, click the item on which to sort, and click **Ascending** or **Descending**. Repeat this process for up to three more sub-sorts, and then click **OK**.

5. Click **Filter**, click in the **Search For The Word(s)** text box, type the words to search on, click the **In** down arrow, click where you want to search, and use the other fields to locate just tasks you want to work with, and click **OK**.

6. Click **Other Settings** to change the font and font size, to turn the Reading Pane off and on, change the grid line and headings displays. In the AutoPreview section, choose how you want to use AutoPreview, if and where you want the Reading pane, make any desired changes in Other Options, and click **OK**.

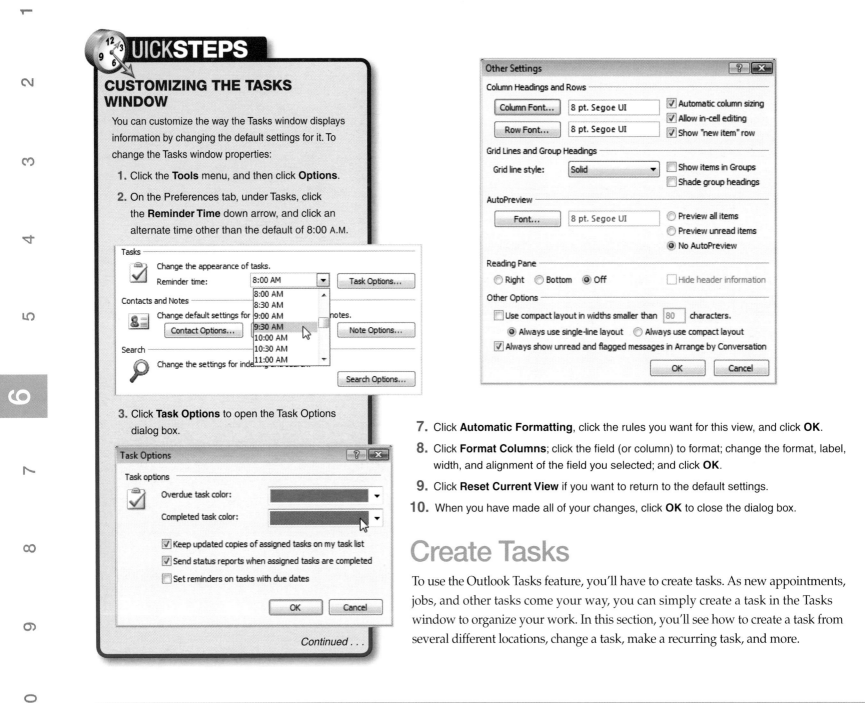

QUICKSTEPS

CUSTOMIZING THE TASKS WINDOW

You can customize the way the Tasks window displays information by changing the default settings for it. To change the Tasks window properties:

1. Click the **Tools** menu, and then click **Options**.

2. On the Preferences tab, under Tasks, click the **Reminder Time** down arrow, and click an alternate time other than the default of 8:00 A.M.

3. Click **Task Options** to open the Task Options dialog box.

Continued . . .

7. Click **Automatic Formatting**, click the rules you want for this view, and click **OK**.

8. Click **Format Columns**; click the field (or column) to format; change the format, label, width, and alignment of the field you selected; and click **OK**.

9. Click **Reset Current View** if you want to return to the default settings.

10. When you have made all of your changes, click **OK** to close the dialog box.

Create Tasks

To use the Outlook Tasks feature, you'll have to create tasks. As new appointments, jobs, and other tasks come your way, you can simply create a task in the Tasks window to organize your work. In this section, you'll see how to create a task from several different locations, change a task, make a recurring task, and more.

CUSTOMIZING THE TASKS WINDOW *(Continued)*

4. Click the **Overdue Task Color** down arrow to display a drop-down list of other colors from which you can choose. Click the color you want to use instead of the default red.

5. Click the **Completed Task Color** down arrow, and change the color of completed tasks to the color you want to use.

6. By default, the Keep Updated Copies Of Assigned Tasks On My Task List check box is selected. Clear the check box by clicking it if you do *not* want your assigned tasks updated.

7. By default, the Send Status Reports When Assigned Tasks Are Completed check box is selected. Clear the check box by clicking it. Both of these items are used primarily by those on Microsoft Exchange Server.

8. Click **Set Reminders On Tasks With Due Dates** to create a reminder on your To-Do Bar to complete your tasks on time.

9. Click **OK** to close the Task Options dialog box. Click **OK** once more to close the Options dialog box.

Create a Task from the Menu Bar

If you have used earlier versions of Microsoft Outlook, adding a new task from the menu bar may be familiar to you.

1. In the Tasks window, click the **File** menu, click **New**, and then click **Task**.

    –Or–

    On the standard toolbar, click **New**.

    Either way, the New Task window opens, as shown in Figure 6-5.

2. In the Task tab Show group, click **Task** if it is not already selected.

3. Click in the **Subject** text box, and type a name for this task. This is all the information you must enter for your task.

4. If you choose, click the **Start Date** down arrow to display a calendar from which you can choose the starting date for this task, or simply type a date.

5. If you have chosen to enter a start date, the due date is automatically the same date. Click the **Due Date** down arrow to display a calendar from which you can choose the date this task is to be completed.

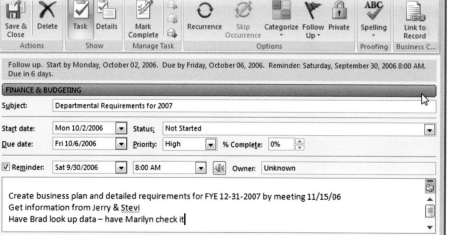

Figure 6-5: **The New Task window helps you enter information about a job you must complete.**

Status:	Not Started
Priority:	Low
	Low
	Normal
	High

6. You can keep track of the progress of this task with the Status, Priority, and %Complete boxes:

- Click the **Status** down arrow to choose the current stage of this task.
- Click **Priority** to set the importance of this task to low, normal, or high.
- Click **%Complete** to enter what percentage of the task is currently complete. You can also use the up and down arrows to scroll among 25%, 50%, 75%, and 100%.

7. If you want to be reminded of this task, click the **Reminder** down arrow, and choose a date on which to be reminded. Type a time for the reminder or choose one from the drop-down list.

8. Click the 🔊 to open the Reminder Sound dialog box:

- Click **Play This Sound** to have that happen.
- Click **Browse** to look for and select another sound file that you want to play as a reminder.
- Click **OK** to close the dialog box.

9. Click **Owner** to type the name of the person who is responsible for this task.

10. Click in the task body to add any additional information or notes about this task.

11. In the Task tab Show group, click **Details** to open the Details window. This window can be used as a basis for billing a client, as documentation for expense reports, or simply as a means of recording all pertinent information about your task.

12. To save the task, in the Task tab Actions group, click **Save & Close**.

TIP

To create a new task from anywhere in Outlook, use the keyboard shortcut **CTRL+SHIFT+K**.

Set Recurring Tasks

If you want to have a task reappear in your To-Do Bar on a regular basis, such as paying your bills each month on the tenth, you need to tell Outlook.

1. From the Task window, open the task you want to recur.

2. On the Task tab Options group, click **Recurrence** to open the Task Recurrence window.

3. Click **Monthly** if you want to have this task appear on a monthly basis. Choose one of the other options if they apply.

4. Click **Day** to set the day of the month on which this task is to appear, and enter how many months. For example, if you want your task to appear on day 10 of every month, type 10 and 1, as seen in Figure 6-6.

Task Recurrence

Recurrence pattern

- Daily
- Weekly
- Monthly
- Yearly

- Day 10 of every 1 month(s)
- The second Tuesday of every 1 month(s)
- Regenerate new task 1 month(s) after each task is completed

Range of recurrence

Start: Tue 10/10/2006

- No end date
- End after: 10 occurrences
- End by: Tue 7/10/2007

OK   Cancel   Remove Recurrence

*Figure 6-6: **The Task Recurrence dialog box is used when you create repeating tasks.***

5. Alternately, you can designate the first, last, or other week and corresponding day of the month.

6. Click **Regenerate New Task _ Month(s) After Each Task Is Completed**, and enter the number of months between appearances if this is a monthly, quarterly, or other repeating task, such as paying your bills.

7. Click **No End Date** if the recurrence of the task is permanent—as in paying bills. If the task occurs for only a specific amount of time, choose the option that applies.

8. Click **OK** to close the dialog box. In the Task tab Actions group, click **Save And Close**.

SKIP A RECURRING TASK

1. From the Tasks window, double-click the recurring task with which you want to work.

2. In the Task tab Options group, click **Skip Occurrence**. The current occurrence of this task will be skipped, and the due date is set to the next regular occurrence.

3. In the Task tab Actions group, click **Save & Close**.

4. If you have set a specific number of occurrences for this task, the number is reduced by one.

END A RECURRING TASK

If you wish to end a recurring task:

1. From the Tasks window, double-click the recurring task you want to end. The Task window will open.

2. In the Task tab Options group, click **Recurrence** to open the Task Recurrence dialog box.

3. Click **Remove Recurrence** at the bottom of the dialog box.

4. In the Task tab Actions group, click **Save & Close**.

Categorize a Task

If a task belongs with other Outlook items in a specific category:

1. From the Task window, open the task you want to categorize.

2. In the Task tab Options group, click **Categorize** to open the Color Category menu.

3. Click the category to which this task belongs. The category appears at the top of the Tasks window.

4. In the Task tab Actions group, click **Save & Close**.

CREATE A TASK IN THE TO-DO BAR

By default, the To-Do Bar appears in all Outlook views. You can easily create a new task in the To-Do Bar itself.

1. In any Outlook view, click the **Task Input Panel**. (You may see this as the Type A New Task text box.)

2. The text box changes to an outlined box with a blinking cursor. Type a quick description for the task, and press **ENTER**.

3. The new task will appear immediately in your Tasks window with today as both the start and due dates. The new task also appears under Today's Tasks in the To-Do Bar.

4. Double-click the new task in the To-Do Bar to make any changes to it.

CREATE A NEW TASK IN THE DAILY TASK LIST IN CALENDAR

When you are working in the Day or Week view in Calendar in Outlook 2007, the Daily Task list can be displayed at the bottom of the Calendar grid. You can quickly add a new task from this list.

1. In the Outlook Calendar window, click **Day** or **Week**.

2. Click the **View** menu, click **Daily Task List**, and click **Normal**. The Daily Task list appears at the bottom of the Calendar grid.

3. Position your mouse pointer in a blank area of the Daily Tasks list, and click the **Click To Add Task** message that appears under your mouse pointer. A text box appears.

NOTE

To change or remove the color category of an existing task, in the Tasks window, right-click the **Color Category** field, and choose **Clear All Categories** or choose another color category.

4. Type a name or subject for your task, and press **ENTER**. The task will be assigned the same start and end dates of the day in which the Daily Task list appears.

5. To change these dates, you can drag the task to the proper date or open the task and make the changes.

ADD A NEW TASK FROM AN E-MAIL MESSAGE

From time to time, you may receive an e-mail that you need to make into a task.

1. In Outlook, from the E-mail view, click the e-mail to select it.

2. Hold down the mouse button and drag the e-mail message to the Task button on the Navigation pane.

3. The New Task window opens with a copy of the e-mail appearing in the task body. Make any changes or additions you need, as described in "Create a New Task from the Menu Bar" earlier in this chapter.

4. In the Task tab Actions group, click **Save & Close** to save the new task.

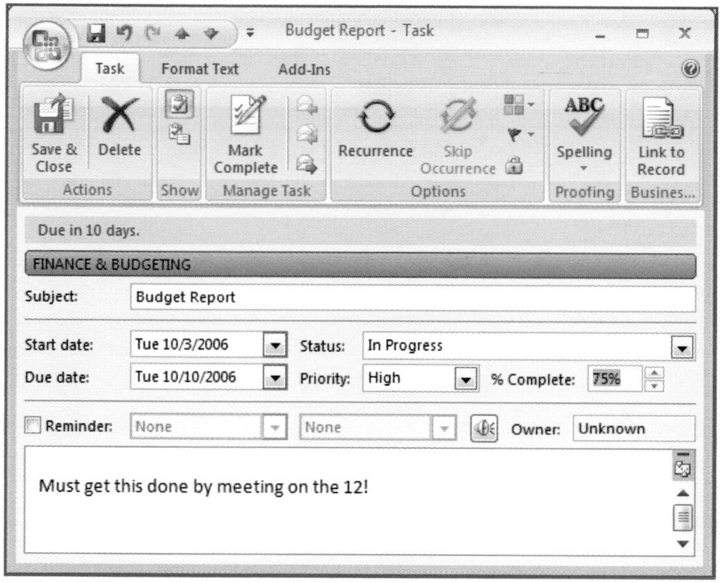

CHANGE A TASK

Some of the tasks that you create will change. The report that was due in a month is suddenly due in a week, and the conference call you had planned for 10:00 A.M. changes to 4:00 P.M. You can easily change and edit your tasks. To change a task:

1. Double-click your selected task from the Tasks window.

–Or–

Double-click the selected task in the To-Do Bar.

In either case, the Task window will open.

2. Make any desired changes to the task. For example, in Figure 6-7, we have changed the start date for the task and changed its percentage complete to 75%.

3. When you're done, in the Tasks tab Actions group, click **Save & Close**.

Assign a New Task

You can easily create a task and assign it to someone else who is using Microsoft Outlook.

Figure 6-7: **You can make any desired changes to a task.**

![Complete next year budget report - Task window. Ribbon with Task, Insert, Format Text, Add-Ins tabs. Actions group (Delete), Show group (Task, Details), Manage Task group (Cancel Assignment, Address Book, Check Names), Options group (Recurrence, Skip Occurrence, Categorize, Follow Up, Private), Proofing group (Spelling).](image)

Reply. Start by Monday, October 02, 2006. Due by Thursday, October 26, 2006.
This message has not been sent.

To... brad@ellison.com

Subject: Complete next year budget report

Start date: Mon 10/2/2006   Status: In Progress

Due date: Thu 10/26/2006   Priority: Normal   % Complete: 75%

☑ Keep an updated copy of this task on my task list
☑ Send me a status report when this task is complete

Brad – I need your data by the 10th – would really appreciate it earlier, but absolute date is the 10th.
Please review your data with Marilyn before you submit it

Figure 6-8: **Assigning a task to another Outlook user is as easy as sending an e-mail.**

TIP

You can assign the same task to several people by simply typing all e-mail addresses in the To text box, just as you would with any e-mail.

TIP

The recipient must accept the task that you send in order for it to be added to his or her Tasks window. You will receive an e-mail receipt from the recipient once the task is accepted.

1. In the Tasks window, click the **File** menu, click **New,** and click **Task Request**. The New Task Request window will open, as shown in Figure 6-8.

2. In the Task tab Show group, click **Task** if it is not selected.

3. Click **To** and enter the name or e-mail address of the person to whom you are assigning the task.

4. Click **Subject** and enter a name for this new task.

5. If you choose, click the **Start Date** and **Due Date** down arrows, and enter the beginning and due dates of this task, respectively.

6. If you choose, click the **Status** and **Priority** down arrows to enter the current status and priority level of this task.

7. If any part of the task has been completed, indicate the percentage in the **%Complete** field.

8. Clear the **Keep An Updated Copy Of This Task On My Task List** check box (which is selected by default) if you do not want to have this task updated.

☑ Keep updated copies of assigned tasks on my task list
☑ Send status reports when assigned tasks are completed
☐ Set reminders on tasks with due dates

9. Click the **Send Me A Status Report When This Task Is Complete** check box (also selected by default) if you don't want to receive a status report.

10. Click in the body of the task, and type any additional information needed by the assignee.

11. If you want this task to be recurring, in the Task tab Options group, click **Recurrence** and follow the steps outlined in "Set Recurring Tasks" earlier in this chapter.

12. Click **Send** to send the task request.

ASSIGN AN EXISTING TASK

1. In the Tasks window, double-click the task you want to assign.

2. In the Task tab Manage Task group, click **Assign Task**. The Assign Task window will open.

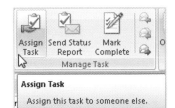

Manage Task

Assign Task

Assign this task to someone else.

3. Click **To** and type the e-mail or name of the person to whom you are assigning this task. The e-mail subject will be the same name as the existing task.

4. Follow steps 5–12 in "Assign a New Task" earlier in this chapter.

TRACK ASSIGNED TASKS

You can track assigned tasks in three ways: automatically keep copies, view assigned tasks, and view a list of people who have received assigned tasks.

To automatically keep copies:

1. In the Tasks window, click the **Tools** menu, and click **Options**.

2. Click **Task Options** to open the Task Options dialog box.

3. Choose **Keep Updated Copies Of Assigned Tasks On My Task List**, **Send Status Reports When Assigned Tasks Are Completed**, and/or **Set Reminders On Tasks With Due Dates**, as appropriate.

4. Click **OK** twice to close first the Task Options and then the Options dialog boxes.

VIEW ASSIGNED TASKS AND RECIPIENTS

To view tasks you have assigned to others:

1. In the Tasks window, click the **View** menu.

2. Click **Current View** and click **Assignment**. The list of assigned tasks is displayed in your Tasks window.

To view a list of people who have received tasks:

1. In the Tasks window, double-click the assigned task you want to view.

2. In the Task tab Show group, click **Details** to see a list of people who have accepted the task. The names will appear in the Update List box.

3. In the Task tab Actions group, click **Save & Close**.

Make a Task Private

In networks that use Microsoft Exchange Server, you can give other people access to your tasks. For example, let's say that you are a team leader for a department. Within your department, several department coordinators may need to access your tasks and enter tasks that you need to complete. This allows others to manipulate and change your tasks, which you can, of course, also work on yourself.

If you are a user on a private network, or one who uses Outlook for Internet e-mail, there is no advantage to making an item private. This feature is designed for networks where other users have specifically been granted permission to see your Tasks window, Calendar, and other Outlook features.

ACCEPTING OR DECLINING A TASK ASSIGNMENT

You can easily accept or decline a task assignment given to you.

1. In the Tasks window, double-click the task to open it.

2. In the Task tab Respond group, click **Accept** or **Decline**. The Accepting Task or Declining Task dialog box appears.

3. If desired, click **Edit The Response Before Sending**; click **OK**; type any notes, questions, or comments in the message box; and click **Send**.

4. If you do not want to include any comments, click **Send The Response Now**.

However, in some instances, you may create a task that you want to keep private in an environment like this. This action will keep people who have permission to view your tasks from seeing that particular task. To make a task private:

1. In the Tasks window, double-click a task to open the Task window.

2. In the Task tab Options group, click **Private**.

3. In the Task tab Actions group, click **Save & Close**. Your task is no longer visible to others.

Manage Tasks

After you have created a task, Outlook provides several tools you can use to manage them, including marking them as completed, choosing whether to display them, deleting, and renaming them, as well as creating status reports on your tasks.

Mark a Task as Complete

Once you finish a task, you can mark it as having been completed. The task will be attached to the day on which you marked it complete, and it will appear with a line drawn through it.

There are several ways in which you can mark a task as complete.

MARK A TASK AS COMPLETE FROM THE TASK WINDOW

1. From the Tasks window, double-click the selected task to open the Task window.

2. Click the **%Complete** box, and select **100%**.

3. In the Task tab Actions group, click **Save & Close**. The task will appear on your Task list with a line drawn through it.

MARK A TASK AS COMPLETE FROM THE TO-DO BAR

1. On the To-Do Bar in any view of Outlook 2007, locate the task.

2. Right-click the task that you want to mark as complete.

3. Click **Mark Complete** on the context menu.

MARK A FLAGGED TASK AS COMPLETE FROM THE TASK WINDOW

1. Locate the task you want to mark as complete.

2. Click the flag. The flag turns into a check mark, and a line is drawn through the task.

Choose to Not Display a Completed Task

Normally, when you complete a task, it remains on the Task list with a line through it. However, a task does not appear on the To-Do Bar after it has been marked as complete.

SET COMPLETED ITEMS NOT TO DISPLAY IN A TASK LIST

In Outlook Tasks, click the **View** menu, click **Current View**, and click **Active Tasks**.

–Or–

Click **Current View** on the navigation bar, and click **Active Tasks**.

Either choice will set your list to display only the active items.

SHOW COMPLETED ITEMS IN THE TO-DO BAR

By default, the To-Do Bar does not display completed items. To change this:

1. In the To-Do Bar, right-click **Arranged By** to open its context menu.

2. Click **Custom** to open the Customize View dialog box.

3. Click **Filter** to display the Filter dialog box.

4. Click **Clear All** to clear the default choices.

5. Click **OK** to close the Filter dialog box.

6. Click **OK** once more to close the custom view dialog box.

SHOW COMPLETED ITEMS IN THE DAILY TASK LIST

1. In Outlook Calendar Day or Week view, click the **View** menu.

2. Click **Daily Task List**, and click **Normal**.

NOTE

If you want to change the status of a task you have marked complete, click the **Status** field in Detailed List view to see a drop-down menu. Choose the status to which you want to change.

NOTE

Be careful *not* to delete tasks that you still need, even if they are completed. Completed tasks provide a record of what has been accomplished, so make sure you no longer need the task before you delete it.

NOTE

You can rename a task from the To-Do Bar by slowly clicking the task name twice, backspacing over the old name, and typing a new name.

3. In the Daily Task list, right-click **Show Tasks On**.

4. If it is not already selected, click **Show Completed Tasks**.

Delete a Task

Once a task has been completed, or should a task fall out of the scope of your responsibility, you can simply delete the task.

There are several ways to delete a task.

1. Right-click the task in the Tasks window, and click **Delete** on the context menu.

   –Or–

   Double-click the task in the To-Do Bar or in any Task list to open the Task window.

2. In the Task tab Actions group, click **Delete**.

   –Or–

   Click the selected task in a Task list, and click **Delete** on the standard toolbar.

   –Or–

   Click the selected task in any list, and press **CTRL+D**.

Rename a Task

As projects go along, it may be necessary to rename a task. You can do this at any time.

1. In Outlook Tasks, in any list view, (or in the Daily Task list in Calendar), click the selected task.

2. Press the **F2** key on your keyboard.

3. Backspace over the old name, and type the new name.

4. Press **ENTER**.

Create Status Reports

Outlook allows you to create a status report for a task, which, in reality, is an e-mail message summarizing the status of your task. You can then send the e-mail to anyone who needs the status information. You can also print a copy for your records.

QUICKSTEPS

LINKING A TASK TO A CONTACT

There may be occasions where you would like to link a task to one of your contacts. Before you can do this, it is necessary to set contacts to appear in your Tasks window.

1. In Outlook Tasks, click the **Tools** menu, and click **Options**.

2. Click the **Preferences** tab, and click **Contact Options**.

3. Click **Show Contact Linking On All Forms**.

Contact Options dialog box:

Contact Options   [?] [⊠]

Name and filing options for new contacts

Select the order you want Outlook to use for new names:

Default "Full Name" order: First (Middle) Last ▾

Select the default setting for how to file new contacts:

Default "File As" order: Last, First ▾

☑ Check for duplicate contacts

Contact Linking

☑ Show Contact Linking on all Forms

Contacts Index options

☐ Show an additional Contacts Index

Additional Contacts Index: Arabic ▾

OK   Cancel

4. Click **OK** to close the Contact Options dialog box.

5. Click **OK** once more to close the Options dialog box.

6. In the Tasks window, double-click the task that you want to link to a contact. The Task window will open.

Continued . . .

1. In the Tasks window, double-click the task on which you want to report. The Task window will open.

2. In the Task tab Manage Task group, click **Send Status Report**. An e-mail message will open, as seen in Figure 6-9.

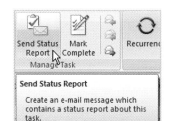

3. Click **To** and type the e-mail address or the name of the person to whom you are sending the report.

4. Click **Cc** if you want to send a carbon copy. Type the e-mail address or the name of the person to whom you want the carbon copy sent.

5. Click **Bcc** and follow the procedure in step 4 for a blind carbon copy. The e-mail subject line is already filled in with "Task Status Report" and the name of your task.

6. Click in the message body, and type any additional comments or notes.

7. Click **Send**.

Figure 6-9: A status report provides a fast and easy way to e-mail progress information on a task.

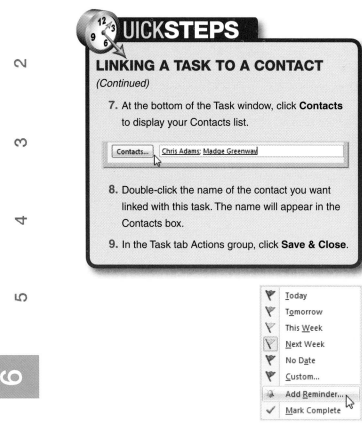

QUICKSTEPS

LINKING A TASK TO A CONTACT
(Continued)

7. At the bottom of the Task window, click **Contacts** to display your Contacts list.

Contacts... | Chris Adams; Madge Greenway

8. Double-click the name of the contact you want linked with this task. The name will appear in the Contacts box.

9. In the Task tab Actions group, click **Save & Close**.

Work with Follow-up Flags

When you add a flag to any item in Outlook 2007, it is a visual reminder that you need to do something with that item. There are several default settings for the follow-up flags in Outlook 2007. Each is based on a date. Table 6-1 explains how the dates work. You can, however, customize the dates for any flag, and you do not need to set a reminder.

When you add a flag to any item, it is shown in the To-Do Bar, the Daily Task list in Calendar, and all Task lists in Tasks.

Add a Flag to an Existing Task

A flag draws your attention to a task. It is a signal that you need to follow up on this item. If you did not mark a task for follow-up when you created it, you can add the flag at any time.

1. In Outlook, click **Tasks** on the Navigation pane to show your Task list.

2. Double-click the task with which you want to work to open the Task window.

3. In the Task tab Options group, click **Follow Up**.

4. Click your selection from the menu.

5. If you want to include a reminder with this task, click **Add Reminder**. The Custom dialog box appears.

Today
Tomorrow
This Week
Next Week
No Date
Custom...
Add Reminder...
Mark Complete

Table 6-1: **Default Settings for Follow-up Flags**

FLAG	START DATE	DUE DATE	REMINDER SETTING
Today	Today's date	Today's date	The reminder will prompt you one hour before the end of your current work day.
Tomorrow	Tomorrow's date	Tomorrow's date	You will be reminded at the start of your next work day.
This Week	Today plus two days, but no later than the last work day of this week.	The last work day of this week.	You are sent a reminder at the start time of today's date plus two days.
Next Week	The first work day of the next work week.	The last work day of the next work week.	You are sent a reminder at the start time of the first work day next week.
No Date	No date is set.	No date is set.	You are reminded today.
Custom	You may choose a start date.	You choose a due date.	You are reminded on the due date you set.

6. Click the **Flag To** down arrow, and choose an option.

7. The Start Date and Due Date fields are filled with information from the existing task. Click the **Reminder** down arrow, and choose the date and time at which you want to be reminded.

8. Click **OK** to save your changes and close the Custom dialog box.

9. In the Task tab Actions group, click **Save & Close**.

Set a Quick Click Flag

You can attach a Quick Click flag to any Outlook item. This flag, which is set to today's date by default, allows you to flag a task, contact, e-mail message, or other item with only one mouse click in the flag column.

To set the type of flag that will be added with Quick Click:

1. In any Task list, right-click in the Flag column.

2. Click **Set Quick Click** on the context menu. The Set Quick Click dialog box will appear.

3. Click the **Flag** down arrow to select the settings for the Quick Click flag.

4. Choose the flag from the drop-down list that will appear upon being clicked.

5. Click **OK** to close the dialog box.

Work with the To-Do Bar

The To-Do Bar has four parts, three of which can be hidden. The Task list remains at all times.

Set the To-Do Bar to Show Only Tasks

Because, by default, all flagged items in Outlook are shown on the To-Do Bar, there may be times when that is too much information. To turn off all items except your tasks:

1. In Outlook 2007, right-click in the top bar of the To-Do Bar.

2. In the resulting context menu, click to remove the check mark next to **Date Navigator** to hide the Date Navigator.

3. Reopen the To-Do Bar context menu, and click to remove the check mark next to **Appointments** to hide your appointments.

4. To show either item, reverse the above procedure.

CHANGE THE SIZE OF THE TO-DO BAR

The To-Do bar can be resized using your mouse.

1. Position your mouse pointer at the left edge of the To-Do Bar.

2. When the pointer changes to parallel lines with arrows ⬌, hold down the mouse button, and drag the To-Do Bar to the width you want.

TURN THE TO-DO BAR OFF AND ON

By default, Outlook 2007 displays the To-Do Bar in every view. However, you can turn it off in the current view. When you next start Outlook, the To-Do Bar will still be turned off in the current view you were using when you last used Outlook.

To turn the To-Do Bar either off or on, from the keyboard, in any Outlook view, press **ALT+F2**.

Chapter 7
Using a Journal and Making Notes

Microsoft Outlook contains two important features that help you stay organized and that can help you manage various pieces of information. These features—Journal and Notes—are designed to help you manage information that you need to record, keep, and use in a variety of ways. In this chapter you'll learn how to use the Journal feature. You'll see how to work with journal entries, print your journal entries, and even share them. You'll also work with the Notes feature in this chapter. You'll see how to organize your notes, print them, and use them with other Outlook features.

Use a Journal

The Outlook Journal is a great way to track and record different kinds of information. Designed for business use, the Journal can help you keep track of associated Office documents, e-mails to a certain contact, phone calls that you make, and other information. In other words, the Journal can help you keep track of your work flow so that you'll know what has been done. In this section you'll explore the Journal, set it up, work with journal entries, and print and share your Journal.

Explore the Journal

The Journal is a standard Outlook feature. You can easily access it from the Go menu and explore its basic structure. As you can see in Figure 7-1, the Journal looks and works much like Tasks, Calendar, and other Outlook features.

Figure 7-1: *Journal entries are a way to collect and organize comments you have on phone calls, e-mail, meetings, and more.*

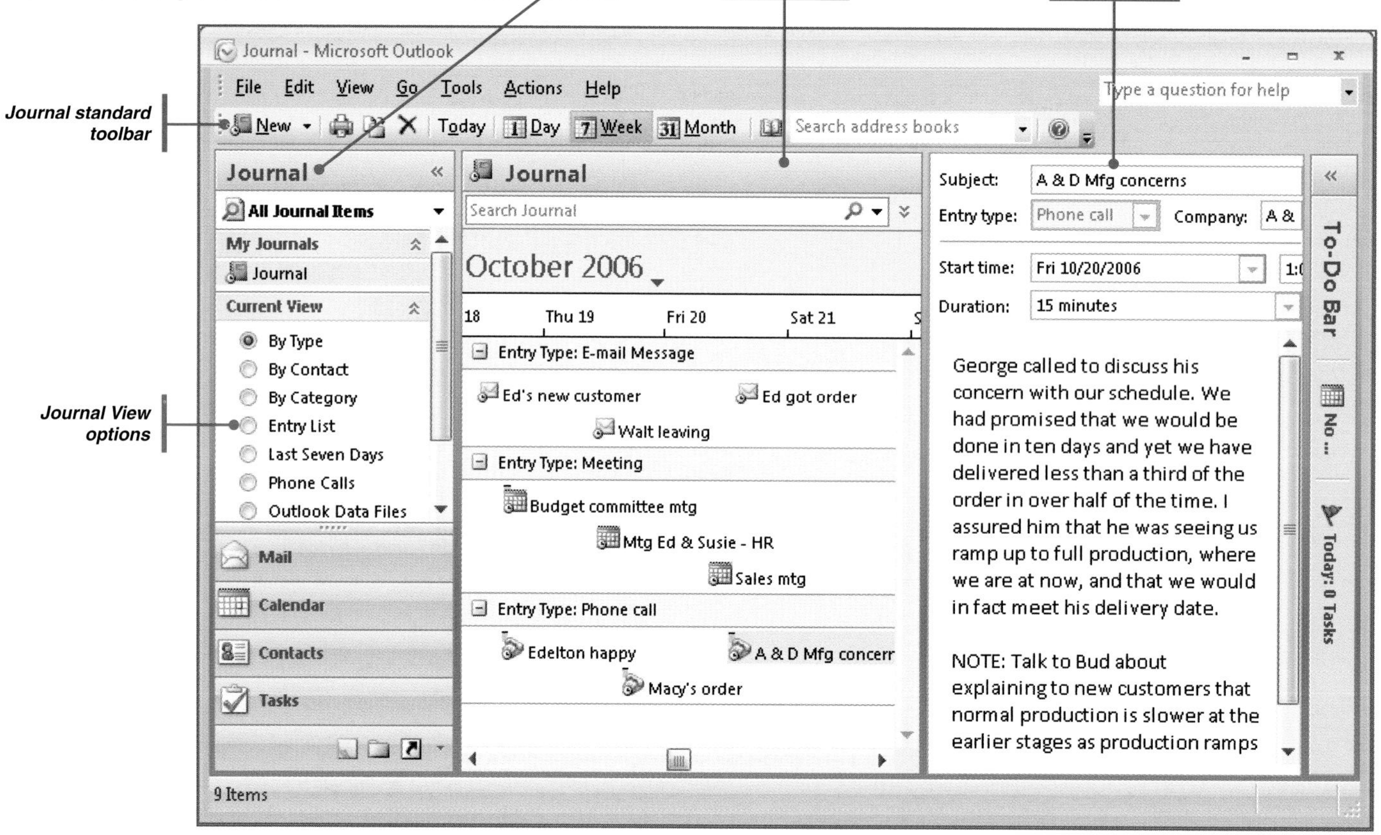

Navigation pane   Journal folder   Reading pane

Journal standard toolbar

Journal View options

NOTE

By default, the Journal is not one of the Outlook view bars in the Navigation pane or in the button bar at the bottom. You can, of course, access the Journal from the Go menu or by using the keyboard shortcut **CTRL+8**. You can also change the Navigation pane to display the Journal by clicking **Configure Buttons** on the right of the button bar, clicking **Navigation Pane Options**, clicking **Journal** to display it on the button bar, and clicking **Move Up** to display the Journal in one of the Outlook view bars.

TIP

You can make changes to the Journal options at any time by clicking **Tools** and then clicking **Options**. In the Options window Preferences tab, click **Journal Options**. You'll see the dialog box in Figure 7-2.

1. Click the **Go** menu, and then click **Journal** (see the "Setting Up the Journal" QuickSteps later in this chapter). You will see the following features:

   ● The **Navigation pane**, on the left, reflects the Journal features you can access, such as the Journal view options, which are explored later in this chapter.

   ● The **Journal folder**, in the middle, by default gives you a timeline view and a listing of any existing journal entries for the portion of the timeline you are looking at.

   ● The **Reading pane**, on the right, displays the content of the selected journal entry.

   ● The **Journal View options** in the Navigation pane allow you to look at your journal in various ways.

   ● The **standard toolbar** on the Journal gives you the option of selecting a one-day, one-week, or one-month view of the Journal folder. You can also zero in on today's journal entries.

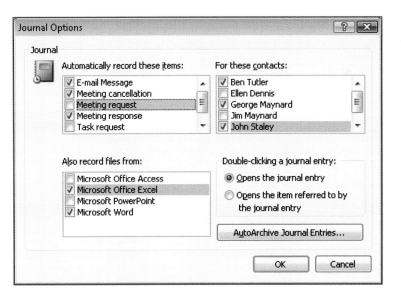

Figure 7-2: *You can select the items that you want the Journal to track, including contact e-mail data.*

UICKSTEPS

SETTING UP THE JOURNAL

If this is the first time you have used the Journal, you'll need to make a decision about how you will use it.

1. If it isn't already displayed, click **Go** and then click **Journal**.

2. A dialog box appears telling you that the Journal can track Office documents, as well as e-mail sent to contacts. However, the Activities tab on the contact's Properties dialog box is the easiest way to track e-mail. So, the question is whether you want to turn the Journal on for this purpose. Click **Yes** if you want to do this. You can turn it off later if you change your mind.

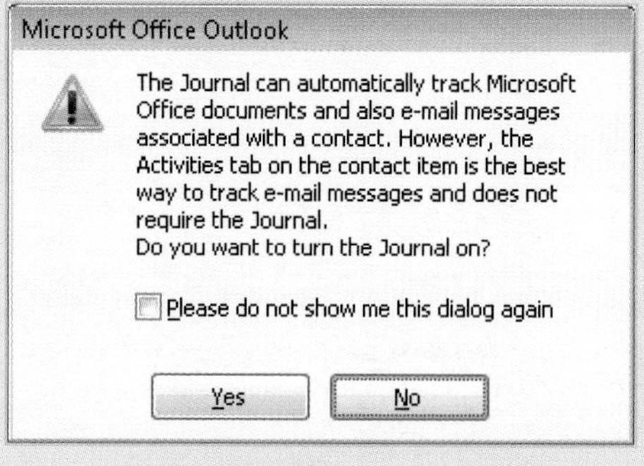

> **Microsoft Office Outlook**
>
> ⚠ The Journal can automatically track Microsoft Office documents and also e-mail messages associated with a contact. However, the Activities tab on the contact item is the best way to track e-mail messages and does not require the Journal.
> Do you want to turn the Journal on?
>
> ☐ Please do not show me this dialog again
>
> [Yes] [No]

3. In the Journal Options dialog box that appears, shown in Figure 7-2, select the contacts you want Journal to track and what items you want to track for those contacts. Notice that you can also track other Microsoft Office documents. Click **OK** when you're done.

Add a Journal Entry

With the Journal open, you can quickly and easily add journal entries as you need them.

> 🗒 New ▾ | 🖨 🗋 ✕
> Journ New Journal Entry

1. Click the **New** button on the standard toolbar.

2. In the Journal Entry window, type a descriptive name for the journal entry in the Subject text box, as shown in Figure 7-3.

3. Click the **Entry Type** drop-down menu, and choose the type of entry you are creating.

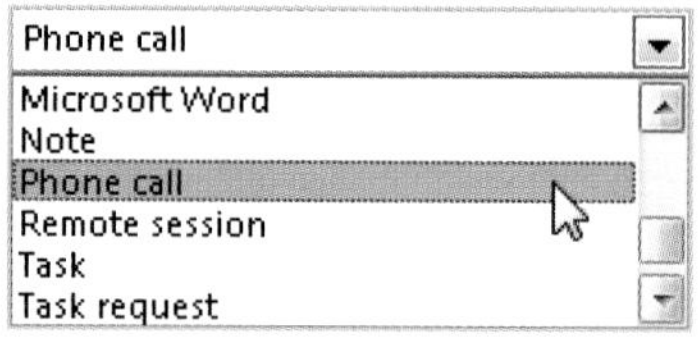

> Phone call ▾
> Microsoft Word ▲
> Note
> **Phone call**
> Remote session
> Task
> Task request ▾

4. Use the drop-down menus to select the start date and time. You can also use the drop-down menu to choose the duration of the event, if desired.

5. Click in the large text box, and type the journal entry you want to make.

6. If you want to time the entry, such as in the case of a telephone call or meeting, click **Start Timer** in the Journal Entry tab Timer group. The results of the timer appear in the

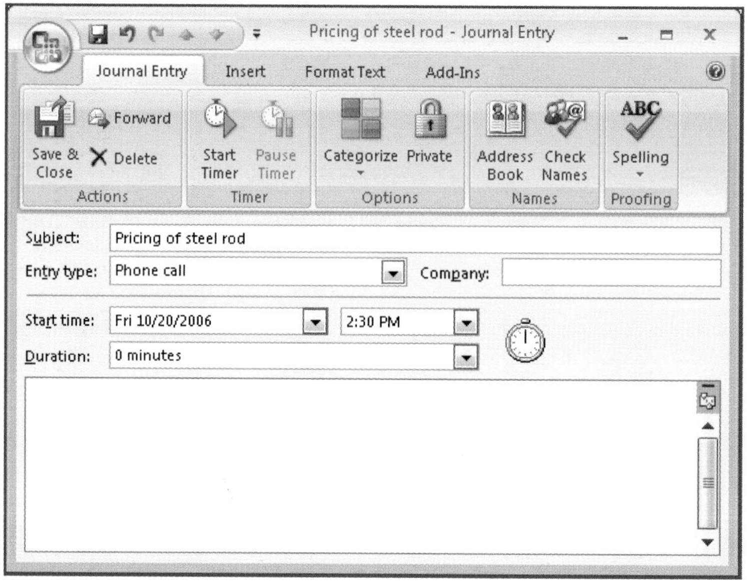

Figure 7-3: *Enter a short but descriptive name for the new journal entry.*

Duration field in even-minute increments. Click **Pause Timer** to stop the timer. You can add time to the existing time in the Duration field by clicking **Start Timer** again; reset the timer by clicking the **Duration** down arrow and clicking **0 Minutes**.

7. Click **Save And Close**. The new journal entry appears in your Journal.

Change a Journal Entry

Journal entries, like most anything else you might record in Outlook, may need to be changed. To do that:

1. In your Journal, right-click the entry you want to change, and click **Open Journal Entry**.

   –Or–

   Double-click the journal entry that you want to change.

2. The Journal Entry window opens. Make any desired changes to it, as shown in Figure 7-4.

3. Click **Save And Close**.

Delete a Journal Entry

You can easily and permanently remove journal entries from your Journal. You can do this by simply deleting the entry item. To delete a journal entry:

Right-click the entry in the Journal, and click **Delete**.

–Or–

Select the entry in the Journal, and click the **Delete** button on the toolbar.

–Or–

Select the entry in the Journal, click the **Edit** menu, and then click **Delete**.

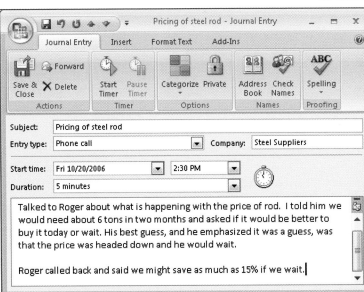

Figure 7-4: **You can change and/or add information to any journal entry.**

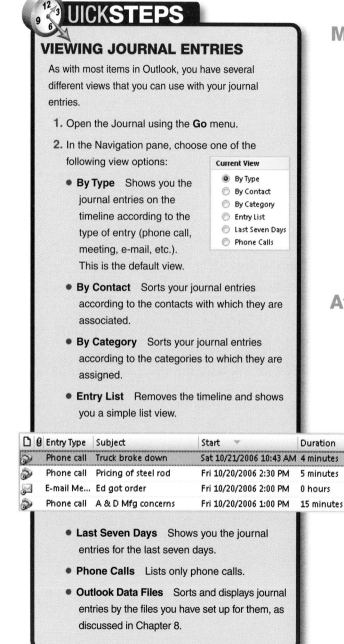

VIEWING JOURNAL ENTRIES

As with most items in Outlook, you have several different views that you can use with your journal entries.

1. Open the Journal using the **Go** menu.

2. In the Navigation pane, choose one of the following view options:

   Current View
   - By Type
   - By Contact
   - By Category
   - Entry List
   - Last Seven Days
   - Phone Calls

   - **By Type** Shows you the journal entries on the timeline according to the type of entry (phone call, meeting, e-mail, etc.). This is the default view.

   - **By Contact** Sorts your journal entries according to the contacts with which they are associated.

   - **By Category** Sorts your journal entries according to the categories to which they are assigned.

   - **Entry List** Removes the timeline and shows you a simple list view.

🗋	🖉	Entry Type	Subject	Start ▼	Duration	Cont...	C..
	🕽	Phone call	Truck broke down	Sat 10/21/2006 10:43 AM	4 minutes		
	🕽	Phone call	Pricing of steel rod	Fri 10/20/2006 2:30 PM	5 minutes		
	✉	E-mail Me...	Ed got order	Fri 10/20/2006 2:00 PM	0 hours		
	🕽	Phone call	A & D Mfg concerns	Fri 10/20/2006 1:00 PM	15 minutes		

   - **Last Seven Days** Shows you the journal entries for the last seven days.

   - **Phone Calls** Lists only phone calls.

   - **Outlook Data Files** Sorts and displays journal entries by the files you have set up for them, as discussed in Chapter 8.

Move a Journal Entry in the Timeline

The time and date values placed on journal entries might change. For example, the phone call you were going to make at 10:00 A.M. might have been moved to 4:00 P.M., and meeting times and dates are certainly subject to change, along with most other Journal items. You cannot directly drag items within the Journal itself, but you can easily change the start date and time for an entry, thus moving it on the timeline.

1. In your Journal, right-click the entry you want to edit, and click **Open Journal Entry**.

   –Or–

   Double-click the entry.

2. In the Journal Entry window, change the start date and time as needed.

3. Click **Save And Close**. The entry item will be updated on the timeline.

Attach Contacts to Journal Entries

You can attach a contact to a journal entry as you are creating a new entry, or you can decide to attach a contact later.

1. For an existing entry, double-click the entry in the Journal. If you are creating a new entry, click the **New** button on the toolbar. In either case, the Journal Entry window will open.

2. In the Journal Entry tab Names group, click **Address Book**. The Select Contacts window opens, as shown in Figure 7-5.

   Address Book   Check Names
   Names

3. If it is not already selected, under **Look In**, click the **Contacts** folder. In the **Items** field, click the desired contact. If you want to select more than one contact, hold down **CTRL** while clicking several noncontiguous contacts, or hold down **SHIFT** while clicking the first and last in a series of contiguous contacts.

4. Click **OK** and then click **Save And Close**.

NOTE

Moving a journal entry does not change the start time of the item, document, or contact for that item.

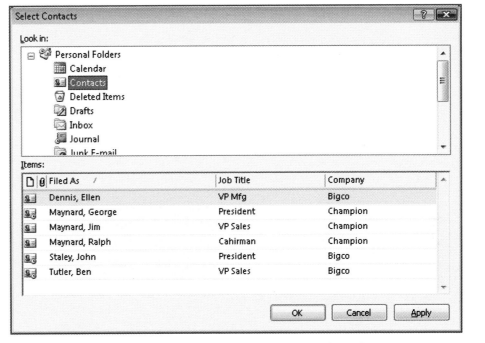

Select Contacts

Look in:

- Personal Folders
  - Calendar
  - **Contacts**
  - Deleted Items
  - Drafts
  - Inbox
  - Journal
  - Junk E-mail

Items:

🗋	🔗	Filed As	Job Title	Company
		Dennis, Ellen	VP Mfg	Bigco
		Maynard, George	President	Champion
		Maynard, Jim	VP Sales	Champion
		Maynard, Ralph	Cahirman	Champion
		Staley, John	President	Bigco
		Tutler, Ben	VP Sales	Bigco

OK   Cancel   Apply

*Figure 7-5: **Choose the contact(s) you want to associate with the journal entry.***

Categorize Private Address Book

Clear All Categories

- Blue Category
- Green Category
- Orange Category
- Purple Category
- Red Category
- Yellow Category
- All Categories...

Assign a Category to a Journal Entry

As with Tasks, you can assign categories to a journal entry. This feature makes it easier for you to keep track of the specific nature of the journal entries.

1. For an existing entry, double-click the entry in the Journal. If you are creating a new entry, click the **New** button on the toolbar. In either case, the Journal Entry window will open.

2. In the Journal Entry tab Options group, click **Categorize**. The drop-down list of categories will appear.

   –Or–

   For an existing journal entry, right-click the entry in the Journal, and click **Categorize** to open a similar drop-down list.

3. Click the desired category you want to assign. If the category is one of the initial color categories, the Rename Category dialog box will appear. Type the name of the category, change the color, and assign a shortcut key. If you have already made the color a specific category, it will be immediately applied to the entry.

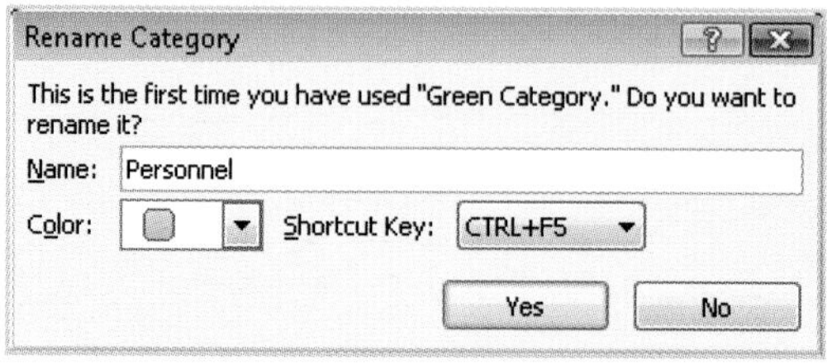

Rename Category

This is the first time you have used "Green Category." Do you want to rename it?

Name: Personnel

Color: [ ] ▼   Shortcut Key: CTRL+F5 ▼

Yes   No

4. If you do not see a category in the drop-down list that accurately identifies your task, click **All Categories** to open the Color Categories dialog box (see Figure 7-6). Click **New** to open the Add New Category dialog box. Type the name of the category, change the color, assign a shortcut key, and click **OK**. Your new category will appear in your category list with a check mark. Click **OK** again, and the new category will be attached to the journal entry.

5. Click **Save And Close**.

TIP

You may need to drag the view bars up a bit to see the Notes option.

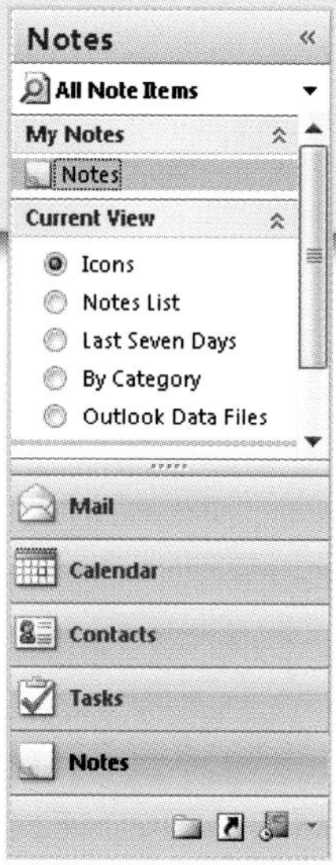

Notes «

All Note Items ▼

My Notes ≫
Notes

Current View ≫
- ⦿ Icons
- ○ Notes List
- ○ Last Seven Days
- ○ By Category
- ○ Outlook Data Files

Mail

Calendar

Contacts

Tasks

Notes

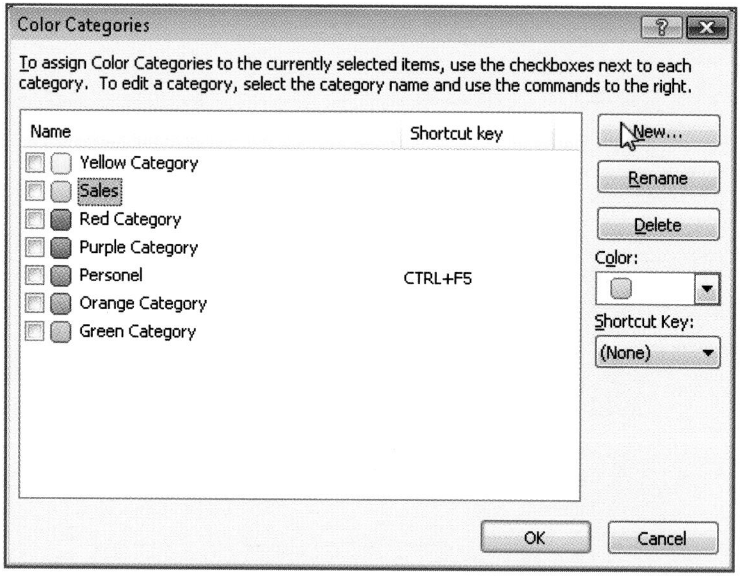

Color Categories

To assign Color Categories to the currently selected items, use the checkboxes next to each category. To edit a category, select the category name and use the commands to the right.

Name	Shortcut key	
☐ Yellow Category		New...
☐ Sales		Rename
☐ Red Category		Delete
☐ Purple Category		
☐ Personel	CTRL+F5	Color:
☐ Orange Category		[ ] ▼
☐ Green Category		Shortcut Key:
		(None) ▼

OK   Cancel

*Figure 7-6: **Assigning categories to journal entries allows you to group entries and more easily find them.***

TIP

If you use Outlook and are connected to a Microsoft Exchange server, you can share your Journal with others and also access the shared Journals of other Outlook users for which you have permission. Start sharing your Journal by clicking **Share My Journal** on the Navigation pane. To access another person's journal, click **Open A Shared Journal** in the Navigation pane. Neither of these options will appear if you are not connected to a Microsoft Exchange server.

Print Journal Entries

You can easily print journal entries, and you can also print files that are attached to those journal entries.

1. To print a memo-style copy of the journal entry, simply right-click the journal entry in the Journal, and click **Print**. The journal entry is sent to your default printer.
2. For additional printing options, select the entry in the Journal, click the **File** menu, and click **Print**.
3. In the standard Windows Print dialog box that appears, choose the print options you would like, as shown in Figure 7-7. Notice the check box that also allows you to print attached files.
4. Make your selections and click **OK** to start printing.

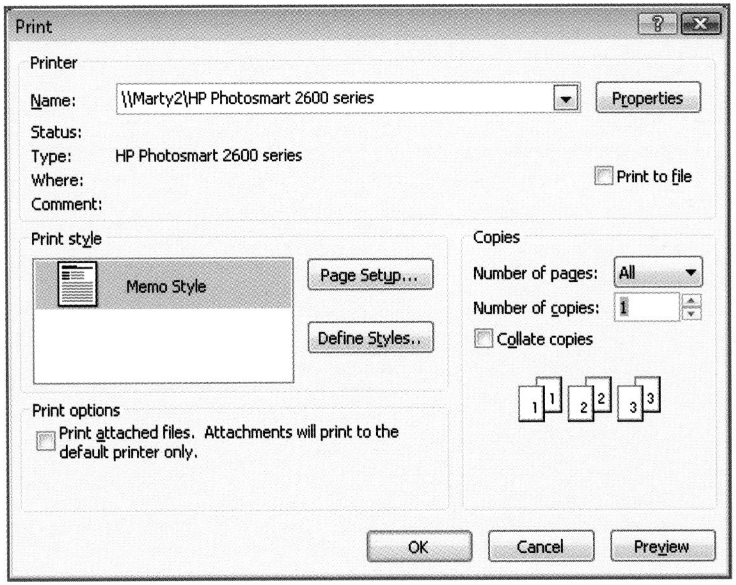

Figure 7-7: ***You can change the default print options as desired.***

Make Notes

If you are like most of us, notes are a way of life. Your desk might be littered with scraps of paper where you can scribble important things quickly. Of course, finding the note you need is another story. The great news is that you can keep all of the notes you want and simply let Outlook take care of them. Instead of scribbled notes on paper, you can use the Notes feature in Outlook to collect and organize them all. In this section, you'll learn how to create, manage, and work with your notes.

Explore Notes

The Notes feature in Outlook is easy to use. To explore the Notes feature:

Click **Go** and then click **Notes**.

–Or–

Click the **Notes** button on the Navigation pane in either the Outlook view bars or in the button bar at the bottom.

The Notes folder appears in the middle pane, as you can see in Figure 7-8. If you have any notes written, they will appear in the task pane. On the toolbar, you can change the icon size of the notes from large icons to small icons, and even to a simple list. You can easily switch between these icon views as desired.

Add a Note

You can quickly and easily create a note whenever you need to. To add a note to your Notes folder:

1. Click the **New** button on the standard toolbar. A note appears. Type the information you want directly on the note.

2. When you're done, click the **Close** button on the note. The note now appears in your Notes folder.

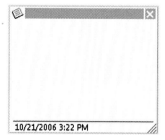

10/21/2006 3:22 PM

TIP

Notes are designed to be short remarks or comments, so don't worry about complete sentences or other grammatical issues. However, you can type just about as much text as you want, if necessary. You can easily drag the note's corner handle and expand the size of the note as needed.

TIP

You can also right-click anywhere within the Notes folder (provided you are not right-clicking an actual note), and click **New Note** to add a note to the folder.

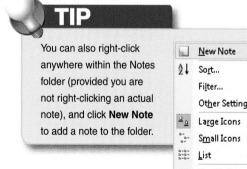

New Note
Sort...
Filter...
Other Settings...
Large Icons
Small Icons
List
Line Up Icons
Customize Current View...

QUICKSTEPS

SETTING UP NOTES

You can make some quick and easy changes to the way notes look.

1. Click **Notes** in the Navigation pane.

2. Click **Tools** and then click **Options**.

3. In the Options dialog box, click the **Note Options** button.

4. In the Note Options dialog box that appears, click the **Color** drop-down arrow, and click a color for your notes. The default is yellow.

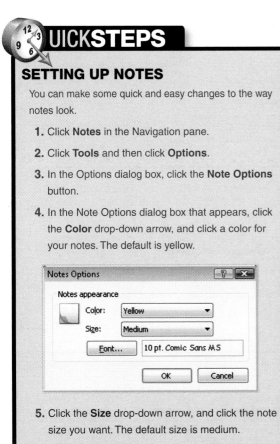

5. Click the **Size** drop-down arrow, and click the note size you want. The default size is medium.

6. Click the **Font** button to select a different font. In the Font window that opens (see Figure 7-9), you can choose the font, font style, size, and any effects you might want to use. Make your selections and click **OK**.

7. Click **OK** to close the Notes Options dialog box, and click **OK** to close the Options dialog box.

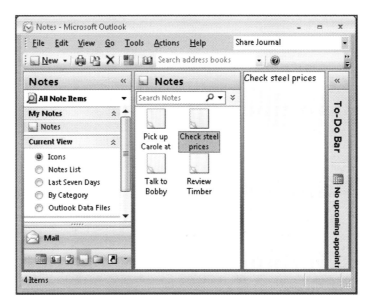

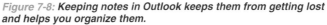

Figure 7-8: *Keeping notes in Outlook keeps them from getting lost and helps you organize them.*

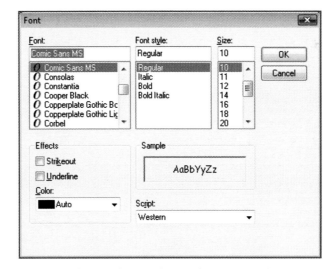

Figure 7-9: *Select a font that is easy for you to read.*

TIP

Notice that there is no Save or Save As option for the notes. Once you click the Close button, your changes are automatically saved. Also, there isn't an Undo feature. To undo a change, you must retype the original material.

Open

🖨 Print

📤 Forward

Categorize ▶ | ‾C‾lear All Categories

✕ Delete | 🟦 Personel
| 🟦 Sales 🔓
| 🟦 Green Category
| 🟦 Orange Category
| 🟦 Purple Category
| 🟥 Red Category
| ⬜ Yellow Category
| ⬛ All Categories...
|
| Set ‾Q‾uick Click...

Change a Note

Editing a note is quick and easy. You can change and update information on any note.

1. In the Notes folder, double-click the desired note.

2. Retype or change the information on the note.

3. Click the **Close** button on the note.

Delete a Note

Notes are designed to be pieces of information that help you stay organized. As such, you'll probably need to update, change, and delete old notes fairly often. To delete a note:

Right-click the note in the Notes folder, and click **Delete**.

–Or–

Select the note and click the **Delete** button on the standard toolbar.

–Or–

Select the note, click the **Edit** menu, and then click **Delete**.

Categorize Notes

As with other Outlook items, you can attach categories to your notes. When you use a category view (which you'll explore later in this chapter), you can easily keep business notes separate from personal notes, and so on. To categorize a note:

1. In the Notes folder, right-click the note and click **Categorize**. The Categories drop-down menu appears.

2. Click the desired category you want to assign. If the category is one of the initial color categories, the Rename Category dialog box will appear. Type the name of the category, change the color, and assign a shortcut key. If you have already made the color a specific category, it will be immediately applied to the entry.

3. If you do not see a category in the drop-down list that accurately identifies your task, click **All Categories** to open the Color Categories dialog box. Click **New** to open the Add New Category dialog box. Type the name of the category, change the color, assign a shortcut key, and click **OK**. Your new category will appear in your category list with a check mark. Click **OK** again, and the new category will be attached to the note.

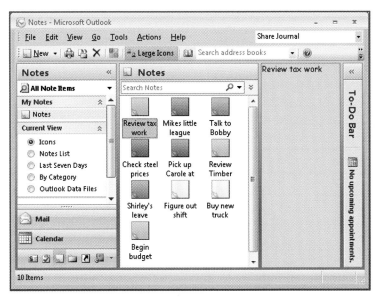

Figure 7-10: **Color-coding gives you a quick way to visually identify related notes.**

Change a Note's Color

By default, your notes are all the same color, depending on the color you originally chose in the Notes Options dialog box. However, if you categorize your notes to better organize them, you can assign the categories any color you choose, thereby color-coding your notes. You might choose to color-code all of your personal notes with one color, all sales notes with another, and all finance notes with a third. Or, you might assign a certain color to urgent notes and another color to those that are not as pressing. No matter what your technique for assigning colors, you can easily use the Categorize feature to change a note's color at any time. With your notes color-coded, it is easy to see the category each note is in, as shown in Figure 7-10. This is simply a by-product of categorization.

Forward a Note

The notes you create in Outlook can easily be attached to e-mail and sent to other Outlook users. This feature enables you to easily share information with someone over e-mail without having to retype the information in the e-mail or having to cut and paste the information. To forward a note:

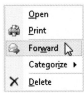

1. In the Notes folder, right-click the note and click **Forward**.

2. A new e-mail message appears with the note included as an attachment, as you can see in Figure 7-11. Enter the recipient's e-mail address, and type your message.

3. Click **Send**.

View Notes

The Notes feature gives you five important options for viewing your notes in the Navigation pane:

● **Icons**   This default view shows your notes as icons, as seen in various illustrations in this section.

● **Notes List**   Displays your notes as a list of items.

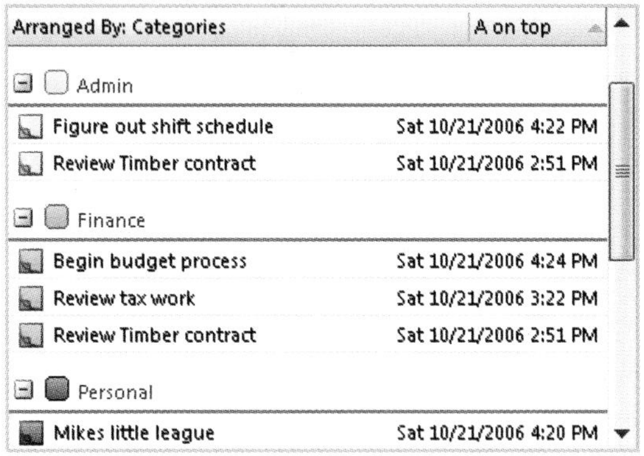

Arranged By: Categories	A on top
☐ ☐ Admin	
🗒 Figure out shift schedule	Sat 10/21/2006 4:22 PM
🗒 Review Timber contract	Sat 10/21/2006 2:51 PM
☐ ☐ Finance	
🗒 Begin budget process	Sat 10/21/2006 4:24 PM
🗒 Review tax work	Sat 10/21/2006 3:22 PM
🗒 Review Timber contract	Sat 10/21/2006 2:51 PM
☐ ☐ Personal	
🗒 Mikes little league	Sat 10/21/2006 4:20 PM

Add New Group
Customize Current View...

- **Last Seven Days**   Displays the last seven days of notes as a list.
- **By Category**   Organizes your notes by category.
- **Outlook Data files**   Sorts and displays notes by the files you have set up for them, as discussed in Chapter 8.

CUSTOMIZE THE CURRENT VIEW

You can customize the current view by working with the options for Notes.

1. Click the current view you want in the Notes Navigation pane.

2. Click **Customize Current View** at the bottom of the Current View list in the Navigation pane.

3. Click the desired area button to make any changes that you want in the Customize View dialog box, shown in Figure 7-12. The function of each buttons is as follows:
   - **Fields** allows you to select the fields you want displayed.
   - **Group By** provides the means to group the items in the view.
   - **Sort** provides the means to sort the items in the view.
   - **Filter** allows you to select certain items to be displayed and exclude others.
   - **Other Settings** provides the means to select the fonts and other display settings.

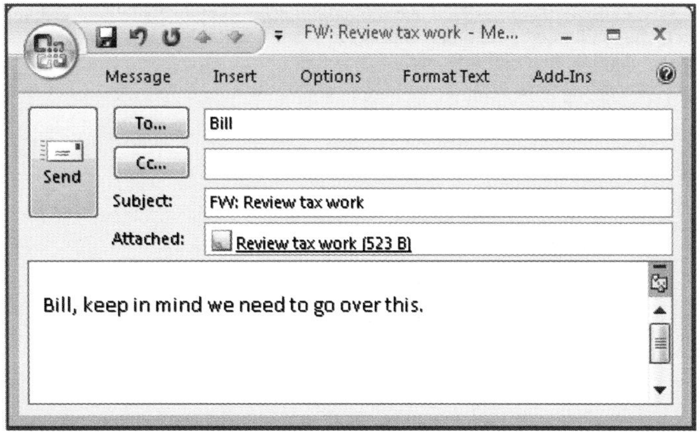

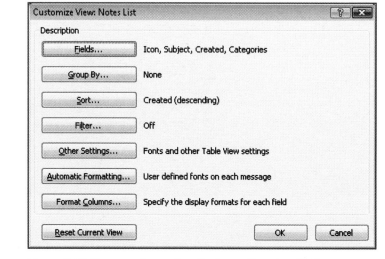

Figure 7-11: **A note can be automatically added to an e-mail message as an attachment.**

Figure 7-12: **You can change the display options by clicking an option button.**

USING NOTES IN OTHER OUTLOOK AREAS

You can drag notes to other areas of Microsoft Outlook, where they will change accordingly:

- To automatically create an e-mail message using a note, drag the desired note to the **Mail** button on the Navigation pane, as shown in Figure 7-13.

- To send a note to your Calendar, drag the note to the **Calendar** button on the Navigation pane. The note is converted to a Calendar item, which you can configure as needed, as shown in Figure 7-14.

- Repeat this same process to turn a note into a Task or a Contact.

- **Automatic Formatting** allows you to select rules for formatting.

- **Format Columns** allows you to select the format, label, width, and alignment of each column.

- **Reset Current View** returns all the settings to the original default setting.

4. When you're done making your changes, click **OK**.

USE THE READING PANE

The Reading pane works with most Outlook features, including Notes. The Reading pane allows you to easily switch between notes and read the full content of a note without having to open it. To use the Reading pane with notes:

1. Click the **View** menu, click **Reading Pane**, and then click **Right, Bottom**, or **Off**.

2. Click a note in order to view its text in the Reading pane.

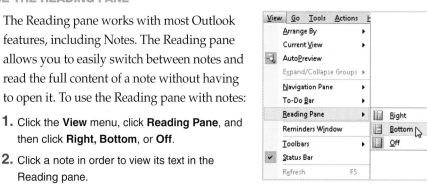

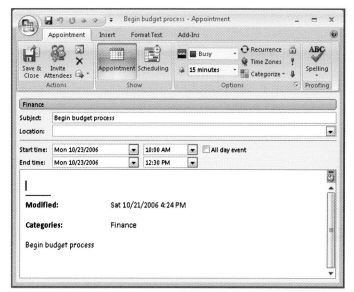

Figure 7-13: **You can drag the note to any Navigation pane option.**

Figure 7-14: **Your note instantly turns into a Calendar item.**

> **TIP**
>
> You can share your notes with others and access their shared notes, provided you are connected to a Microsoft Exchange server and have the appropriate permissions. Start sharing your notes by clicking **Share My Notes** on the Navigation pane. To access another person's notes, click **Open Shared Notes** in the Navigation pane. Neither of these options will appear if you are not connected to a Microsoft Exchange server.

> **TIP**
>
> You can print multiple notes at the same time. In the Notes folder, hold down the **CTRL** key on your keyboard, and click the notes you want to print. If your notes are a contiguous list, hold down the **SHIFT** key, and click the first and last note in the list. This creates a "multiple selection" of notes, which you can then print together in either of the two ways described in "Print Notes."

> **TIP**
>
> When you drag a note to Mail, Calendar, Tasks, or Contacts, the information is taken from the note to generate the desired item. However, your original note remains in your Notes folder; it is not moved or deleted.

Print Notes

You can easily print your notes, when desired.

1. To print a memo-style copy of the note entry, simply right-click the note, and click **Print**. The note is sent to your default printer.
2. For additional printing options, select the note you want to print in the Notes folder, click **File**, and then click **Print**.
3. In the standard Windows Print dialog box that appears (see Figure 7-15), choose the print options you would like, such as the style, the number of copies, the default printer, and so forth.
4. Make your selections and click **OK** to start printing.

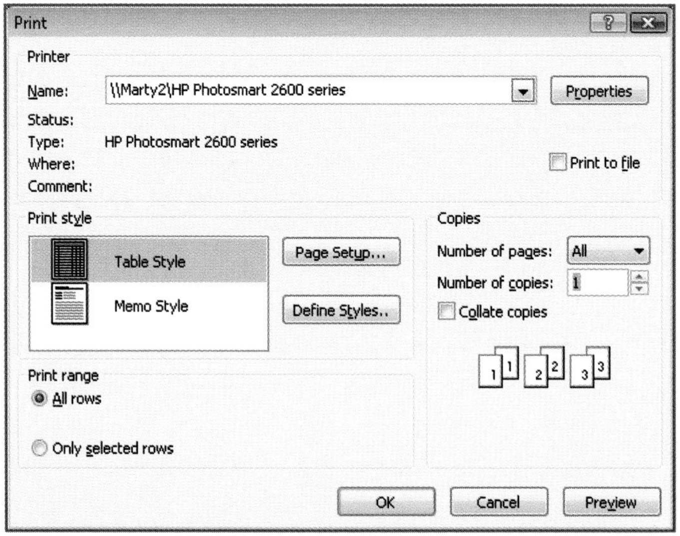

Figure 7-15: ***You can print notes in either table or memo style.***

Chapter 8

Managing Files and Folders

As you send and receive e-mail and work with your Outlook data, you'll need to organize and work with data files. Microsoft Outlook makes data management easy. In this chapter you'll see how to work with folders and manipulate files in Outlook. You'll also see how to make Outlook secure by setting security options and encrypting private messages.

Work with Folders

Outlook manages data by storing information in folders, specifically, your personal folders. When you use e-mail, you see folders such as Inbox, Outbox, Deleted Items, Sent Items, and so forth. However, you are not limited to these basic folders. You can create and work with additional folders so that you can easily store e-mail messages and files in an organizational system that works best for you. In this section you'll see how to create different kinds of folders, share them, and work with them in a variety of ways.

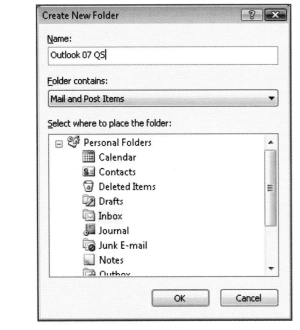

Figure 8-1: *A new Outlook folder can contain only a specific kind of information and must be located within Outlook's Personal Folders hierarchy.*

Create a Normal Folder

You can create basic folders within Outlook so that you can store e-mail messages and files. You may wish to create folders based on work and family correspondence, or you can create any structure that is helpful and meaningful to you. To create a normal folder:

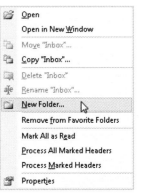

1. Click the **File** menu, click **New**, and then click **Folder**.

   –Or–

   Right-click your **Inbox** and, on the context menu, click **New Folder**.

2. In the Create New Folder dialog box, shown in Figure 8-1, enter a name for the folder. Click the **Folder Contains** drop-down menu, and choose the type of items you will store in the folder, such as Mail And Post Items. Finally, select the location where you want to store the folder, such as a subfolder within your Inbox.

3. When you're done, click **OK**. The folder will appear in the place where you chose to store it.

Create a Search Folder

Search folders are a helpful feature of Outlook. Using search folders, you can store messages and easily search them for certain types of content, for example, or based on the sender or another attribute. In short, search folders enable you not only to store large numbers of messages, but also to sort easily through and find certain kinds of messages.

Search folders aren't really folders at all. They are virtual folders that search all of your other Outlook folders and give you a report of the messages and information you are looking for, rather than being just a collection of messages that are in one place at one time. This feature allows you to find any message that you want and to show it in the search folder, although the original message isn't actually moved there. To create a search folder:

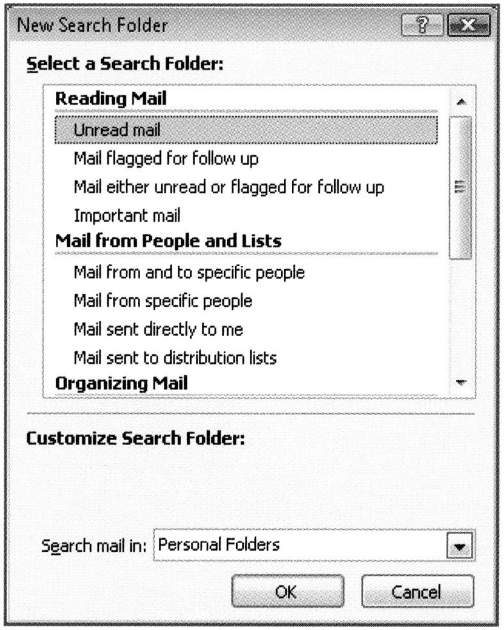

New Search Folder

Select a Search Folder:

Reading Mail
> Unread mail
> Mail flagged for follow up
> Mail either unread or flagged for follow up
> Important mail

Mail from People and Lists
> Mail from and to specific people
> Mail from specific people
> Mail sent directly to me
> Mail sent to distribution lists

Organizing Mail

Customize Search Folder:

Search mail in: Personal Folders

OK   Cancel

Figure 8-2: **Search folders allow you to search Outlook folders for a wide variety of criteria and to create your own folders.**

Mail   «

Favorite Folders   ⊼
> Inbox
> Unread Mail
> Sent Items

Mail Folders   ⊼

All Mail Items   ▼

☐ Personal Folders
> Deleted Items
> Drafts
> ⊞ Inbox
> Junk E-mail
> Outbox
> ⊞ RSS Feeds
> Sent Items
> ☐ Search Folders
>   Categorized M
>   Unread Mail   ▼

Mail

Calendar

1. Click **File**, click **New**, and click **Search Folder**.

2. In the New Search Folder window, shown in Figure 8-2, choose one of the following options:

   - **Reading Mail:**
     - **Unread Mail**   Any mail you have not read in any folder.
     - **Mail Flagged For Follow-Up**   Any mail that is flagged for follow-up in any folder.
     - **Mail Either Unread Or Flagged For Follow-Up**   Unread mail or mail that has been flagged for follow-up in any folder.
     - **Important Mail**   Mail that has been sent with high importance.

   - **Mail From People And Lists:**
     - **Mail From And To Specific People**   Mail from and to specific people in any folder.
     - **Mail From Specific People**   Mail from specific people in any folder.
     - **Mail Sent Directly To Me**   Mail that was sent directly to you (rather than by means of a distribution list or as a Cc or Bcc).
     - **Mail Sent To Distribution Lists**   Mail that was sent to a distribution list.

   - **Organizing Mail:**
     - **Large Mail**   Messages above a specific file size.
     - **Old Mail**   Mail older than a specific date.
     - **Mail With Attachments**   Mail that has an attachment.
     - **Mail Received This Week**   Mail that you have received this week.
     - **Mail With Specific Words**   Mail that contains specific words.

   - **Custom:**
     - **Create A Custom Search Folder**   Allows you to create a custom folder that searches for the parameters you specify.

3. Once you have selected the kind of search folder you want, click **OK**. The type of mail you searched for will appear in the Subject pane.

Rename Folders

Folder names should be easily recognizable. To that end, you can change the name of a folder you have created at any time.

COPYING AND MOVING FOLDERS

You can easily copy and move folders around as needed.

COPY A FOLDER

1. Right-click the folder in your Personal Folders hierarchy that you want to copy. (You may need to click the **Go** menu and then click **Folder List** to see your personal folders in the Navigation pane.)

2. Click **Copy** *folder name*.

3. In the Copy Folder window, shown in Figure 8-3, choose the location to which you want to copy the folder.

4. Click **OK**. The folder and its contents are copied to the desired location.

5. Click the new folder and then slowly click the name twice, type the name you want for the folder, and press **ENTER**.

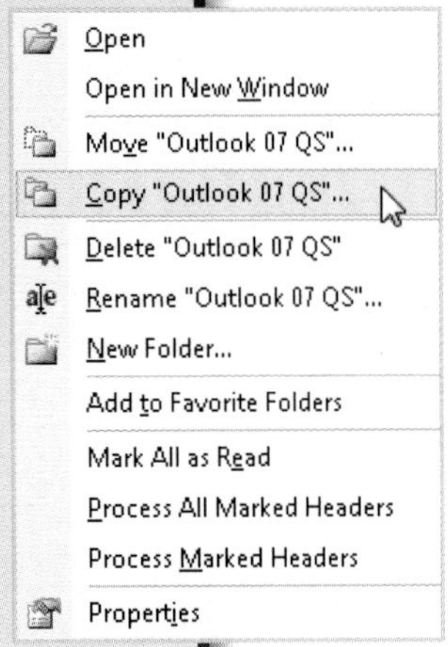

MOVE A FOLDER

You can move the folders you create within your personal folders, but you cannot move the system-created folders such as Inbox, Outbox, and Sent Items.

1. In the Navigation pane, right-click the folder you want to move. (You may need to click **Go** and click **Folder List** to see your personal folders in the Navigation pane.)

2. Click **Move** *folder name*.

3. In the Move Folder window, choose the location to which you want to move the folder, and click **OK**. The folder and its contents are moved to the desired location.

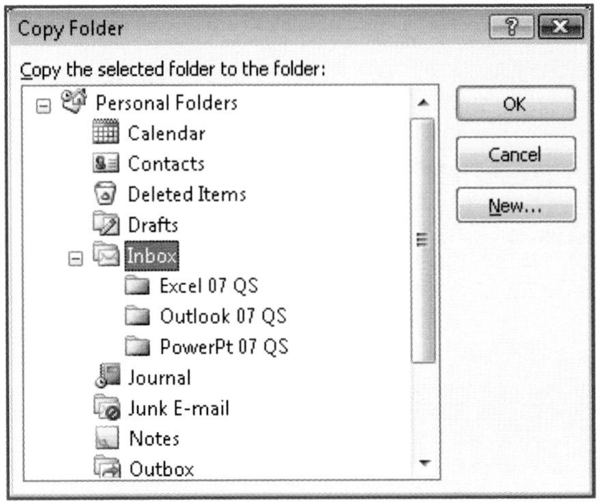

Figure 8-3: *Select a folder location where you want to place the copied folder.*

You cannot change the name of the system folders, such as Inbox and Sent Items.

1. Right-click the folder in the Navigation pane, and click **Rename** *folder name*. (You may need to click **Go** and click **Folder List** to see your personal folders in the Navigation pane.) Your cursor appears on the folder name.

2. Type a new name for the folder, and press **ENTER**.

Delete Folders

You can delete the folders you have created, but not the system folders. When deleting a folder, you can move all of the folder's contents to another folder, if you still want to keep the folder contents. If not, the folder contents are moved to the Deleted Items folder.

1. In the Navigation pane, right-click the folder you want, and click **Delete** *folder name*. (You may need to click **Go** and click **Folder List** to see your personal folders in the Navigation pane.)

2. Click **Yes** in response to the warning message that appears.

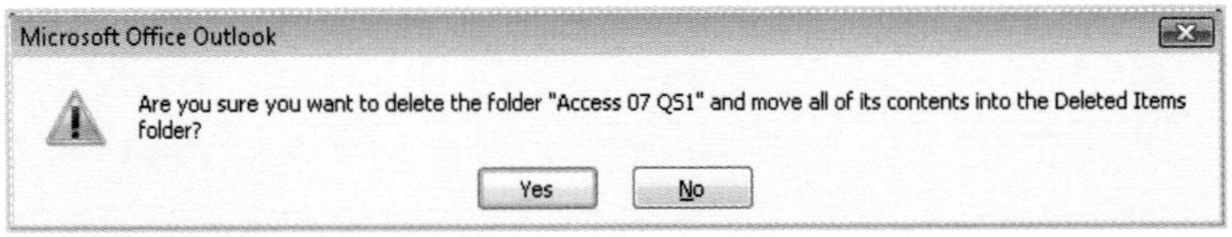

Set Folder Properties

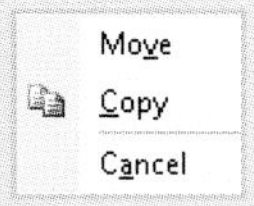

Like all folders in Windows, Outlook folders have some basic properties that you can configure as needed. The tabs described below are available with most, but not all, Outlook folders.

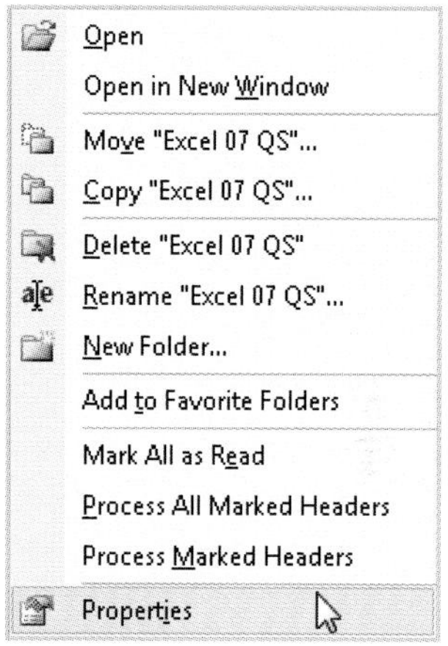

1. Click **Go** and click **Folders List**.

2. Right-click the desired folder and click **Properties**. You have the following options:

   - On the **General** tab, shown in Figure 8-4, you see the name of the folder and its general properties. You can enter a description and choose to show the number of total items in the folder or the number of unread items in the folder. By default, Microsoft Exchange views are automatically set to be created. You can click **Folder Size** to find out how much disk space your folder is taking up.

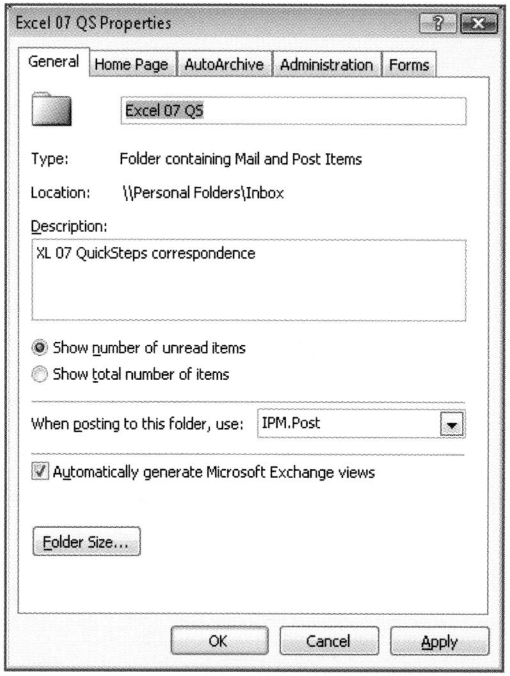

Open
Open in New Window
Move "Excel 07 QS"...
Copy "Excel 07 QS"...
Delete "Excel 07 QS"
Rename "Excel 07 QS"...
New Folder...
Add to Favorite Folders
Mark All as Read
Process All Marked Headers
Process Marked Headers
Properties

Excel 07 QS Properties

General | Home Page | AutoArchive | Administration | Forms

Excel 07 QS

Type: Folder containing Mail and Post Items
Location: \\Personal Folders\Inbox
Description:
XL 07 QuickSteps correspondence

● Show number of unread items
○ Show total number of items

When posting to this folder, use: IPM.Post

☑ Automatically generate Microsoft Exchange views

Folder Size...

OK   Cancel   Apply

Figure 8-4: **You can get basic information about your folder on the General tab.**

You can also copy a file by selecting it and pressing **CTRL+C**, paste it by pressing **CTRL+V**, and cutting it (to move the file) by pressing **CTRL+X**.

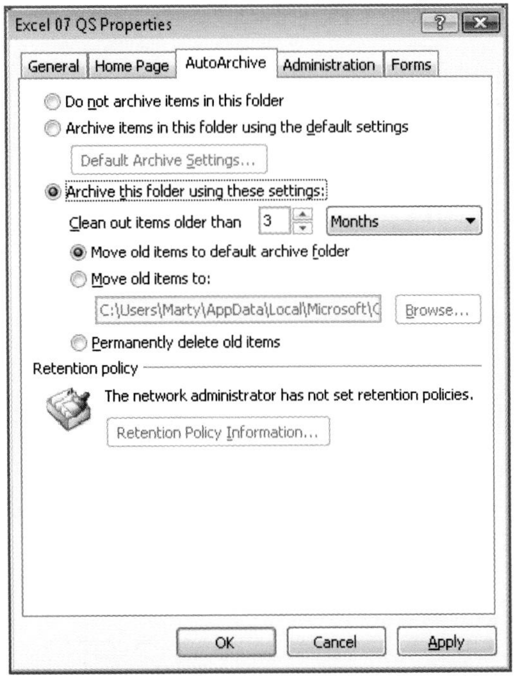

Figure 8-5: *The AutoArchive settings give you the flexibility to automatically archive folder items in a way that works best for you.*

- The **Home Page** tab allows you to configure a default home page for the folder, if your folders are Web-enabled (which is common for folders found on a company intranet).

- On the **AutoArchive** tab, shown in Figure 8-5, you can choose the method of archiving you want to use with this folder. By default, the Do Not Archive setting is selected. However, you can choose to automatically have the folder archived based on Outlook's default settings, or you can configure your own archive settings for the folder, as I have done in Figure 8-5.

- On the **Administration** tab, the basic folder view is the Normal setting, which is probably your best configuration. The other options on this tab are only available if you are on a Microsoft Exchange network.

- On the **Forms** tab, you can choose to associate any default forms or forms you have created (see Chapter 9) with this folder. Click **Manage** to choose the forms you want to associate with or make available in that folder.

3. Click **OK** when you are done making any desired changes.

Manipulate Files

Just as you can work with individual folders in Outlook, you can also work with individual files and groups of files that are stored in those folders. In this section, you'll see how to manipulate files and work with them by copying, renaming, sharing, deleting, grouping, and sorting files. You'll also see how to import and export files in Outlook.

Delete Files

You can delete individual files from within Outlook as needed. Let's say you have a folder that contains several older e-mail messages. You do not want to delete the entire folder, but you do want to delete all the unneeded messages from the folder. In this case, you can individually select the messages that you want to delete. Deleted messages are moved to your Deleted Items folder.

COPYING AND MOVING FILES

You can easily copy and move files between Outlook folders in basically the same manner as with standard Windows files.

COPYING FILES

1. Click **Go** and click **Folders List**. In the Navigation pane, expand and select the desired folder. The folder contents appear in the Folder pane.

2. In the Folder pane, select the file that you want to copy, click the **Edit** menu, and click **Copy**, as shown in Figure 8-6.

3. You can now paste the copied file into any Outlook or Windows folder by locating and selecting the folder, clicking **Edit**, and clicking **Paste**.

MOVING FILES

1. Click **Go** and click **Folders List**. In the Navigation pane, expand the desired folder and select it. The folder contents appear in the Folder pane.

2. Select the folder that contains the file you want to move.

3. In the Folder pane, right-click the file you want to move, and, on the context menu that appears, click **Move To Folder**. The Move Items dialog box will appear.

4. In the Move Items window, choose the Outlook folder where you want to move the file, and click **OK**.

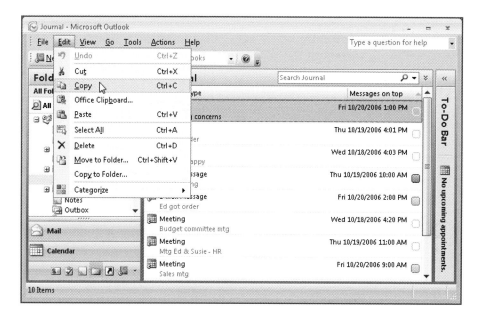

Figure 8-6: **Select the file you want to copy, and then use the Edit menu to copy it.**

1. In the Navigation pane, select the folder that contains the file you want to delete. You may need to click **Go** and click **Folder List** to see your personal folders in the Navigation pane.

2. In the Folder pane, right-click the file and click **Delete** in the standard toolbar, or click the **Edit** menu and click **Delete**.

Group Files

You can have Outlook automatically group files for you as a part of Outlook's standard grouping arrangement, or you can manually group items. For example, you might want all e-mail from a specific person grouped into one folder, or you might want e-mail that contains attachments to be grouped into one folder. The choice is yours, but you can easily group items in almost any way that you need.

CREATE A CUSTOM GROUPING

1. Click the **View** menu, click **Arrange By**, and then click **Custom**.

2. In the Customize View dialog box, click **Group By**.

3. In the Group By dialog box, if it is selected, clear the **Automatically Group According To Arrangement** check box. Then select the desired check boxes, and use the drop-down menus to determine how you want to group items within Outlook, as shown in Figure 8-7.

4. Click **OK** when you're done.

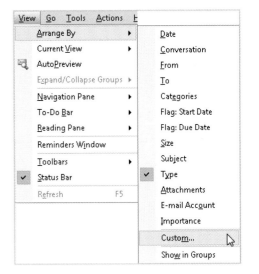

UNGROUP ITEMS

Should you need to ungroup items at any time, you can easily do so.

1. Click **View**, click **Arrange By**, and click **Custom**.

2. In the Customize View dialog box, click **Group By**.

3. In the Group By dialog box, click the **Group Items By** drop-down menu, click **None**, and click **OK**.

Sort Files

Outlook has the capability to sort files that you receive in your Inbox. This feature can automatically help you manage your e-mail, and is particularly helpful if you typically receive a large volume of e-mail.

Group By [dialog box]

Automatically group according to arrangement

Group items by

Company — Ascending / Descending

Show field in view

Then by

Contacts — Ascending / Descending

Show field in view

Then by

(none) — Ascending / Descending

Show field in view

Then by

(none) — Ascending / Descending

Show field in view

Select available fields from:

Frequently-used fields

Expand/collapse defaults:

As last viewed

OK / Cancel / Clear All

*Figure 8-7: **You can group files by up to four items, such as attachments and categories.***

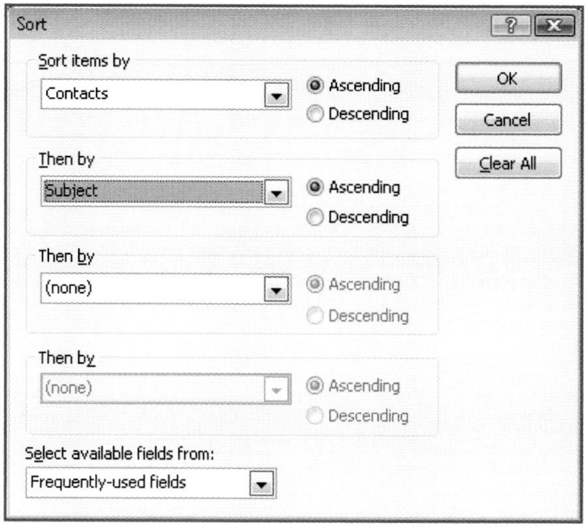

Sort [dialog box]

Sort items by

Contacts — Ascending / Descending

Then by

Subject — Ascending / Descending

Then by

(none) — Ascending / Descending

Then by

(none) — Ascending / Descending

Select available fields from:

Frequently-used fields

OK / Cancel / Clear All

*Figure 8-8: **You can sort files in any folder by up to four levels of criteria.***

1. Click **View**, click **Arrange By**, and click **Custom**.

2. In the Customize View dialog box, click **Sort**.

3. In the Sort dialog box, shown in Figure 8-8, do the following:

   - Click the **Sort Items By** down arrow, and click a sort item, such as **Attachment**, **Contacts**, **Cc**, and so on.

   - Choose more sort criteria in the additional drop-down list boxes as needed.

4. Click **OK** when you are done, and click **OK** again on the Customize View window. Your items in the current view are now sorted as you specified.

Import and Export Files

You can import and explore Outlook files from a variety of sources and in a variety of formats.

IMPORT FILES

1. Click **File** and then click **Import And Export**.

2. In the Import And Export Wizard, choose what you would like to import, as shown in Figure 8-9. Make your selection and click **Next**. You have the following options:

   - **Import A VCARD File (.vcf)** allows you to import to your Contacts folder an Outlook vCard that you have received.

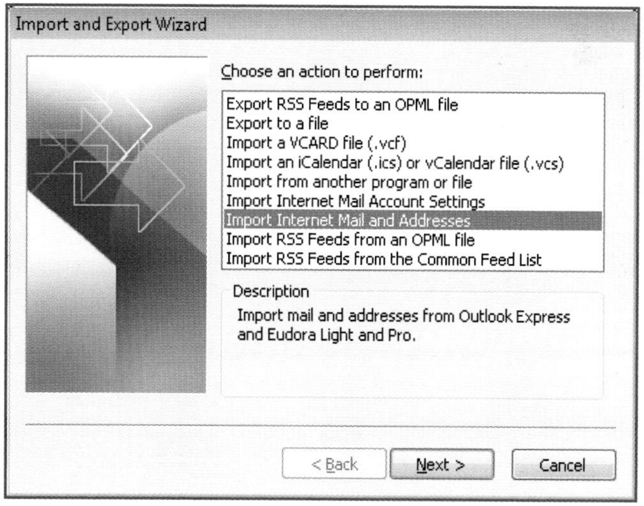

Import and Export Wizard

Choose an action to perform:

Export RSS Feeds to an OPML file
Export to a file
Import a VCARD file (.vcf)
Import an iCalendar (.ics) or vCalendar file (.vcs)
Import from another program or file
Import Internet Mail Account Settings
Import Internet Mail and Addresses
Import RSS Feeds from an OPML file
Import RSS Feeds from the Common Feed List

Description

Import mail and addresses from Outlook Express and Eudora Light and Pro.

< Back / Next > / Cancel

*Figure 8-9: **You can import a number of different kinds of files, including those created by Outlook Express, Eudora, ACT!, and Lotus Organizer.***

The options you see in the Sort dialog box allow you to have up to four levels of sorting. For example, in Figure 8-8, the files are sorted first by your contacts and then by subject within each contact. This sorting feature can be helpful in locating items.

- **Import An iCalendar Or vCalendar File (.vcs)** imports information from an iCalendar or vCalendar file directly into your Calendar.
- **Import From Another Program Or File** allows you to import items from other e-mail programs, such as ACT!, Lotus Organizer, and so forth. You can also import text and database files, as well as personal folders (.pst) from another Outlook program.
- **Import Internet Mail Account Settings** allows you to import settings from Outlook Express or Eudora e-mail programs.
- **Import Internet Mail And Addresses** allows you to import Internet mail and e-mail addresses directly from Outlook Express or Eudora e-mail programs.
- **Import RSS Feeds From An OPML File or The Common Feed List** allows you to bring syndicated information to which you subscribe and receive through RSS (Real Simple Syndication) into Outlook (See Chapter 10.)

3. Complete the steps as instructed by the wizard to import the desired files.

EXPORT FILES

Just as you can import files, you can also export files so that they can be used with other programs, or as a way to back up your Outlook files.

1. Click **File** and click **Import And Export**.

2. In the Import And Export Wizard, click **Export To A File**. Click **Next**.

3. Choose the kind of file you want to export to. You can choose personal folder file (.pst), which allows your files to be imported by other Outlook programs, or you can choose file types for other programs. See the other e-mail program for details about the kinds of files it will import so that you make the best decision depending on what you want to do. Click **Next**.

4. Select the folder within Outlook that you want to export, as shown in Figure 8-10. If you choose a parent folder, it will include the subfolders beneath it.

5. If you are exporting to a personal folder file (.pst) and want to filter out some of the messages that you are exporting, click **Filter**, which opens the Filter window. Here, you can search for particular words in specified fields in order to filter out certain messages. For example, you can filter out messages that have certain subjects in the Subject line, messages sent directly to you, and so on. Click the **More Choices** tab for additional filtering options, and then click **OK** when you're done.

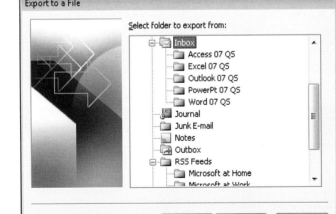

Figure 8-10: **You can choose to export both individual folders and a folder with all of its subfolders.**

6. Click **Next**. Choose an export location and file name for the file. Choose how you want to replace previously exported items and duplicate items, and click **Finish**.

7. The Create Microsoft Personal Folders dialog box appears so that you can choose to create the desired folder where the items will be exported. If you want to accept the default name, just click **OK**. Also, notice that you can password-protect the exported file so that no one can open it without your password.

Create Microsoft Personal Folders	
File:	D:\QuickSteps\Outlook07\Outlook061023.pst
Name:	Personal Folders
Format:	Personal Folders File
Password	
Password:	
Verify Password:	
☐ Save this password in your password list	

OK   Cancel

8. Make your selections and click **OK**. The files are exported. This process may take some time, depending on the number of files that must be exported.

Make Outlook Secure

Outlook 2007 has a completely new set of security options that you can configure to keep your e-mail, Calendar, Journal, and other Outlook items secure. In this section, you'll see how to set the security options, how to encrypt messages, and how to protect your computer against viruses that may be transmitted through e-mail.

Set Security and Privacy Options

Outlook 2007 shares with the rest of the Microsoft Office 2007 family of programs the *Trust Center*, where you can set a variety of security and privacy options. The Trust Center allows you to view and manage add-in programs;

NOTE

It is important to point out that the security provided by Outlook and Microsoft Office is just one level of security against threats from the Internet. You probably also want to enable the Windows Personal Firewall (see the companion book *Windows Vista QuickSteps* for further information on the Windows Firewall and other security measures at that level). You may also wish to purchase additional security software or hardware for maximum protection from companies such as McAfee, Symantec, Zone Alarm, and WatchGuard for a third level of protection.

set options that affect your privacy; determine if and how you want to secure your e-mail; and how you want to handle attachments, downloads, and macros. We'll explore securing your e-mail in the next section, and then look at virus protection from macros in the upcoming QuickSteps. This section explores the other settings in the Trust Center.

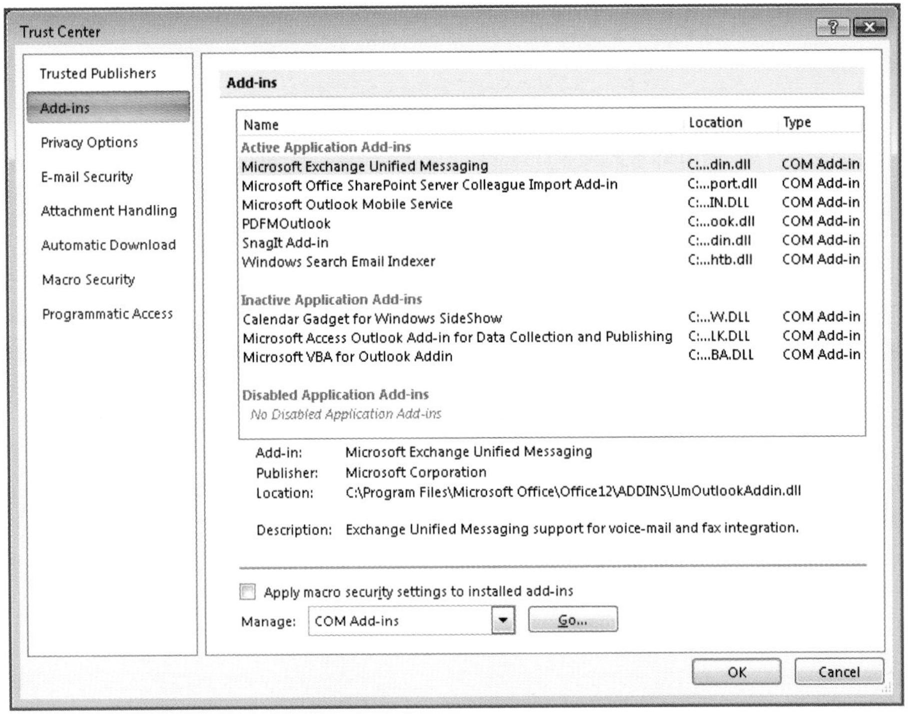

To open and explore the Trust Center:

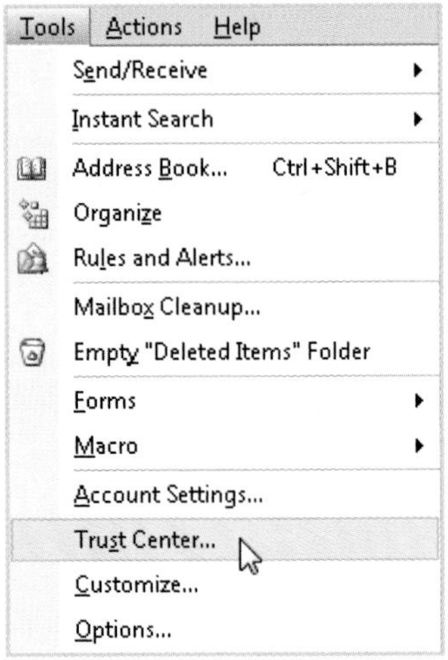

Trust Center

Name	Location	Type
Active Application Add-ins		
Microsoft Exchange Unified Messaging	C:...din.dll	COM Add-in
Microsoft Office SharePoint Server Colleague Import Add-in	C:...port.dll	COM Add-in
Microsoft Outlook Mobile Service	C:...IN.DLL	COM Add-in
PDFMOutlook	C:...ook.dll	COM Add-in
SnagIt Add-in	C:...din.dll	COM Add-in
Windows Search Email Indexer	C:...htb.dll	COM Add-in
Inactive Application Add-ins		
Calendar Gadget for Windows SideShow	C:...W.DLL	COM Add-in
Microsoft Access Outlook Add-in for Data Collection and Publishing	C:...LK.DLL	COM Add-in
Microsoft VBA for Outlook Addin	C:...BA.DLL	COM Add-in
Disabled Application Add-ins		
No Disabled Application Add-ins		

Left column: Trusted Publishers, Add-ins, Privacy Options, E-mail Security, Attachment Handling, Automatic Download, Macro Security, Programmatic Access

Add-in: Microsoft Exchange Unified Messaging
Publisher: Microsoft Corporation
Location: C:\Program Files\Microsoft Office\Office12\ADDINS\UmOutlookAddin.dll

Description: Exchange Unified Messaging support for voice-mail and fax integration.

Apply macro security settings to installed add-ins

Manage: COM Add-ins   Go...

OK   Cancel

*Figure 8-11: **Most add-ins are from trusted publishers like Microsoft and Adobe, but it is a good idea to keep an eye on them just in case.***

Tools menu:
Tools   Actions   Help
Send/Receive ▶
Instant Search ▶
Address Book...   Ctrl+Shift+B
Organize
Rules and Alerts...
Mailbox Cleanup...
Empty "Deleted Items" Folder
Forms ▶
Macro ▶
Account Settings...
Trust Center...
Customize...
Options...

1. Click the **Tools** menu, and then click **Trust Center**. In the Trust Center window, click **Trusted Publishers** in the left column. A list of trusted software publishers will appear. It is likely that the list is empty. You add a publisher to the list when you install software or a macro by clicking **Trust All Documents From This Publisher** in the Security Alert dialog box that appears. In the Trust Center page, you can remove a publisher from the list and view a publisher's credentials by selecting a publisher in the list and clicking the relevant button at the bottom of the page.

2. Click **Add-Ins** in the left column of the Trust Center. A list of installed add-ins will appear, as shown in Figure 8-11.

NOTE

The Research Options button on the Privacy Options page allows you to select the reference sources that will be searched when you choose to do a search.

COM Add-Ins

Add-Ins available:

- Calendar Gadget for Windows SideShow
- Microsoft Access Outlook Add-in for Data Collection and Publishing
- ✓ Microsoft Exchange Unified Messaging
- ✓ Microsoft Office SharePoint Server Colleague Import Add-in
- ✓ Microsoft Outlook Mobile Service
- ✓ Microsoft VBA for Outlook Addin
- ✓ PDFMOutlook
- ✓ SnagIt Add-in

OK
Cancel
Add...
Remove

Location: C:\PROGRA~1\MICROS~4\Office12\ADDINS\UMOUTL~1.DLL

Load Behavior: Load at Startup

Add-ins are pieces of program code that add functionality to another program. The add-ins are placed on the list when they are installed. You should see a Security Notice dialog box that allows you to enable or disable the add-in or to trust this publisher, as mentioned previously.

3. To manage add-ins, click **Go** at the bottom of the page. The COM Add-Ins dialog box appears, where you can make an add-in active or inactive by selecting or clearing the check box, respectively, or add and remove an add-in with the buttons on the right.

4. Click **Privacy Options** in the left column of the Trust Center. Select which of the Microsoft programs you want to sign up for, all requiring varying degrees of disclosure on your part. For example, if you sign up for the Customer Experience Improvement Program, you will be expected to divulge some information about what you do with Microsoft Office.

5. Click **Attachment Handling** to add properties to attachments, replay with changes, turn off and on the ability to preview attachments, or specify which preview tools are enabled.

6. Click **Automatic Downloads** and determine how you want to handle the downloading of pictures in e-mail.

7. Click **Programmatic Access** to enable Microsoft security to work in conjunction with your antivirus software to determine the level of warning you will be given when a program is trying to access your address book or send messages in your name.

8. Click **OK** to close the Trust Center.

Secure E-mail

You can secure your e-mail by encrypting it so that no one else can read it, and you can add a digital signature to your mail so that the recipient knows you sent it and no one has changed it. Encryption is the process of making an e-mail message unreadable to anyone who is not authorized to view it. Encryption takes a plain-text e-mail message and scrambles it so that it is unreadable. Your recipient must have a private key that matches a public key you used to write the message in order to decrypt and read the message.

TIP

See "Protecting Against Viruses" later in this chapter to find out how to use the Macro Security feature in the Trust Center.

8

TIP

In case you are wondering, Outlook uses the 3DES or Triple DES encryption algorithm, which is a standard form of encryption used in the United States and other countries.

NOTE

If you attempt to encrypt and send a message and you do not have a certificate, you will get a message that Outlook could not send the message for that reason. The message will also tell you to open the Tools menu, click Trust Center, click E-mail Security, and click Get A Digital ID, or to use a different mail account that has a certificate. This will give you a list of commercial services that, for a fee, will validate your identity and issue you a digital ID, which is valuable when you are working with people you don't know. To unencrypt the message until you have the proper certificate, click **Change Security Settings**.

Invalid Certificate   ✕

⚠ Microsoft Office Outlook cannot sign or encrypt this message because you have no certificates which can be used to send from the e-mail address   . You can do either of the following:

Get a new digital ID to use with this account. On the Tools menu, click Trust Center, click E-mail Security, and then click Get a Digital ID.

Use the Accounts button to send the message using an account that you have certificates for.

[Change Security Settings...] [OK]

If you are on a private Microsoft Exchange network, messages can be encrypted and sent and automatically decrypted by other users on the Exchange network. However, if you are sending messages over the Internet to another Outlook user, that user must have a private key that matches your public key in order to read the message. You can do this in a few different ways:

- **Send a digitally signed message** to the recipient. The recipient can then add your e-mail name to his or her Contacts list, which imports your certificate with a private key.

- **Attach your certificate** (.cer) file to a message you send to the recipient. The recipient can then import the .cer file and add it your contact card. The certificate can be used to exchange keys.

- **Create a contact with your .cer file**, and then send the contact card to the recipient.

No matter which way you choose to go, the recipient must have your .cer file in his or her Outlook program so Outlook can use that to exchange keys to decrypt any encrypted messages you send.

ENCRYPT AN INDIVIDUAL MESSAGE

You can choose to encrypt an individual message as needed.

1. Create a new e-mail message addressed to the desired recipient.

2. In the Message tab Options group, click the **Dialog Box Launcher** in the lower-right corner.

3. In the Message Options dialog box that appears (shown in Figure 8-12), click **Security Settings**. The Security Options dialog box appears.

4. Click the **Encrypt Message Contents And Attachments** check box.

5. Click **OK** and click **Close** to return to your message.

6. Click **Send**. The message will be encrypted and sent.

ENCRYPT ALL OUTGOING E-MAIL

You can also choose to encrypt all outgoing mail, which saves you from having to configure each e-mail message with encryption. However, keep in mind that this setting will encrypt every e-mail that you send and that everybody who receives your e-mail will need to have a key to open it.

QUICKSTEPS

PROTECTING AGAINST VIRUSES

Computer viruses are a major headache in the computing world, and e-mail and Internet usage are major pathways for your computer to become infected. Outlook provides *minimal* protection against viruses. Outlook is not equipped to scan your e-mail and remove viruses, so when Outlook tells you that it can help with virus protection, it really does mean that it "helps" only.

Outlook provides virus protection through macro security options. Different files, especially Microsoft Word files, can contain *macros,* which are little programs, and viruses can be implanted in macros. This is a common way for viruses to be spread. Outlook's macro security simply disables macros that are not from secure or trusted sources, thus reducing the likelihood of getting a macro virus. Outlook, by default, disables macros that are unsigned and warns you about signed macros. You can change those settings if you wish.

1. In Outlook, click **Tools**, click **Trust Center**, and click **Macro Security** in the left column.

2. Under **Macro Security**, on the right, click one of the four options for handling macros. The second option is the default.

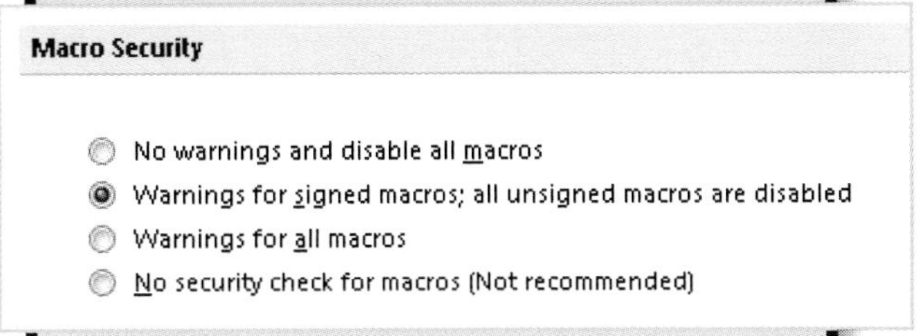

Macro Security

○ No warnings and disable all macros
◉ Warnings for signed macros; all unsigned macros are disabled
○ Warnings for all macros
○ No security check for macros (Not recommended)

3. Click **OK**.

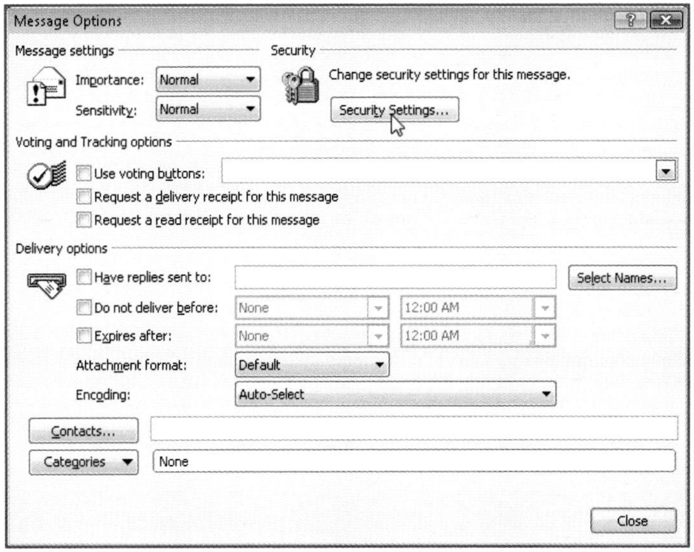

Figure 8-12: **You can encrypt an individual message through the Message Options dialog box.**

1. In Outlook, click **Tools**, click **Trust Center**, and click **E-mail Security**.

2. In the Trust Center E-mail Security page, under **Encrypted E-mail**, click the **Encrypt Contents And Attachments For Outgoing Messages** check box, as shown in Figure 8-13.

3. Click **OK**.

ADD A DIGITAL SIGNATURE TO E-MAIL

A digital signature identifies you, proves the message and its attachments were not changed, and includes a certificate and public key. For an individual message:

1. In the Message tab Options group, click the **Dialog Box Launcher** in the lower-right corner.

2. In the Message Options dialog box that appears, click **Security Settings**.

3. Click the **Add Digital Signature To This Message** check box.

4. Click **OK** and click **Close** to return to your message.

TIP

The second or third options for macro protection give you the best protection. You can still use macros, but in either case, you are warned before you use them; in the second case, they are not allowed if they are not signed.

NOTE

Keep in mind that Outlook only helps reduce the *likelihood* of a macro virus; it is not a full antivirus program. You should install and use antivirus software on your computer. Visit http://www.mcafee.com or http://www.symantec.com to learn more about antivirus programs.

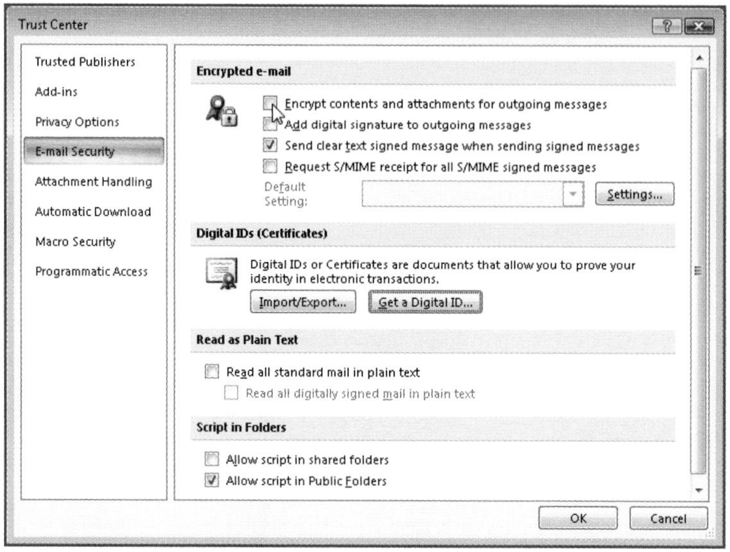

Trust Center

Trusted Publishers
Add-ins
Privacy Options
E-mail Security
Attachment Handling
Automatic Download
Macro Security
Programmatic Access

Encrypted e-mail

☐ Encrypt contents and attachments for outgoing messages
☐ Add digital signature to outgoing messages
☑ Send clear text signed message when sending signed messages
☐ Request S/MIME receipt for all S/MIME signed messages
Default Setting: [　　　　　　　▼] [Settings...]

Digital IDs (Certificates)

Digital IDs or Certificates are documents that allow you to prove your identity in electronic transactions.
[Import/Export...] [Get a Digital ID...]

Read as Plain Text

☐ Read all standard mail in plain text
☐ Read all digitally signed mail in plain text

Script in Folders

☐ Allow script in shared folders
☑ Allow script in Public Folders

[OK] [Cancel]

*Figure 8-13: **It is unlikely that you will want to encrypt and/or digitally sign all your mail, but you may want to use the ability to encrypt individual messages in the e-mail message window.***

To add a digital signature to all your messages:

1. In Outlook, click **Tools**, click **Trust Center**, and click **E-mail Security**.

2. In the Trust Center E-mail Security page, under **Encrypted E-mail**, click the **Add Digital Signature To Outgoing Messages** check box.

3. Click **OK**.

Chapter 9
Using Forms, Labels, and Mail Merge

You've seen that Outlook is a lot more than a mail program. In this chapter we'll expand on that and you'll see how to modify existing forms and create custom forms, how to create and use templates in many Outlook views, and how to set up Outlook to perform a mail merge, as well as how to print both labels and envelopes.

Use Forms

Much of Outlook is built around forms: message forms, appointment forms, contact forms, and many others. *Forms* provide the means to collect information. Forms are built around *fields,* which are individual pieces of information collected by the form, such as the addressee and subject in the e-mail message form shown in Figure 9-1.

9

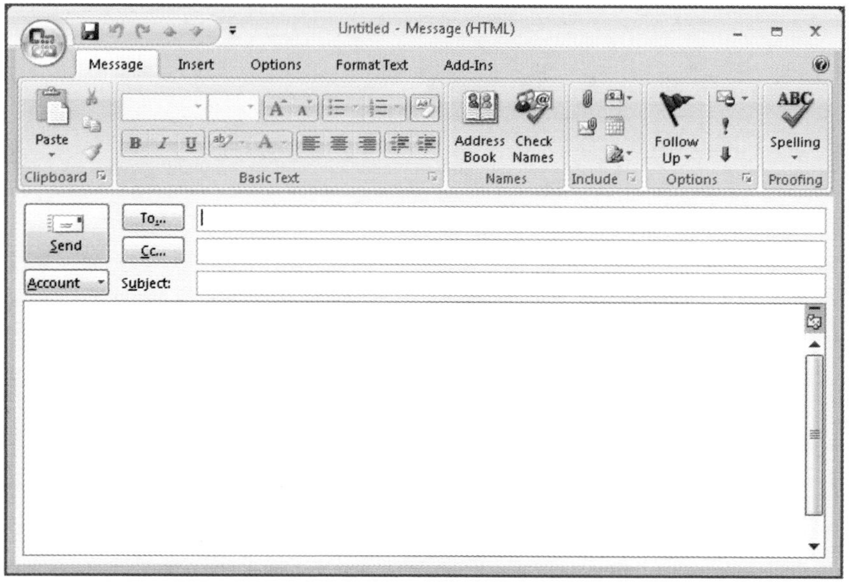

Figure 9-1: *Most of what is done in Outlook is done with forms.*

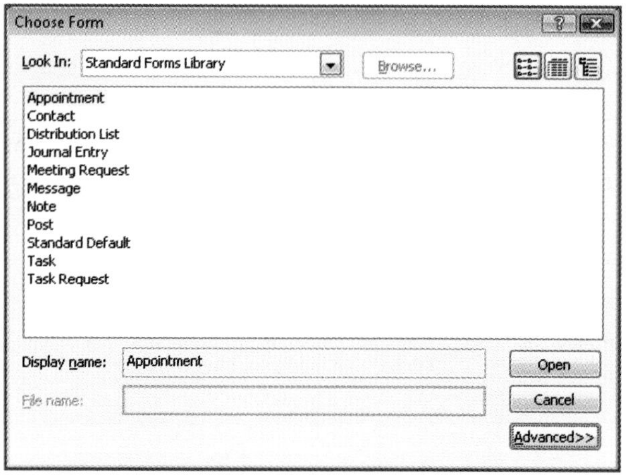

Figure 9-2: *Outlook uses 11 standard forms to perform its functions.*

Explore Outlook Forms

In earlier chapters you saw how to use various forms from within each of the views. You can also see all the forms together.

1. Open Outlook in one of the ways described in Chapter 1.

2. Click the **Tools** menu, click **Forms**, and click **Choose Form**. The Choose Form dialog box appears, as shown in Figure 9-2.

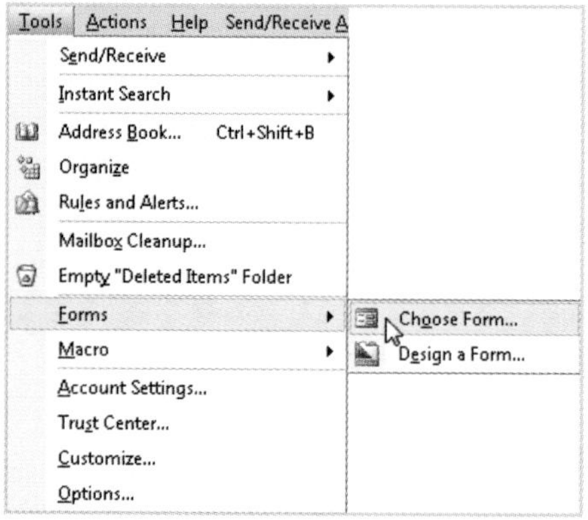

3. Click one of the forms, and click **Advanced**. You'll see a description of the form, who created it, and the message class, which is used in programming for Outlook.

4. Open a form by clicking it and then clicking **Open**.

   –Or–

   Double-click the form.

5. Click **Close** to close the form.

Modify a Standard Form

You can modify any of the standard forms and then use the revised form in the same way you did before it was modified.

1. From Outlook, click the **Tools** menu, click **Forms**, and click **Design A Form**.

2. Click the **Look In** drop-down list, and click the folder that holds the form you want to use. This is particularly useful for the message form, which is used in several different folders.

Form design ribbon   **Add pages**   **Design-related tools**   **Add predefined fields**

Figure 9-3: Opening an existing form in Design mode allows you to add, delete, change, and move fields, as well as add pages with new fields on them.

Place and move fields on grid

Create new fields

3. Click the form you want to modify, and click **Open**. The form will open in Design mode and, if you can add fields to the form, the Field Chooser dialog box will appear beside it (see Figure 9-3).

4. In the Developer tab Design group, select whether you want to change the form as the sender will see it (click **Edit Compose Page**) or as the recipient will see it (click **Edit Read Page**).

5. Choose from among the following changes that can be made on the form:

- Click a field whose size you want to change. A shaded border with *sizing handles* (small black or white squares) appears around the field. Drag one of the sizing handles to change the size of the field.

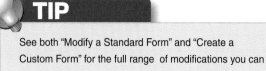

TIP

See both "Modify a Standard Form" and "Create a Custom Form" for the full range of modifications you can make to a form.

New Field

Name:	
Type:	Text
Format:	Text

OK   Cancel

- Click a field you want to delete, and press **DELETE**.

- Click the field categories drop-down list at the top of the Field Chooser dialog box, click a category, and drag a predefined field to the place on the form where you want it.

- To insert a new field in the form, click **New** in the Field Chooser dialog box. In the New Field dialog box that appears, enter a name, select a type and format, and click **OK**. Drag the new field to the place on the form where you want it.

- Click the **Office Button**, and click **Save As**. Click **Browse Folders** and select the folder in which you want to save the form. Enter the file name for the form, click **Save**, and close the form.

Create a Custom Form

Creating a custom form is the same as modifying a form, because Outlook does not allow you to start with a blank form. You can do that very easily, though, by starting with an existing form, deleting all the fields you don't want—possibly all of them—and adding the fields you want. Also, there are a number of additional tools on the Developer ribbon you can use to customize a form, including the Form Design toolbar.

USE THE DEVELOPER TAB

The Developer tab and ribbon in the Form Design window allow you to perform the following functions:

- Program small scripts and macros to add automation to a form.

- Publish the form to a server so that you or anyone else with access can use it.

- View Visual Basic Script code you have added to the form.

- Display or rename a page.

- Create a new form region or rename a current one.

- Choose to edit the page as the sender or the reader will see it.

- Open and close the Field Chooser and the Control toolbox.

- Open the Properties dialog boxes for a field.

- Position and align fields.

To perform these functions, the Developer tab has a number of unique options, as shown in Figure 9-4.

The more important options on the Developer tab are as follows:

- **Design group:**

  - In the **Page** drop-down list, the **Display This Page** and **Rename Page** options allow you to display add-on pages named P.2 through P.6 (which are turned off, by default, indicated by the parentheses) and to rename them from "Message" (or whatever name the standard tab is) and "P.x" to your choice. If your ending form contains one new page, you would turn the page on to use it in the final form. When the new form is opened, it will contain only the pages you have included in the modified form.

  - The **Form Region** drop-down list allows you to create, save, reopen, and close a form region, which provides for the inclusion of Web pages and ActiveX controls on a form. Each region is a separate page.

  - The **Separate Read Layout** check box, when selected (which it is by default), specifies a separate layout for the page as it will be read that is distinct from the layout for the page displayed while the sender is creating it. When this check box is not selected, only one layout is used—the one the sender will see. If you select this check box and then clear it again, both layouts are the same (the compose layout). See "Use Separate Compose and Read Layouts" later in this chapter.

  - **Edit Compose Page** and **Edit Read Page** allow you to select which of the two form layouts you want to edit when Separate Read Layout is selected.

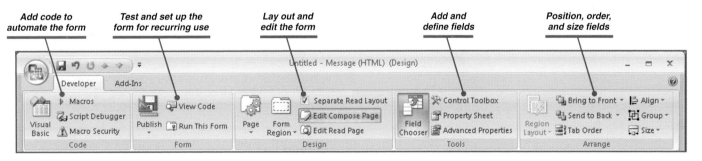

Figure 9-4: *The Developer tab provides a number of form design tools.*

- **Tools group:**

  - The **Control toolbox** contains tools you can use to build a form, as described in "Use the Control Toolbox" later in this chapter.

  - **Property** and **Advanced Properties** allow you to enter detailed specifications, including the name, position, font, color, initial value, and any validation rules you want to establish for a field.

- **Arrange group:**

  - **Region Layout** allows you to specify that a layout will automatically resize itself when the form is resized, or you can manually resize a layout to a fixed form size that you set.

  - **Bring To Front** and **Send To Back** moves a selected field toward the reader ("front") or away from the reader ("back").

  - **Tab Order** allows you to specify the order in which the user will progress from one field to the next. See "Change the Tab Order" later in this chapter.

  - **Align** opens a menu that helps you align multiple fields when they are selected together. This includes options for aligning each of the four sides and centering, as well as options to turn on and use the Snap To Grid, which is a "magnetic" property that causes fields to automatically align to the grid intersections.

  - **Group** and **Ungroup** allow you to combine two or more fields and then move and place them without disturbing the layout within the group.

  - **Size** allows you to make two or more selected objects the same size in width, height, or both and to fit objects within a given space or to the grid.

POSITION AND ALIGN TWO FIELDS

To align two fields, first use the Properties dialog box and then the alignment tools on the Developer ribbon.

1. From Outlook, click the **Tools** menu, click **Forms**, and click **Design A Form**. Double-click the existing form that will be the foundation of a new form.

2. Delete any existing fields you do not need. Drag two new fields from the Field Chooser dialog box to the new form, and purposely make them unaligned and of different sizes.

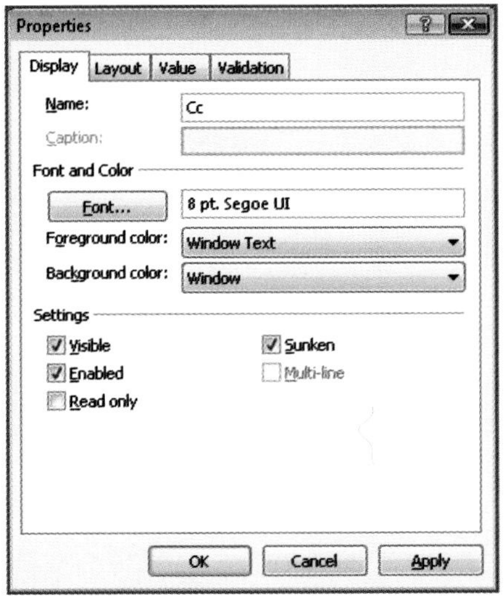

Figure 9-5: *You can align and similarly size two fields by making all but one of their coordinates the same.*

It works best if the label and content fields are sized and aligned separately. It is also helpful to align fields that are all in a vertical column or all in a horizontal row. Finally, if you are having problems sizing and aligning three or more fields, do them two at a time, with one of the two the way you want all the fields.

3. Click the field that will remain in its current position, and make sure its left edge is where you want it. In the Developer tab Tools group, click the **Property Sheet** icon to open the Properties dialog box, as shown in Figure 9-5.

4. Click the **Layout** tab, note the four position numbers, and close the dialog box. You could simply use those coordinates to align and size the fields, but there is an easier way.

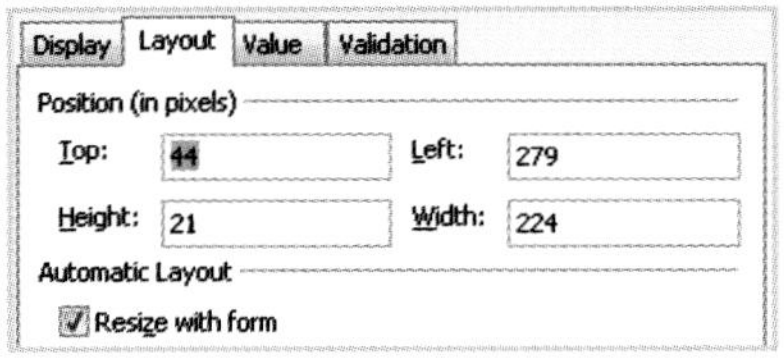

5. Click the field that will remain in its current position, and make sure its left edge is where you want it. It is important that the field that will stay constant be selected first.

6. Hold down **SHIFT** while clicking the second field. Note that the first field has white selection handles, while the second field has black selection handles.

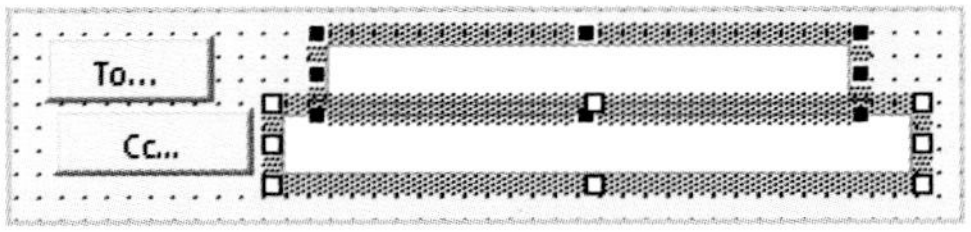

7. In the Developer tab Arrange group, click the **Align** drop-down arrow, and click **Left**. In the same group, click the **Size** drop-down arrow, click **Make Same Size**, and click **Both**. Note that the field with the black handles was the one that moved in both instances.

8. Repeat steps 5–7 with the two field labels, and then with each of the labels and their fields. The result should be four perfectly sized aligned fields, like this:

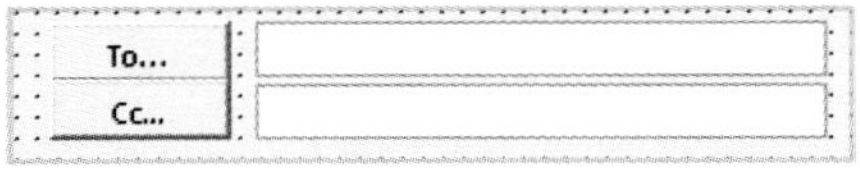

USE THE DESIGN TABS

Beneath the ribbon in the content area, the Form Design window has a number of new tabs, depending on the type of form. For example, the message form contains eight new tabs in addition to the single Message tab on the standard form. Of the

TIP

You can use either **CTRL** or **SHIFT** to select multiple fields, but there is a difference. When you use **CTRL**, the *first* field selected is the one that will move when you align them and will have black selection handles after both fields are selected; the fixed field will have white selection handles. If you use **SHIFT** to select multiple fields, the *last* field selected is the one that will move and will have the black selection handles.

eight new tabs, five are additional blank pages for the form. The three other tabs specify additional aspects of the form:

(P.2)	(P.3)	(P.4)	(P.5)	(P.6)	(All Fields)	(Properties)	(Actions)

- **All Fields** allows you to define new fields (by clicking **New** at the bottom of the window) and specify the initial or default value of a field.

- **Properties** allows you to specify the form's categories, version, form number, icons, contact, and description.

- **Actions** contains the user actions that are implemented for the form, such as reply and forward.

Use the Control Toolbox

The Control toolbox is used to add new fields and labels to a form. The Control toolbox is opened with the Control Toolbox button in the Developer tab Tools group, and it contains 15 tools, as shown in Figure 9-6. For example, you can use the Control toolbox to create a combo box and a label.

1. In Outlook, click the **Tools** menu, click **Forms**, and click **Design A Form**. Double-click an existing form that will be the foundation of a new form.

2. Delete any existing fields you do not need, and otherwise make room, such as moving fields, to add a new label and combo box. In the Developer tab Tools group, click **Control Toolbox** ⚙ Control Toolbox . (If the window is not maximized, you will only see the icon in the Tools group.)

3. Click the **Label** tool. Then, on your form, place the label by clicking to the left of where you want the combo box to be.

4. With the label selected, click the label again until the text box border has slanted lines and the insertion point is available. Then, if there is existing text in the label, drag across the existing text, and type the label you want.

5. In the Control toolbox, click the **Combo Box** tool, and drag a combo box from the right edge of the label to make a box about two inches long and a quarter of an inch wide.

6. Right-click in the new combo box, and click **Properties** from the context menu to open the Properties dialog box. In the Display tab, type the name you want in the Name text box.

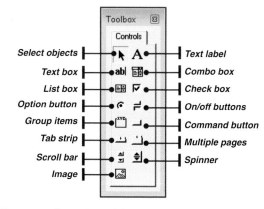

Figure 9-6: Controls and features are added to a new form from the Control toolbox.

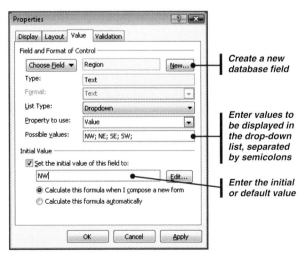

7. Click the **Value** tab, and click the **New** button to create a new field in the Outlook field list. In the New Field dialog box, type the field name in the Name text box, type the type of field in the Type field, and choose the format you want in the Format drop-down list.

8. Click **OK** to close the New Field dialog box. In the Properties dialog box, on the Value tab, click in the **Possible Values** text box, and type the values that are to be displayed in the drop-down list, separated by semicolons.

9. Click the **Set The Initial Value Of This Field To** check box, click in the text box, and type the value from the drop-down list that you want to be the default. If you have numbers in the default value, place quotation marks around the value. When you are done, your dialog box should look something like that shown in Figure 9-7.

10. Click OK to close the Properties dialog box. To see how your new combo box works, in the Developer tab Form group, click **Run This Form**. You should see the default value in the combo box, and if you open the box, you should see the alternatives that you entered. This is what ours looked like:

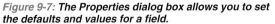

11. Click the **Close** button to close the sample form that was opened and return to the Design view. With the new combo box still selected, hold down **CTRL** and click the field's label. In the Developer tab Arrange group, click the **Group** down arrow, and click **Group** to group the label and the combo box together.

12. Click the **Office Button**, click **Save As**, locate the folder in which you want to save the form, type a name for the form, and click **Save**.

Change the Tab Order

The tab order of a form is the order in which you go from field to field as you are filling out the form by pressing **TAB**. How this works is important, because the tab order should follow, as much as possible, how users would logically

Create a new database field

Enter values to be displayed in the drop-down list, separated by semicolons

Enter the initial or default value

Figure 9-7: The Properties dialog box allows you to set the defaults and values for a field.

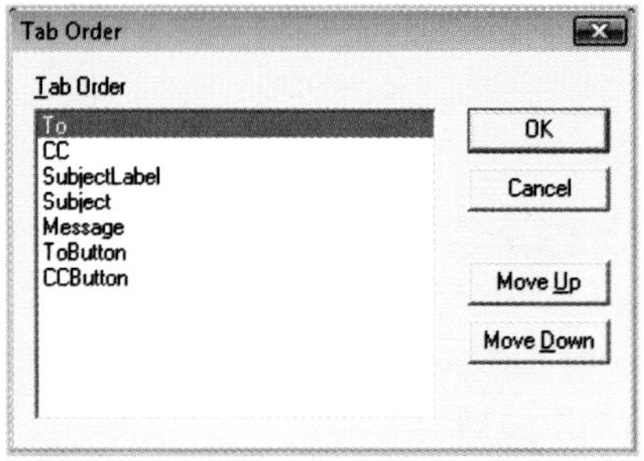

move through the form if they were to click each field. With the Form Design window open:

1. In the Developer tab Arrange group, click **Tab Order** to open the Tab Order dialog box.

2. In the Tab Order dialog box, the fields in a form are listed in the order in which they will be selected as you go through the form. You can change the order by moving fields up and down the list.

3. Click a field you want to change, and move it by clicking **Move Down** or **Move Up**.

4. Click **OK** to close the Tab Order dialog box.

Use Separate Compose and Read Layouts

Outlook allows you to have a form for the person who initially fills it out be different from the form for the person who reads it. When you create a form, you can choose to have the *compose page*—the form the way you fill it out—be different from the *read page*—the form the way it will be read. You can initiate this feature in the Form Design window, in the Developer tab Design group, by making sure that **Separate Read Layout** is selected. When this is selected, you will have two options enabled that allow you to switch between the compose page and the read page.

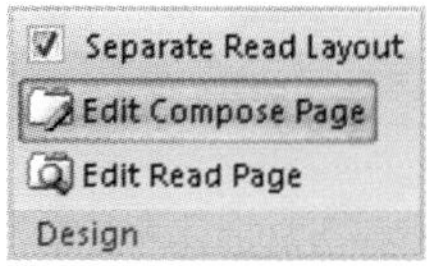

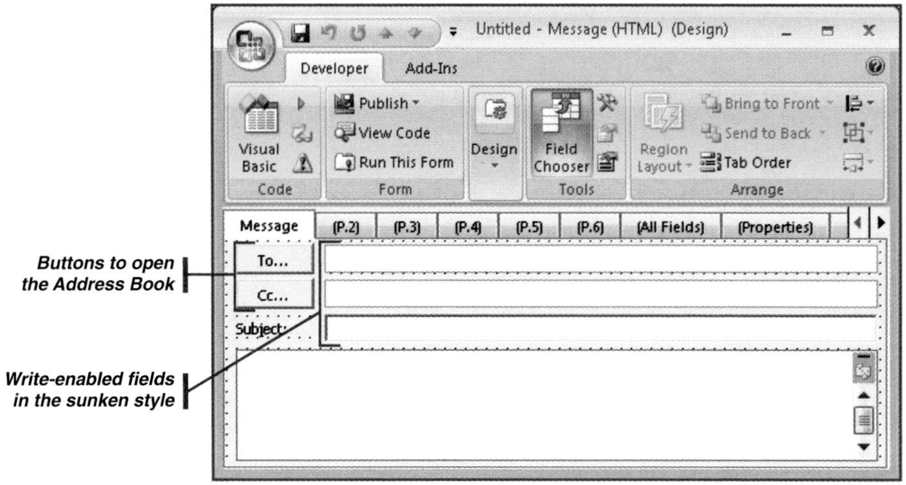

The easiest way to see the difference between a compose page and a read page is by using the standard Outlook e-mail message form. The way you first see the form in Design view is as the compose page, as shown in Figure 9-8. In the Developer tab Design group, click **Edit Read Page**, and you will see a number of changes, as shown in Figure 9-9.

Buttons to open the Address Book

Write-enabled fields in the sunken style

*Figure 9-8: **A message form in compose layout provides special fields useful to the person creating it.***

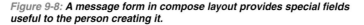
9

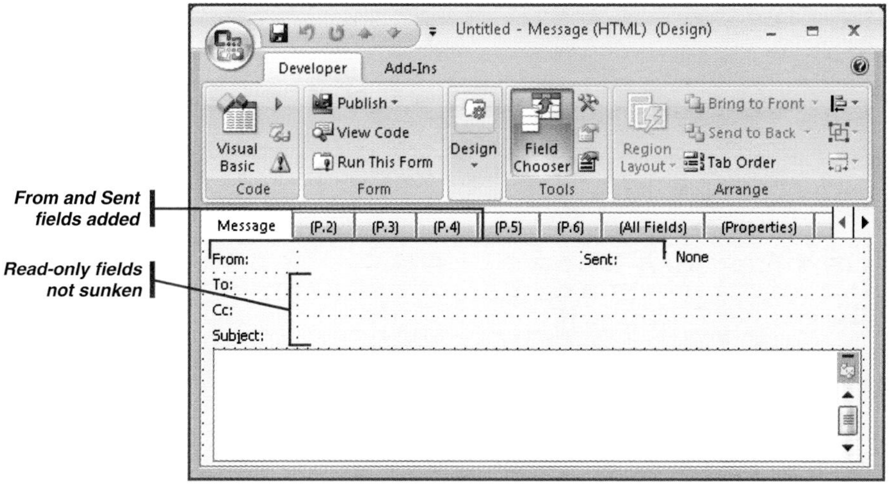

From and Sent fields added

Read-only fields not sunken

Figure 9-9: *A message form in read layout allows it to be tailored for the person who will be receiving it.*

NOTE

Separate read and compose layouts allow you to tailor a form to a specific audience and to add features that are important to either the person filling out the form or the person reading it, but not to both.

Publish a Form

When you are ready for people to start using a form, you need to *publish* it. Publishing a form puts it into a different state than just saving it. When you save a form and then reopen and use it, you are using the original and only copy of the form. If you publish the form and then open and use it, you are using a copy and not the original. Every time you use a published form, you are using a copy of the form. To publish a form that is open in the Form Design window:

1. In the Developer tab Form group, click **Publish** and then click **Publish Form**.

2. Click the folder you want to use (Personal Forms Library is recommended), type the name of the form in the Display Name box (it is automatically repeated in the Form Name box, but you can change it), and click **Publish**, as shown in Figure 9-10.

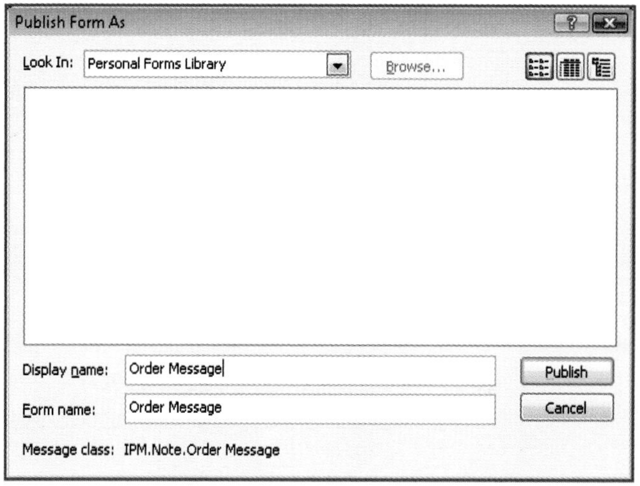

Figure 9-10: *Publishing a form allows it to be used over and over.*

TIP

You can do many things with forms when they are tied to one or more of the Outlook views. For example, you can tie a schedule reminder message to the Calendar or tie a task list confirmation to Tasks.

TIP

Any of the built-in Outlook forms you see by clicking **New** and then clicking **Choose Form** can be customized by you and then saved under a new template name.

QUICKSTEPS

CREATING AND USING A TEMPLATE

A *template* is a blank message form with custom text in the body of the message that can be used as a standard e-mail message. For instance, you might set up a standard reply to professional inquiries you receive. A template uses the same fields as the standard form, whereas the custom forms we've been discussing change those fields.

CREATE A TEMPLATE

Templates are an easy way to send a lot of repetitive e-mail. If you are sending the same message to three or more people, you should probably create a template.

1. From the Outlook window, with the Inbox open, click the **New Mail Message** toolbar button to open a new message window.

2. Leave the To and Cc text boxes blank, type the **Subject** text, and type the template's message text.

Continued . . .

3. If you are asked if you want to save the form definition with the form, click **Yes**. (It's very important to save the form definition information with the message if you're going to send it to someone who doesn't have the form and is not connected to your Exchange Server.)

4. When you are done, close your Form Design window, clicking **Yes** when asked if you want to save your changes.

Use a Custom Form

Using a custom form is easy.

1. In the Outlook window, with the Inbox open, click the **New Mail Message** down arrow on the toolbar, and click **Choose Form**. Click the **Look In** down arrow, click **Personal Forms Library**, and you will see the display name of your custom form.

2. Double-click your form and it will open, ready to be filled in, as you can see in Figure 9-11.

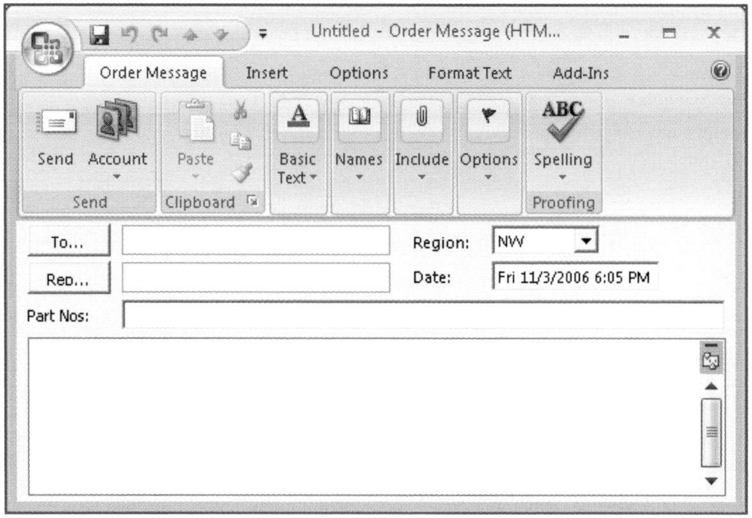

*Figure 9-11: **Custom forms can be handy for such things as order confirmations.***

CREATING AND USING A TEMPLATE (Continued)

3. Click the **Office Button**, click **Save As**, and click **Browse Folders**. Drag **Folders** to the top of the navigation pane, and navigate to and open your Templates folder (this often is C:\Users*yourname*\App Data\Roaming\Microsoft\Templates).

4. Accept the text from your template's subject line as the file name. Under Save As Type, click **Outlook Template (*.oft)**, and click **Save**. The new template will be saved.

5. Click **Close** to close your message window, and click **No** when asked if you want to save the file (that is, if you want to save it in your Inbox, which you don't—you've already saved it as a template).

USE A TEMPLATE

1. Click the **New Mail Message** down arrow in the toolbar, and click **Choose Form**. The Choose Form dialog box appears.

2. In the Look In drop-down list, click **User Templates In File System**. The template you just created should be displayed.

3. Double-click your template name, and it opens as a new message window, with the subject line and body filled in according to the template. All you need to do is fill in the To information and click **Send**, as you can see in Figure 9-12. Of course, you can modify or add to the text.

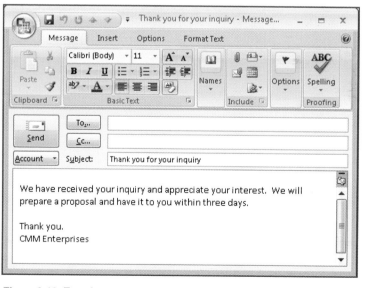

Figure 9-12: *Templates can speed up the handling of a large volume of e-mail.*

NOTE

If your contacts are in more than one folder, you either need to perform multiple mail merges (one with each of the folders designated as the data source), or you must create one folder to combine the contacts, either by merging the folders or by creating a new folder and copying the contacts to it.

Perform a Mail Merge

Performing a mail merge allows you to merge a form letter with your Outlook contacts, thereby sending each contact a unique letter addressed just to him or her. This can be done with all contacts in a folder or just a subset of them. This section discusses sending form letters to a subset of your contacts, although the steps for sending form letters to all of your contacts are much the same—and simpler.

There are three steps to performing a mail merge using the Contacts list in Outlook with a Microsoft Word document. First, within Outlook, you prepare the contacts you wish to use in the mail merge, and then you export them in a form that Word can use with its Mail Merge feature. Second, in Word, you create the document that will be used to perform the mail merge. Finally, you perform the mail merge itself in Word.

Prepare Contacts

If you are only going to perform a mail merge on some of your contacts, it is a good idea to first create a new folder to hold the contacts you wish to include in the mail merge. Then, in Word, you select that folder as your data source. To create a new folder and export it:

1. In Outlook, click **Contacts** in the Outlook view bars.

2. Click the **New Contact** down arrow, and click **Folder**. The Create New Folder dialog box appears.

3. Type the name for the new folder, and make sure that **Contact Items** is selected under Folder Contains and that **Contacts** is highlighted under Select Where To Place The Folder, as shown in Figure 9-13.

4. Click **OK**. Your new folder appears in the list of Contacts folders at the top of the Folder list.

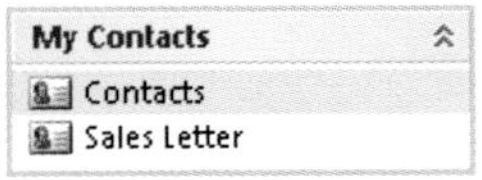

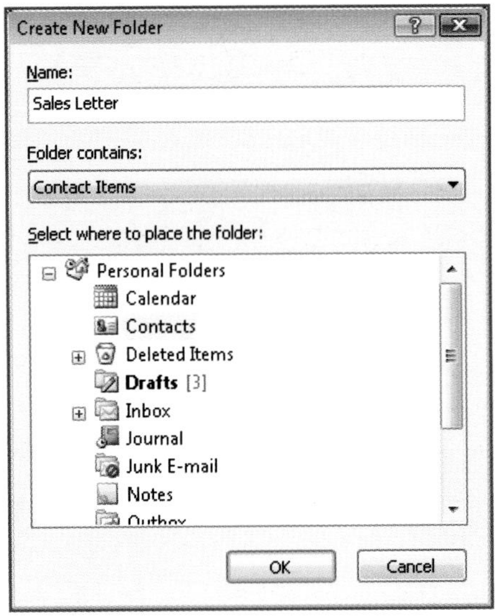

Figure 9-13: *Creating a special folder for a mail merge allows you to easily send mail to the same people in the future.*

UICKSTEPS

SELECTING CONTACTS

You can select contacts to use in a mail merge in four ways: manually, using Outlook's Mail Merge feature, using Outlook's filters, or using Word's Mail Merge feature. The first three are discussed here. The fourth is discussed in "Prepare a Mail Merge Document in Word" Later in this chapter.

SELECT CONTACTS MANUALLY

To add contacts to a mail merge folder:

Right-drag contacts from your main Contacts folder to your new mail merge folder, and click **Copy**.

–Or–

Select several contacts, either by holding down CTRL while clicking the contacts you want or by holding down SHIFT while clicking the first and last members of a contiguous range of contacts. These can then be dragged to the new folder or used directly in Outlook's Mail Merge feature.

USE OUTLOOK'S MAIL MERGE FEATURE

This technique is often used when you are ready to do the mail merge in "real time." You have the contacts and the document you are going to send them, and you are ready to move right into the actual merge. In this approach, you link your contacts (either in the Contacts folder or your own folder of selected contacts) to a Word document containing the mail merge text.

1. In Outlook Contacts, click the **Tools** menu, and click **Mail Merge**. The Mail Merge dialog box appears, as shown in Figure 9-14.

2. Either click **All Contacts In Current View**, which can be filtered (see "Use Outlook Filtering") or click **Only Selected Contacts** when contacts have been manually selected (see "Select Contacts Manually").

Continued . . .

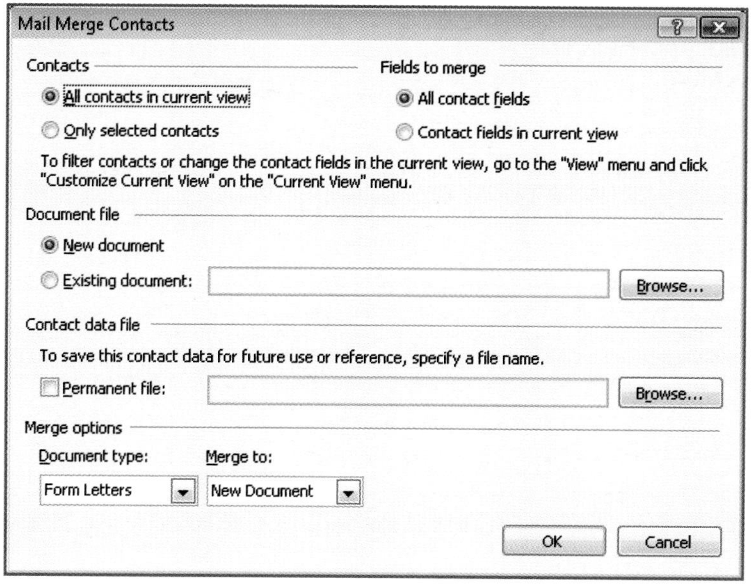

*Figure 9-14: **Outlook will help you set up your contacts for a mail merge and then will open Word, to access the document, and do the merge.***

Prepare a Mail Merge Document in Word

You can approach a mail merge from Outlook and then use Microsoft Word just to produce a document, or you can start from Word and just use Outlook to supply the contacts. Since this book is on Outlook, we will use the first approach and assume you have used Outlook's Mail Merge feature (see the "Selecting Contacts" QuickSteps) to prepare your contacts and then opened Word to create a new mail merge document. You should, therefore, have Word open on your screen to type the document and place field names where you want the Outlook contact information.

1. In Word type the body of a new letter, or paste an existing one that you will be sending to your selected contacts. Leave blank the areas that will contain the recipient's name and address.

QUICKSTEPS

SELECTING CONTACTS *(Continued)*

3. Click either **New Document** or an **Existing Document**, which you can then identify.

4. Click **Permanent File** and browse to or type the file name you wish to use.

5. Select the merge options, such as form letters, labels, or envelopes to a new document, printer, or e-mail that are correct for you, and then click **OK**.

Outlook will prepare your contact data, open Microsoft Word, and create a new mail merge document linked to your contact data and ready for you to type the message contents. See "Prepare a Mail Merge Document in Word" later in this chapter.

USE OUTLOOK FILTERING

Outlook's filtering capability allows you to select the contacts you want to use in a mail merge. The filtered contacts are placed in a file within a new folder you create specifically for the mail merge.

1. With the Contacts list still open, click the **View** menu, click **Current View**, and click **Customize Current View**.

2. Click **Filter** in the Customize View dialog box. In the Filter dialog box, type the criteria to select only the contacts you want, and then click **OK** twice.

3. Click the **Edit** menu, and click **Select All**. Right-drag the contacts to the new folder you created, and click **Copy** in the context menu to keep the contacts also in the Contacts folder.

4. Click your new folder in the Folder list to see the selected contacts, as shown in Figure 9-15. This folder can now be used to merge contacts into a Word document.

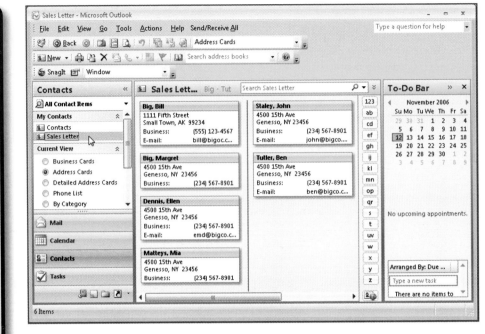

Figure 9-15: ***Use one of several options within Outlook to select contacts for use in a mail merge.***

2. When the body of the letter is the way you want it, return to the top of the page. In the Mailings tab Write & Insert Fields group, click **Address Block**. The Insert Address Block dialog box appears.

3. Review the default settings. In most cases, they work well. Click **Match Fields**. Make sure the field on the right matches the required information on the left. Click **OK** twice when ready.

4. Under the address block that just appeared, leave a blank line or two. Then, in the Mailings tab Write & Insert Fields group, click **Greeting Line**. The Insert Greeting Line dialog box appears. Select the options that are correct for you, and click **OK**.

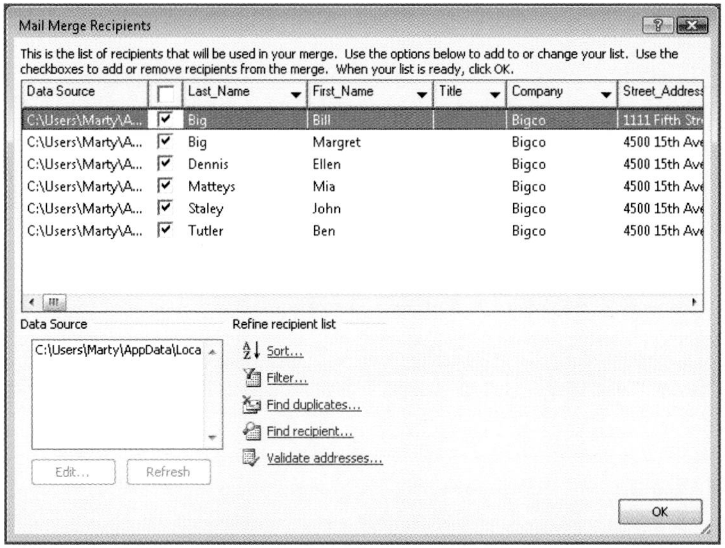

*Figure 9-16: **Word provides a means of filtering, sorting, and selecting contacts in the Mail Merge Recipients dialog box.***

5. In the Mailings tab Start Mail Merge group, click **Edit Recipient List**. Here you can make a final selection of your recipients, as shown in Figure 9-16. Use the check boxes on the left to select individuals; click a column heading to sort the list on that column; click the down arrow in a column heading to select a particular entry in the column, including "blanks" and "nonblanks"; click the data source in the lower-left, and then click **Edit** to change an individual record. When you have the recipients the way you want them, click **OK**.

6. In the Mailings tab Preview Results group, click **Preview Results** to display your contacts merged with the letter, as shown in Figure 9-17 (if your Word window is narrow and there is a down arrow under Preview Results, you'll need to click **Preview Results** a second time in the drop-down options). Use the arrows in the middle of the Mail Merge toolbar to look at more contacts.

7. When the document is as you want it, click **Save** on the Quick Access toolbar.

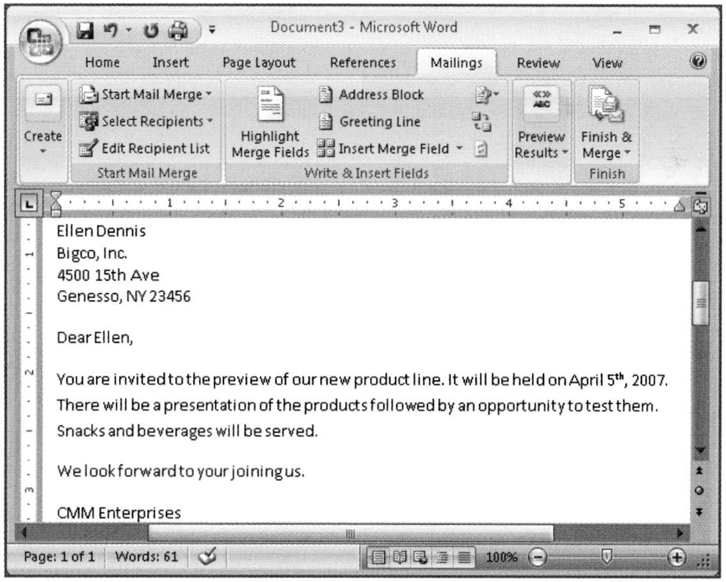

*Figure 9-17: **A well-done mail merge letter is impossible to tell from an individually typed letter.***

Perform a Mail Merge

When you perform a mail merge, you can print letters, mailing labels, or envelopes, or you can send e-mail messages, all to Outlook contacts. Once you have the document and contacts the way you want them, run tests—first of the data and then of the merge—to see if any fields are missing in the data and if the merge is picking up the right fields. When you are satisfied with the results, print the actual letters, labels, or envelopes, or send the e-mail.

1. In the Mailings tab Preview Results group, click **Auto Check For Errors** to see if there are any needed fields missing. In the Checking And Reporting Errors dialog box, click **Simulate The Merge And Report Errors In A New Document**, and click **OK**. You will get either a message of errors in the data or a message that there are no errors.

2. When you have fixed any errors, in the Mailings tab Finish group, click **Finish & Merge**, click **Edit Individual Documents**, accept the default selection (**ALL**) to merge all records, and click **OK**. A new document will be created containing all of the letters you want created. Use the **Next Page** and **Previous Page** controls in the lower-right area of the Word window to look at the succession of letters you have created.

3. When you are ready to print your merged letters, click **Print** on the Quick Access toolbar of the new merged document you created in step 2.

   –Or–

   In place of creating the individual merged documents in step 2, in the Mailings tab Finish group, click **Finish & Merge** and then click **Print Documents**, or click **Send E-mail Messages**.

4. If you wish, save your new merged document, and once more save the original mail merge document.

Print Labels

Printing labels is done the same way as the mail merge. First, you prepare your data file in Outlook (which you've already done while preparing for the mail merge). Then switch to Word, create a blank document, and perform a mail merge.

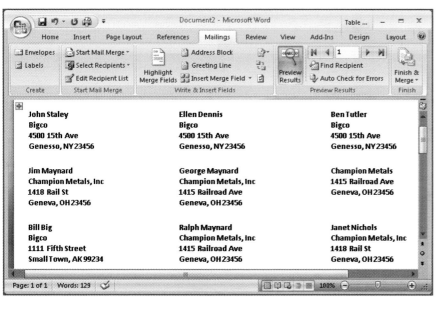

1. If you haven't already prepared a Contacts file for the mail merge, follow the steps described in "Prepare Contacts" and in the "Selecting Contacts" QuickSteps earlier in this chapter to get a data file for the names and addresses.

2. In Word, open a new, blank document. Then, in the Mailings tab Start Mail Merge group, click the **Start Mail Merge** down arrow, and click **Labels**. The Label Options dialog box appears.

3. Select the label vendor and product number you want to use (Avery 5160 or its equivalent is a common 30-per-sheet address label), and click **OK**.

4. In the Mailings tab Start Mail Merge group, click **Select Recipients** and click **Select From Outlook Contacts**. Double-click the contacts folder you want to use, make any needed selections or changes in the Mail Merge Recipients dialog box (shown earlier in Figure 9-16), and click **OK**. Your Word page will be filled with label fields.

5. Click in the upper-left corner label (the first label on the sheet—the insertion point may already be there). Then, in the Mailings tab Write & Insert Fields group, click **Address Block**. Make any needed changes to the address block, check for any unmatched fields, and click **OK**.

6. In the Mailings tab Write & Insert Fields group, click the **Update Labels** icon 📄. The address block will be added to all labels.

7. In the Mailings tab Preview Results group, click **Preview Results** (if your Word window is narrow and there is a down arrow under Preview Results, you'll need to click **Preview Results** a second time in the drop-down options), and you will see the labels populated with your contact list, as you can see in Figure 9-18.

8. Scroll through the preview document. After making sure your blank labels are correctly loaded in your printer, in the Mailings tab Finish group, click **Finish & Merge** and then click **Print Documents**. If you want to save your merged labels document for later use, click **Save** in the Quick Access toolbar, enter a name, select a folder, and click **Save**.

*Figure 9-18: **Word has a Mail Merge Wizard that can lead you through all types of mail merges, including letters, labels, and envelopes.***

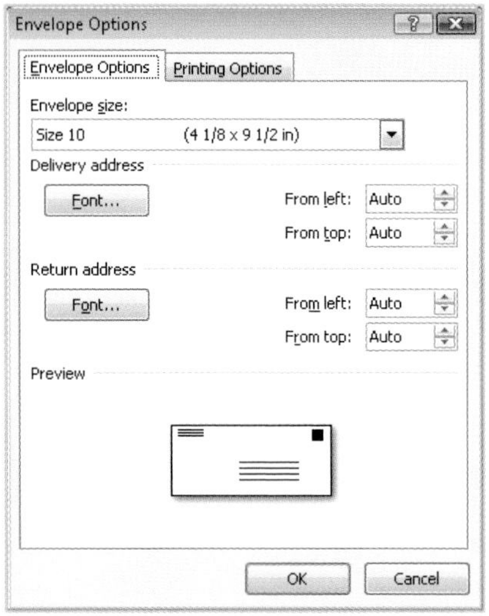

Print Envelopes

You may want to print names and addresses directly onto envelopes. As with the mail merge and printing labels, printing envelopes first requires that you create a Contacts data file. This is described earlier in "Prepare Contacts" and in the "Selecting Contacts" QuickSteps. After that, create a Word envelope merge document.

1. In Word, open a new, blank document. In the Mailings tab Start Mail Merge group, click the **Start Mail Merge** down arrow, and click **Envelopes**. The Envelope Options dialog box will appear.

2. Make any needed changes, and click **OK**. An envelope-shaped document will be displayed.

3. In the Mailings tab Start Mail Merge group, click **Select Recipients** and click **Select From Outlook Contacts**. Double-click the contacts folder you want to use, make any needed selections or changes in the Mail Merge Recipients dialog box (shown earlier in Figure 9-16), and click **OK**.

4. With the insertion point in the addressee area in the middle of the envelope, click **Address Block** in the Mailings tab Write & Insert Fields group. Make any needed changes to the address block, check for any unmatched fields, and click **OK**.

5. Click in the upper-left corner of the envelope displayed in Word, and type the return address if the envelopes aren't preprinted.

6. In the Mailings tab Preview Results group, click **Preview Results** (if your Word window is narrow and there is a down arrow under Preview Results, you'll need to click **Preview Results** a second time in the drop-down options), and you will see your first address appear on the envelope, as shown in Figure 9-19.

7. After making sure your envelopes are loaded correctly in your printer, in the Mailings tab Finish group, click **Finish & Merge** and then click **Print Documents**. If you want to save the merged envelopes document for later use, click **Save** in the Quick Access toolbar, type a name, select a folder, and click **Save**.

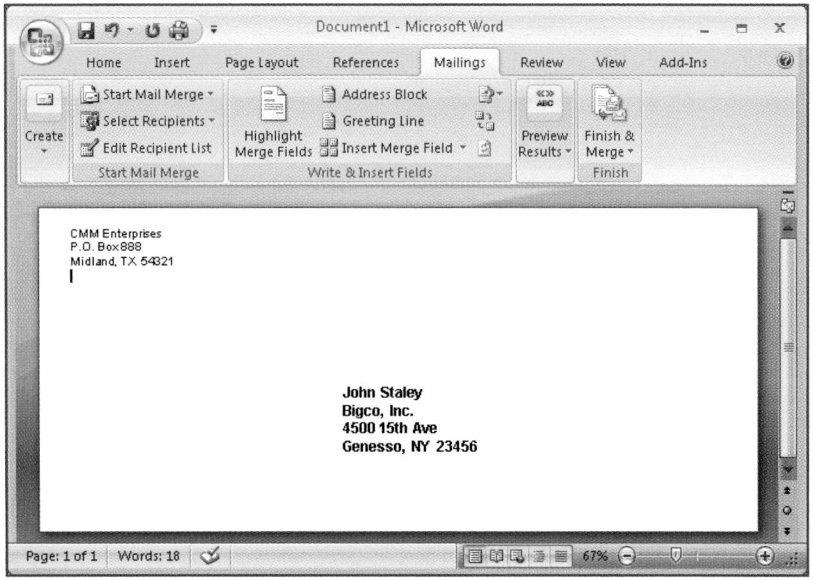

*Figure 9-19: **Generating Mail Merge envelopes is almost the same as creating labels.***

Chapter 10

Using Outlook in Other Ways

Being a part of Microsoft Office and the Microsoft family brings a number of features and capabilities to Outlook that extend what it can do and how it functions. In this chapter you'll see some of those features and capabilities, including using Outlook with instant messaging, with RSS (real simple syndication) feeds, and with a potpourri of extensions. These supplementary applications, such as Office Clipboard and using features from Microsoft Word, help integrate Outlook with fellow members of the Office suite or, in the case of using Outlook as a Web browser, with the Windows product line.

Use Instant Messaging with Outlook

If you're addicted to instant messaging, you'll be glad to know that Outlook can launch you right into a conversation. If you've never used instant messaging, now's the time to try it, because Outlook 2007 has instant messaging built into it.

10

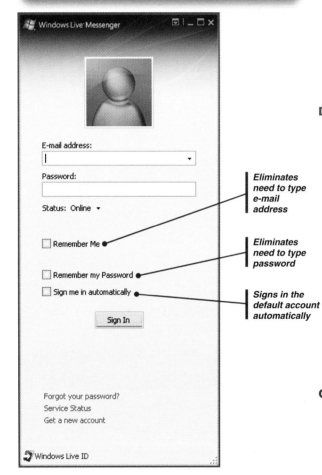

Figure 10-1: Other persons using the same computer can use their Passport accounts to sign on to instant messaging.

You just might get hooked on this quick and easy tool for making plans, solving problems, or catching up. You can do it with one person or with several at a time. If you have a Microsoft Passport or MSN Hotmail account, as explained in Chapter 2, you're ready to go. If not, get one and come back when you're ready.

Set Up Instant Messaging

Get some IM-savvy friends to send you the e-mail addresses they use for IM. If an address is different from the person's regular e-mail address, enter it the IM Address field in your Contacts list. Send yours to your friends, too, of course. Once you have done that, you can proceed to enter the world of IM-ing. If you haven't used Windows Live Messenger, now's the time to start.

DOWNLOAD WINDOWS LIVE MESSENGER

In Windows Vista you need to first download Windows Live Messenger.

1. If you haven't installed Windows Live Messenger, click **Start**, click **All Programs**, and click **Windows Live Messenger Download**. Click **Get It Free**, click **Save**, select a file location, and click **Save** again.

2. When the download completes, click **Open Folder**, double-click the program, and click **Run** to install it. Follow the remaining instructions to complete the installation.

3. When installation is complete, Windows Live Messenger will start (see Figure 10-1). Type your Microsoft Passport e-mail address and password, click the options you want, and click **Sign In**. The Windows Live Messenger window opens (see Figure 10-2).

4. If you have previously installed Windows Live Messenger and it didn't automatically start when you started Windows, click **Start**, click **All Programs**, and click **Windows Live Messenger**. The Windows Live Messenger window will open, as shown in Figure 10-2. A Welcome To Windows Live Messenger message may appear, informing you about using music, radio, and software. Click **Close**.

CREATE A NEW IM CONTACT

1. Click **Add A Contact** on the right of the toolbar in the Windows Live Messenger window. The Add A Contact dialog box appears, as you can see in Figure 10-3.

2. Type the contact's instant messaging address (usually the same as his or her e-mail address, but not always); choose whether to type a personal e-mail invitation, a mobile phone number for text messaging, and a nickname; and select a group.

10

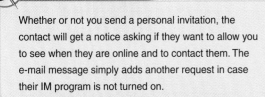
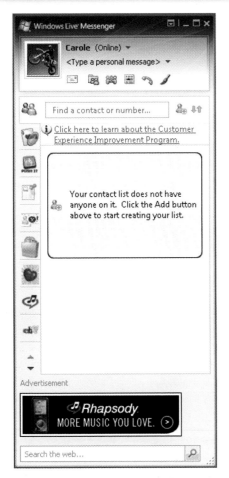

Figure 10-2: Windows Live Messenger offers access to video, audio, games, telephone service, and text messaging.

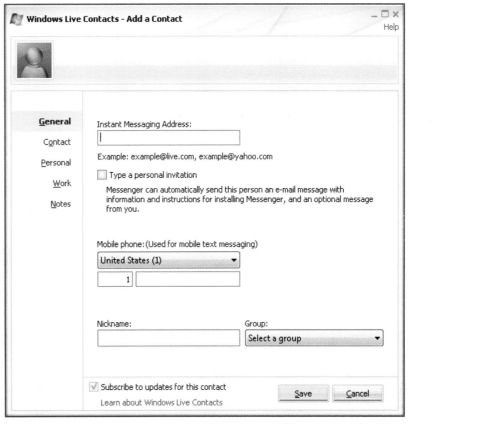

Figure 10-3: Your IM contacts have to be added manually, since there is not a way to transfer them from Outlook.

3. If you want to add further information about this contact while still in the Add A Contact dialog box, such as the full name, phone numbers, and address, click one of the options on the left, type the information you want to enter, and click **Save** when you are done.

Activate Instant Messaging in Outlook

You can also access instant messaging from within Outlook without affecting your ability to do so from Windows Live Messenger. Using IM from Outlook allows you to easily access Outlook's features at the same time. Start by activating IM in Outlook.

NOTE

As you create IM contacts, they will be automatically notified that you have done so and will see an option to add you to their list of contacts.

Windows Live Messenger [x]

Carole   has added you to his/her contact list.

Do you want to:

○ Allow this person to see when you are online and contact you

○ Block this person from seeing when you are online and contacting you

Remember, you can make yourself appear offline temporarily to everyone at any time.

☑ Add this person to my contact list.

View Profile   [OK] [Cancel]

NOTE

A Smart Tag is a small button that appears in Microsoft Office products to allow you to perform some function related to a piece of information next to the button. In this case, when you point to a person's name in an e-mail field, a green Windows Messaging button will appear if that person has been entered as an IM contact.

The appearance of the button tells you if the person is online. Clicking the button opens a menu of various options, including replying with an instant message.

To: ○ ▼ Marty Matthews

Cc: Marty Matthews - Available

Subje: Schedule a Meeting...

         Send Mail

         Reply with Instant Message

         Reply All with Instant Message

         Additional Actions   ▶

         Send Options...

         Outlook Properties

---

1. Start **Outlook**, click the **Tools** menu, click **Options**, and click the **Other** tab.

2. Under Person Names, click the **Display Online Status Next To A Person Name** check box, if it is not already selected, and click **OK**.

Person Names

☑ Display online status next to a person name

☑ Display online status in the To and Cc fields only when mouse pointer rests on a person name

Use Instant Messaging from Outlook

See if the person is online by pointing to his or her name in any of these locations:

- New message window
- Reading pane return address
- Opened message

1. Right-click a Smart Tag for someone who is online, and click **Reply With Instant Message**. An IM window will open.

2. Start typing a greeting or message in the lower pane. It will be reflected in the upper pane along with any replies from your contact. When you're ready, click **Send**.

3. When you're finished, close the window.

MAKE IT A PARTY

Several people can talk at a time when you are using IM, provided that you have already set them up as IM contacts. Get a conversation going with one other person, and then:

1. Click **Invite Someone To This Conversation** in the very left of the toolbar (if you haven't set up another person as an IM contact, the Invite Someone icon will not appear on the toolbar). The dialog box lets you see which of your IM contacts is currently online.

2. Select the person and click **OK**.

3. Continue conversing as before.

STATE YOUR AVAILABILITY

Click the down arrow to the left of your display name, and select a status.

Marty (Online) ▼
- Online
- Busy
- Be Right Back
- Away
- In a Call
- Out To Lunch
- Appear Offline

Implement RSS Feeds

RSS, or *Really Simple Syndication*, allows you to receive and store in one place information from a number of sources on an on-going basis. The information can be from any source on the Web that has implemented RSS and to which you have subscribed, often for free, but sometimes at a cost. Normally, the information is from sites that frequently update their content, such as news organizations like CNN, MSN, and CNET, or active blogs (Web logs or online journals) from both individuals and companies. The information frequently consists of short summary text headings in the form of a link that you can click to download and read the full article; but increasingly, the RSS feed includes larger blocks of text, pictures, and even multimedia content, which are called *podcasts*.

10

The primary reason for RSS feeds is that they allow you to collect information from a number of sources without having to visit many different sites. You subscribe to the feed, and it is automatically downloaded for you by the program handling the RSS feed. You might do this because of a particular interest you have, or a desire to stay informed, or because it supports your work.

You can receive RSS feeds from many sources using a number of different programs, including Internet Explorer and the Windows Sidebar in Windows Vista. Outlook allows you to subscribe, receive, read, organize, store, and delete RSS content. The process is similar to how e-mail is handled:

- Locate and subscribe to an RSS feed.
- Outlook creates a folder for that feed under the RSS Feeds folder in the navigation pane.
- Outlook periodically goes out to the RSS publisher's server and downloads any new or updated articles.
- On your own schedule, you can open the folder, read the new content, move it to new folders, or delete it. You can also forward it to someone else and flag it.

Locate and Subscribe to RSS Feeds

You can locate RSS feeds by having the Internet address, or URL, sent to you in an e-mail message, see it in an article or publication, and find an RSS link in a Web site. Also, you can do searches on Google or MSN, or look at lists of RSS feeds by clicking the **RSS Feeds** folder in Outlook or at http://www.search4rss .com and http://www.syndic8.com.

USE AN RSS LINK IN AN E-MAIL

If someone sends you a link with the URL for an RSS feed, such as the one in Figure 10-4, you can add it to Outlook's RSS folders.

1. In Outlook, with the Inbox open, click the message with the RSS link, drag across the link to select it, and press **CTRL+C** to copy the link to the Clipboard.

2. Click the **Tools** menu, click **Account Settings**, click the **RSS Feeds** tab, and click **New** just below the tabs. The New RSS Feed dialog box will appear.

3. Press **CTRL+V** to paste the link into the dialog box, and click **Add**. The RSS Feed Options dialog box will appear, as shown in Figure 10-5.

Inbox - Microsoft Outlook
File Edit View Go Tools Actions Help Send/Receive All
Type a question for help
Back
Messages
New Reply Reply to All Forward Send/Receive
Search address books
Mail
Favorite Folders
Inbox (2)
Sent Items
Mail Folders
All Mail Items
Outbox
RSS Feeds
Microso
Microso
MSNBC.
Sent Items
Search Folc
Inbox
Search Inbox
Arranged By: Date
Today
Senator Elizabeth D...
Thank You!
Shifty 3:44 PM
Cooking site
Yesterday
Marty Matthews Th...
Talk
ShermansTravel Thu...
BULLETIN: Discover ...
Cooking site
Shifty
Sent: Fri 11/17/2006 3:43 PM
To: marty
Look at this
site: http://www.stylegourmet.com/reviews/cookbooks.xml
XML
shifty
14 Items

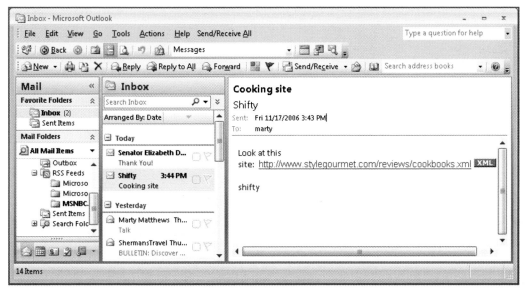

***Figure 10-4:** You can get an RSS feed in an e-mail from a friend.*

4. Consider changing the folder, automatically downloading enclosures, downloading the full article, and using the publisher's recommended update frequency; and make the needed changes. Under most circumstances, the default settings shown in Figure 10-5 are recommended.
5. When you are ready, click **OK** and click **Close**. You'll see the new RSS feed folder added to your RSS Feeds folder.

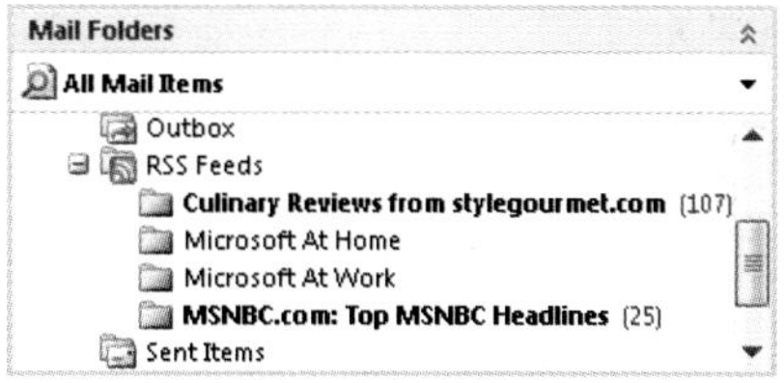

Mail Folders
All Mail Items
Outbox
RSS Feeds
Culinary Reviews from stylegourmet.com (107)
Microsoft At Home
Microsoft At Work
MSNBC.com: Top MSNBC Headlines (25)
Sent Items

NOTE

In case you want to check the settings for current RSS feeds or to change or remove them, you can also display the RSS Feed Options dialog box by double-clicking an RSS entry in the Account Settings dialog box.

CAUTION

RSS feeds can potentially download a lot of information that can both clog your Internet connection and take up a lot of room on your hard disk. Start out by downloading as little as possible and look at the impact that causes before choosing to download attachments or full articles.

RSS Feed Options
Use the choices below to configure options for this RSS feed.
General
Feed Name: Culinary Reviews from stylegourmet.com
Channel Name: Culinary Reviews from stylegourmet.com
Location: http://www.stylegourmet.com/reviews/cookbooks.xml
Description:
Delivery Location
Items from this RSS feed will be delivered to the following location:
Change Folder
Personal Folders\RSS Feeds\Culinary Reviews from stylegourmet.com
(C:\Users\Marty\AppData\Local\Microsoft\Outlook\Outlook.pst)
Downloads
Automatically download Enclosures for this feed
Download the full article as an .html attachment to each item
Update Limit
Update this feed with the publisher's recommendation. Send/Receive groups do not update more frequently than the recommended limit to prevent your RSS feed from possibly being cancelled by the content provider.
Current provider limit: 1 hour
OK
Cancel

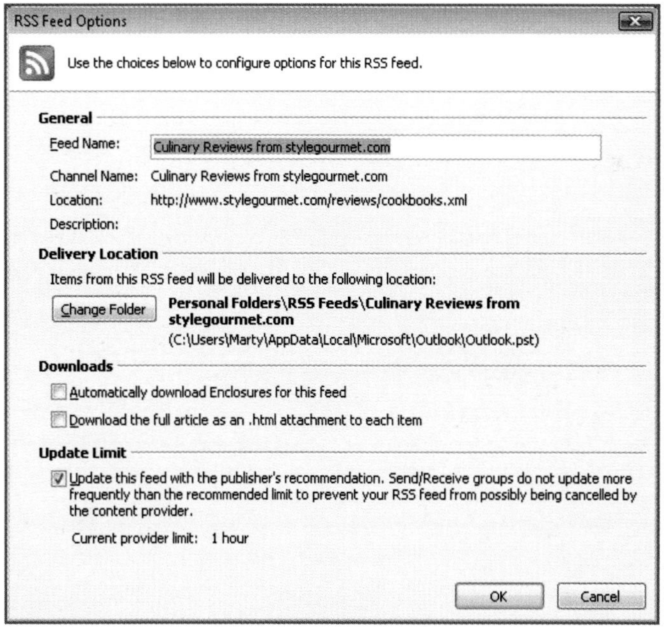

***Figure 10-5:** When you add an RSS feed to Outlook, you can determine how you want feeds handled.*

USE AN RSS LINK IN INTERNET EXPLORER 7

Internet Explorer 7 and Outlook 2007 work together to capture and use RSS feeds. The feeds can be added in either program, and, once captured, can be accessed in either program.

1. In Internet Explorer 7, open the Web site in which you want to capture an RSS feed.

2. Click the **RSS Feeds** down arrow to the right of the Home icon in the tab bar, and click the feed you want.

   –Or–

   In the Web site, click one of the RSS icons:

3. In both cases, the RSS feed will open. At the top will be a box explaining RSS feeds and asking if you want to subscribe. If you do, click **Subscribe To This Feed**. An Internet Explorer dialog box will appear.

4. Change the name, select or create the folder you want for the feed, and click **Subscribe**. Close Internet Explorer and return to Outlook. You should see your new RSS feed in the list of folders under RSS Feeds.

Read and Work with RSS Articles

Reading and working with RSS articles is exactly like reading and working with e-mail messages.

SELECT AND VIEW RSS ARTICLES

1. In Outlook, click the **Mail** view bar.

2. In the All Mail Items folder, click the plus sign (+) opposite RSS Feeds to open the folder.

3. Click the RSS feed you want to view, and it will open in the folder pane.

4. Click the article that you want to read.

5. If the reading pane isn't already open, click the **View** menu, click **Reading Pane**, and click **Right**, unless you want it on the bottom. The RSS article will appear in the reading pane for you to read, as shown in Figure 10-6.

FLAG AND FORWARD RSS ARTICLES

1. Click the RSS article in the folder pane that you want to flag and/or forward.

2. To quickly forward it, click the **Forward** button on the toolbar. Address the message and click **Send**.

   –Or–

CNN.com

You are viewing a feed that contains frequently updated content. When you subscribe to a feed, it is added to the Common Feed List. Updated information from the feed is automatically downloaded to your computer and can be viewed in Internet Explorer and other programs. Learn more about feeds.

Subscribe to this feed

TIP

To view your RSS feeds in Internet Explorer 7, click **Favorites Center** (the star icon) on the far left of the tab bar. A toolbar is displayed below it. Click **Feeds**. You can then click the feed you want to view.

Favorites | Feeds | History

Microsoft Feeds
CNN.com
Culinary Reviews from stylegourmet.com

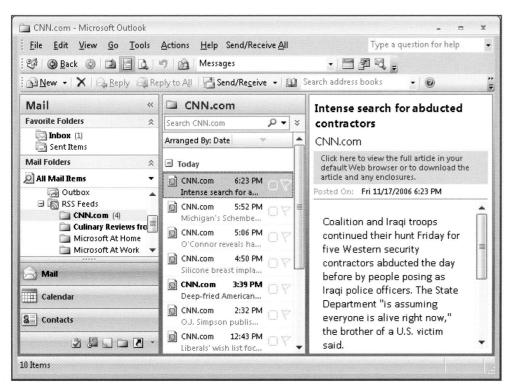

Figure 10-6: RSS feed articles look, behave, and are treated just like e-mail messages.

Click the **Actions** menu to open it. Then:

- If you want to flag the article, click **Follow Up** and click a date on which you want to be reminded.

- If you want to forward the article, click **Forward** to open an e-mail message form. Address the message and click **Send**.

–Or–

Double-click the RSS article in the folder pane to open the article in its own window (see Figure 10-7). In the RSS Article tab Options or Respond groups, click **Follow Up** or **Forward**, and proceed as above.

DELETE RSS ARTICLES

1. Click the RSS article in the folder pane that you want to delete.

2. Click **Delete** on the standard toolbar.

   –Or–

   Press **Delete**.

Transfer RSS Feeds

As you build up a collection of RSS feeds, you may want to share those feeds with others. You can do that for a single feed or for a group of feeds.

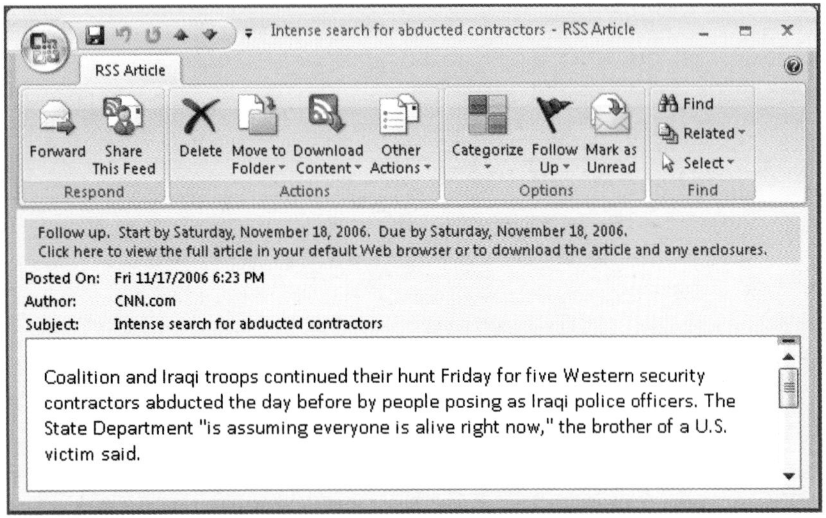

Figure 10-7: The RSS article window has a number of tools you can use to work with RSS articles.

SEND AN RSS FEED

To send an RSS feed to another person:

1. Right-click an article from the RSS feed you want to send, and click **Share This Feed**. An e-mail message will open with the RSS feed attached.

   –Or–

   Double-click an article from the RSS feed you want to send to open the article in its own window. In the RSS Article tab Respond group, click **Share This Feed**.

2. Address the e-mail message, add any comments you want (as shown in Figure 10-8), and click **Send**.

3. Upon receiving an RSS feed in an e-mail, the recipient simply clicks **Add This RSS Feed** to have it added to the list of feeds in Outlook.

QUICKSTEPS

ORGANIZING RSS ARTICLES

By default, RSS articles are placed in the originating feed folder. That may work for some RSS feeds, but for others, you may want to separate the articles into categories or some other segregation. This especially true for general news feeds, where it is almost required that you provide some organization for the articles you keep. Do this by first adding folders, and then by moving the articles to the folders.

CREATE ADDITIONAL FOLDERS

Set up the folder structure you need to organize a particular RSS feed.

Continued . . .

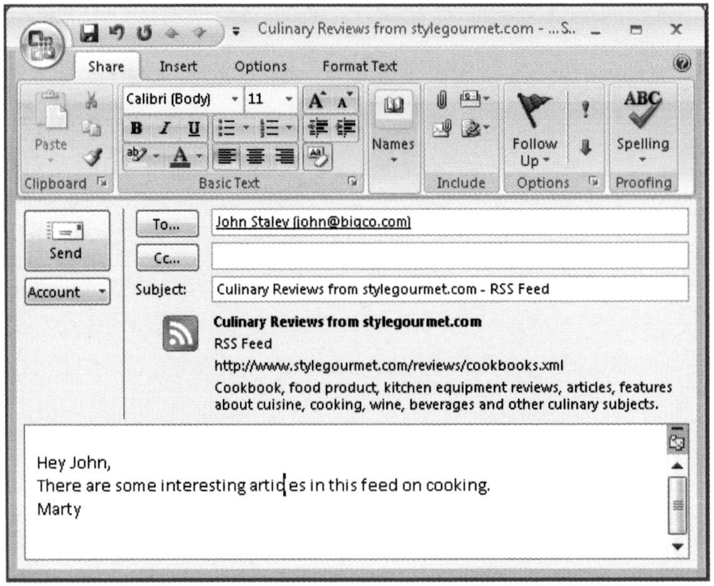

Figure 10-8: An RSS feed in an e-mail is just a specialized attachment.

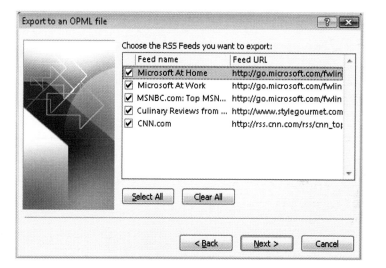

⏰ QUICKSTEPS

ORGANIZING RSS ARTICLES
(Continued)

1. Right-click the folder for the feed, and click **New Folder**. The Create New Folder dialog box appears.

2. Type the name of the new folder, click the parent folder that will contain the new folder (as shown in Figure 10-9), and click **OK**.

3. Repeat steps 1 and 2 as needed to create the folder structure you want.

MOVE ARTICLES TO FOLDERS

Once you have the folder structure in place, you then have to get the articles into the folders.

1. To display and identify the articles that you want to move into another folder, click the folder containing the RSS feeds. The folder pane displays the potential articles to be moved.

2. Drag an article from the folder pane to the desired folder in the Folder list in the navigation pane.

3. Repeat step 2 as needed to move the articles you want segregated.

SEND SEVERAL RSS FEEDS

If you want to send several RSS feeds in a single transaction, the best approach is to export feeds to an .opml file, e-mail that file or copy it to a shared folder or removable media (CD, DVD, or flash memory stick), and then have the recipient import the file to his or her Outlook program.

1. In Outlook, click the **File** menu, and click **Import And Export** (if Business Contact Manager is installed, you must then click **Outlook**). The Import And Export Wizard opens.

2. Click **Export RSS Feeds To An OPML File**, and click **Next**. A list of your RSS feeds appears. By default, all your RSS feeds are selected to be exported.

3. Click the feeds you do not want to export to deselect them, and click **Next**.

Figure 10-9: By setting up a folder structure and separating out your RSS feed articles, you'll be better able to find what you want in the future.

4. Click **Browse** and locate the folder to store the file in. Type the file name for the exported file, click **Save**, and then click **Next**.

5. To move the exported file to a shared folder or removable drive, open Windows Explorer, locate the folder where the file is stored (by default, this is the Documents or My Documents folder), and drag the file to the folder or drive.

6. To send the file as an attachment in an e-mail message, in Outlook, with Mail selected, click **New**; type an address, subject, and message; drag the file to the message, and click **Send**.

IMPORT RSS FEEDS

When you receive an .opml file in an e-mail, it will be just another file that you need to first store on the receiving computer and then import into Outlook.

1. In Outlook Mail, double-click the message with the .opml file to open the message.

2. In the Message tab Actions group, click **Other Actions** and click **Save Attachments**. Click **Browse Folders**, locate and open the folder in which you want to store the file (the default is Documents or My Documents), change the file name if desired, and click **Save**. Close the e-mail message.

Import and Export Wizard

Choose an action to perform:

Export RSS Feeds to an OPML file
Export to a file
Import a VCARD file (.vcf)
Import an iCalendar (.ics) or vCalendar file (.vcs)
Import from another program or file
Import Internet Mail Account Settings
Import Internet Mail and Addresses
Import RSS Feeds from an OPML file
Import RSS Feeds from the Common Feed List

Description

Import RSS feed information from an OPML file.

[< Back]   [Next >]   [Cancel]

3. Click the **File** menu, and click **Import And Export** (if Business Contact Manager is installed, you must then click **Outlook**). The Import And Export Wizard opens.

4. Click **Import RSS Feeds From An OPML File**, and click **Next**. Click **Browse**, locate and double-click the file, and click **Next**.

5. Click the check boxes of the feeds you want to import, and click **Next**. When you are told the feeds have been added to Outlook, click **Finish**. Close the e-mail message.

6. In the Mail Folders in the navigation pane, click **RSS Feeds** and see that your new feeds have been added.

Cancel an RSS Feed

If you are not getting what you want from an RSS feed and want to discontinue receiving its articles, you can either cancel the feed and keep the articles, or cancel the feed and delete the articles.

CANCEL A FEED AND KEEP ARTICLES

1. In Outlook Mail, click the **Tools** menu, click **Account Settings**, and click the **RSS Feeds** tab.

```
Account Settings

RSS Feeds
    You can add or remove an RSS feed. You can

  E-mail | Data Files | RSS Feeds | SharePoint Lists

  New...    Change...   X Remove

  Feed Name

  CNN.com
  Culinary Reviews from stylegourmet.com
  Microsoft At Home
  Microsoft At Work
  MSNBC.com: Top MSNBC Headlines
```

2. Click the name of the feed you want to remove, click **Remove**, and click **Yes** when asked to confirm the removal. The folder for the feed and the articles will remain in Outlook, but no more articles will be downloaded.

3. Repeat step 2 to remove several feeds, or use **SHIFT** or **CTRL** to select several feeds, and then click **Remove**. Click **Close** to close the Account Settings dialog box.

CANCEL A FEED AND DELETE ARTICLES

1. In Outlook Mail, under Mail Folders in the navigation pane, click **RSS Feeds** to display the folders of individual feeds.

2. Right-click the folder to be deleted, click **Delete**, and then click the folder name. Click **Yes** when asked to confirm the removal.

–Or–

Click the folder and either press **DELETE** or click **Delete** in the standard toolbar.

Use Other Extensions of Outlook

Looking across the Office and Microsoft family of products, you can see that many add features to Outlook. Among those discussed here are the Office Clipboard, browsing the web with Outlook, and using Outlook's electronic business cards.

Use the Office Clipboard

The Microsoft Office Clipboard connects all the programs in the Office suite, letting you copy items from various programs and paste them into others. That means you can lift a paragraph and a picture out of Word, a slide out of a PowerPoint presentation, or a graph from Excel. Then you can select from the Clipboard the items that best serve your needs and paste them into an Outlook message.

1. Start a Microsoft Office 2007 program other than Outlook, and either create or open a document with that program, such as:

- An Excel workbook

- A Word document

- A PowerPoint presentation or slide

- An Access database

- A Publisher publication

2. In the Home tab Clipboard group, click the **Clipboard Dialog Box Launcher**, which, in this case, opens the Clipboard task pane on the right, as shown in Figure 10-10.

3. Select an item in the document you opened, and copy it by:

Clicking **Edit** and clicking **Copy**.

–Or–

Pressing **CTRL+C**.

4. Start Outlook and, with Mail open, click **New** to create a new message.

5. Click in the message body, and in the Message tab Clipboard group, click the **Dialog Box Launcher**. The Clipboard task pane opens next to the message.

6. Click the desired item on the Clipboard. This "pastes" the item into the message where the cursor was located, as shown in Figure 10-11.

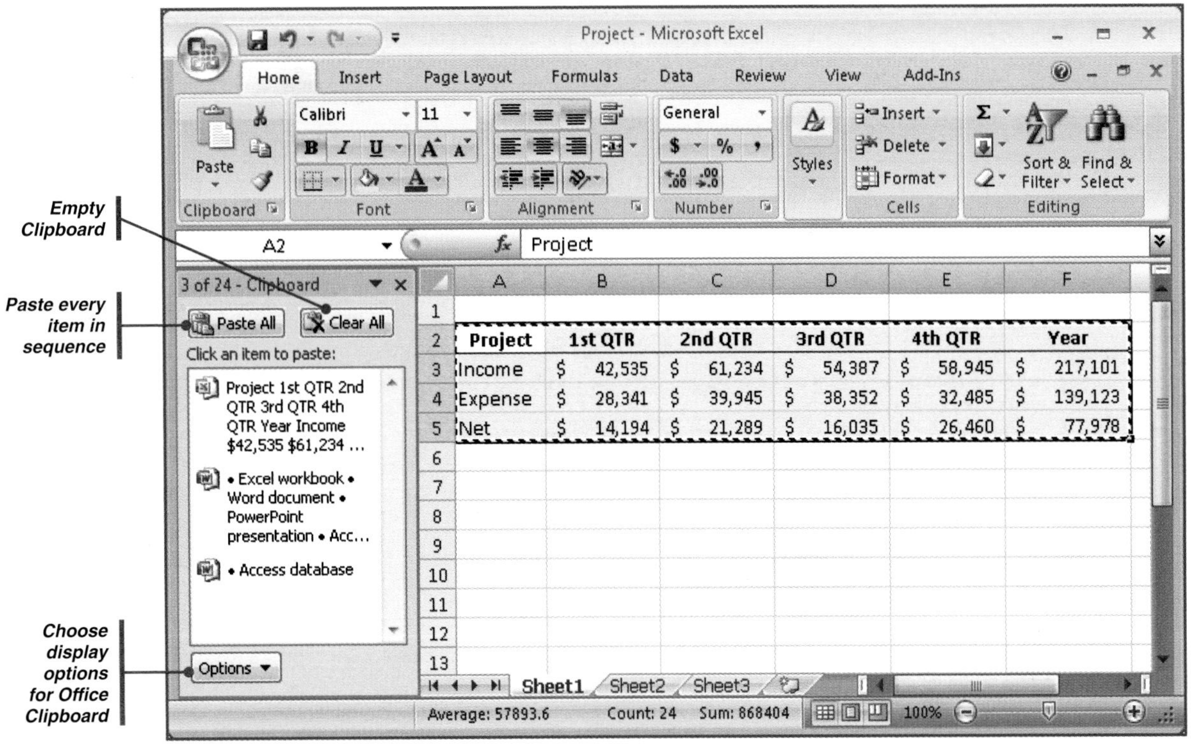

Empty Clipboard

Paste every item in sequence

Choose display options for Office Clipboard

Figure 10-10: The Clipboard displays copied items in thumbnail size, with their source program identified.

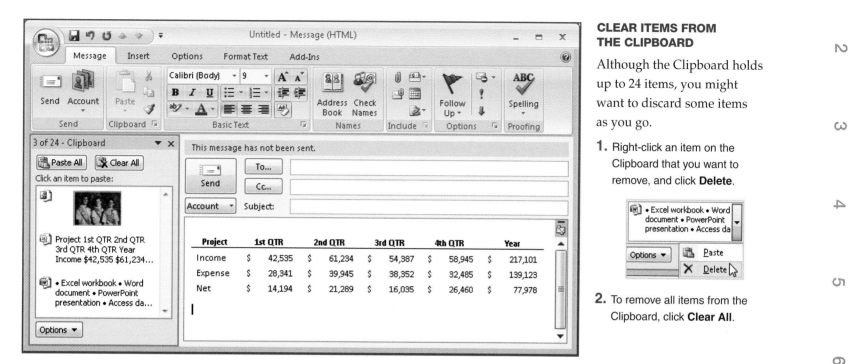

Figure 10-11: You can use the Clipboard task pane to paste several items at the same time, but you can also copy or cut and paste a single item between Office (and many other) programs by simply using CTRL+C or CTRL+X and CTRL+V.

CLEAR ITEMS FROM THE CLIPBOARD

Although the Clipboard holds up to 24 items, you might want to discard some items as you go.

1. Right-click an item on the Clipboard that you want to remove, and click **Delete**.

2. To remove all items from the Clipboard, click **Clear All**.

Browse the Web

Use the Outlook folder pane as a browser window and gain immediate access to the Internet by adding the Web toolbar.

1. Click the **View** menu, click **Toolbars**, and click **Web**.

2. Type the URL for an Internet site in the Address text box, and then press **ENTER**. The folder pane becomes a browser window displaying Web pages, as shown in Figure 10-12.

3. Return to an Outlook view by clicking any folder or button in the Navigation pane.

4. Remove the Web toolbar by clicking the **View** menu, clicking **Toolbars**, and clicking **Web**.

QUICKSTEPS

USING MICROSOFT WORD FEATURES

Unlike previous versions of Outlook, Outlook 2007 only uses Microsoft Office Word 2007 to create and edit e-mail messages. This gives you access to many special features in Word. See Chapter 3 for information on basic e-mail editing. Several of the more useful features in Word that you can use are AutoCorrect, AutoFormat, and the Table menu.

USE AUTOCORRECT

AutoCorrect, which automatically corrects many common typing and spelling errors, is turned on from the Outlook window or from the Message window.

1. In Outlook, click the **Tools** menu, click **Options**, click the **Mail Format** tab, and click **Editor Options**. The Editor Options window opens.

   –Or–

   In Outlook Mail, click **New** to open the Message window. Click the **Office Button**, and click **Editor Options**. The Editor Options window opens.

2. In either case, click **Proofing** in the task pane, and click **AutoCorrect Options**. The AutoCorrect In Email dialog box appears (see Figure 10-13).

3. Click **Show AutoCorrect Options Buttons**, if it isn't already selected and if you want to be able to point to an affected word, see the bar indicating a correction, and be able to select other options.

4. Set the other options for correction conventions as you see fit.

Continued . . .

Figure 10-12: *A fully functioning Web page can be displayed in Outlook.*

Create Electronic Business Cards

Electronic business cards encapsulate personal information in a way that can be easily transferred to others, either as an attachment to an e-mail message or as an e-mail signature. Electronic business cards look like their paper equivalent, and you can customize them with photos and logos, as well as text. When you receive someone else's electronic business card, you can save it to a Contacts folder and forward it to others. When you create a new entry in your Contacts folder, you are creating an electronic business card.

QUICKSTEPS

USING MICROSOFT WORD FEATURES *(Continued)*

5. If it isn't already selected and you want to use it, click **Replace Text As You Type** to use that feature.

6. Scroll through the list of common typographical errors, select any you do not want, and click **Delete**.

7. Type your common personal typos and their corrections in the Replace and With text boxes, and click **Add**.

USE AUTOFORMAT

In the AutoCorrect In Email dialog box, click the other tabs to see additional popular options, such as:

- **AutoFormat** automatically applies formatting, such as typographical quotation marks, superscripted ordinals (1st), fraction characters (½), and em-dashes (—).

- **Math AutoCorrect** replaces written math symbols with the actual symbol. For example, it replaces "\pi" with "Π," "/int" with "∫," or "/div" with "÷."

- **AutoFormat As You Type** defines styles based on formatting you set, automatically creates bulleted and numbered lists, and turns e-mail addresses and URLs into hyperlinks when you press **SPACEBAR**.

Continued . . .

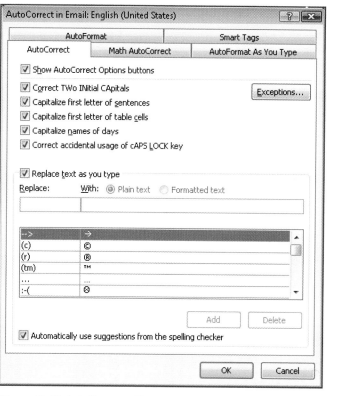

Figure 10-13: AutoCorrect will automatically make changes to your text as you type.

CREATE YOUR OWN ELECTRONIC BUSINESS CARD

Start the construction of an electronic business card by choosing a layout and background; follow this by adding a picture, logo, or other graphic element; and finish by adding text fields.

1. In Outlook, click **Contacts** in either the view bars or the button bar. In Contacts, click **New**.

2. In the Contact tab Options group, click **Business Card**. The Edit Business Card dialog box will appear.

3. To change the layout, click the **Layout** down arrow, and select a different position, text only, or a background image.

USING MICROSOFT WORD FEATURES *(Continued)*

- **Smart Tags** tell Outlook (really Word) to flag certain words or phrases in an e-mail so that you can do something. For example, if you type an e-mail address, you can add it to your Address Book. If you type a date, you can schedule a meeting.

Click **OK** to close the AutoCorrect In Email dialog box.

MAKE A TABLE

Use Word's Table menu to organize information into a grid that will display properly, even for recipients who don't use Word.

1. In an Outlook Message window, in the Insert tab Tables group, click in the message pane, click **Table**, and drag across the squares to give you the table size you want.

   –Or–

   Click **Insert Table**, type or use the spinner to enter numbers of columns and rows to start with, and click **OK**.

2. Add or delete columns and rows, and format the table using the Table Tools Design and Layout tabs that appear on the ribbon, as shown in Figure 10-14.

			Shapes
			SmartAr
Table	Picture	Clip Art	Chart

3x3 Table

- Insert Table...
- Draw Table
- Convert Text to Table...
- Excel Spreadsheet
- Quick Tables

Figure 10-14: The Outlook Message window has the full power of Microsoft Word formatting available to it.

Investment	Ownership	Possible Return
$10,000,000	5%	0 — 5% of net
$15,000,000	7.5%	0 — 7.5% of net

4. To insert an image, click **Change**, locate the folder with the image you want to use, and double-click the image. Adjust the image area and alignment as you see fit.

5. Under Fields, select the first field you want on the card. If this is not the first field in the list, click the up arrow to move it to the top.

6. With the first field selected, type what you want in the first field in the text box on the right, and apply any of the formatting attributes above the text box.

7. Repeat steps 5 and 6 for the remaining fields you want on the card. If there is a field in the list that you don't want, click it and click **Remove**. If you want to use a field that is not on the list, click **Add** and click the field name.

8. See Figure 10-15 for an example of a finished card. When you are ready, click **OK** to save the electronic business card, and click **Save & Close** to close the Contact window.

SEND AN ELECTRONIC BUSINESS CARD

You can send an electronic business card with an e-mail message.

1. In Outlook Mail, click **New** to open a new message form. Type an address, subject, and message as normal.

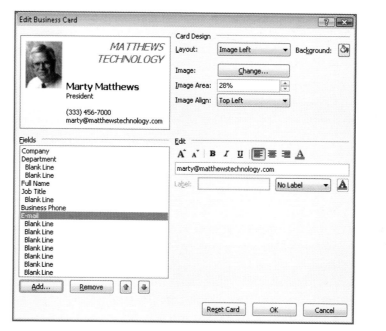

Figure 10-15: Outlook provides a very comprehensive tool for creating and editing electronic business cards.

2. In the Message tab Include group, click **Insert Business Card**, and then click the name you want (the list shows the last 10 business cards you inserted). If you don't see the name you want, click **Other Business Cards**, click the name you want, and click **OK**.

3. The card will be added as a .vcf attachment to the e-mail message, as shown in Figure 10-16. When you are ready, click **Send**.

INCLUDE AN ELECTRONIC BUSINESS CARD IN YOUR SIGNATURE

You can add your electronic business card to your e-mail signature and automatically include it in all the e-mail you send.

1. In Outlook Mail, click **New** to open a new message form. In the Message tab Include group, click **Signature** and then click **Signatures**.

2. In the E-mail Signature tab, click **New**. Type a name for the signature, and click **OK**.

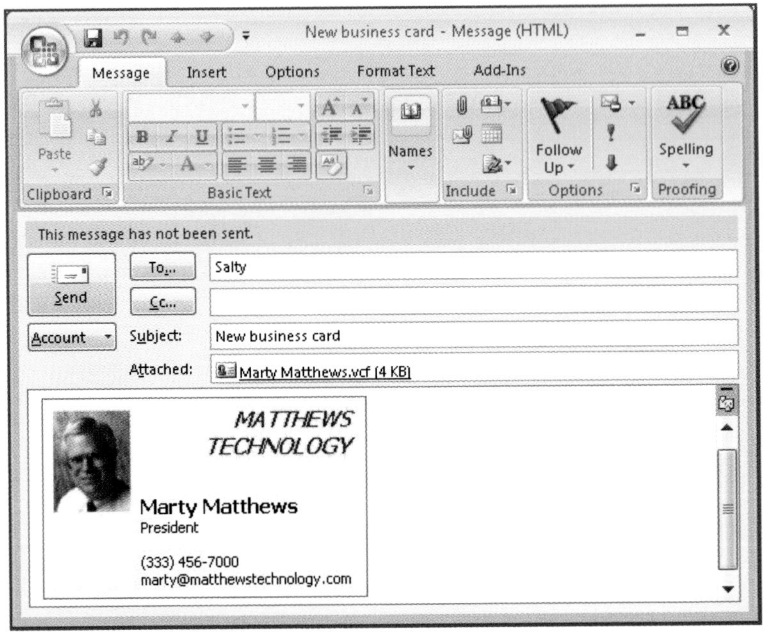

Figure 10-16: Including an electronic business card in an e-mail is a fast way to give the recipient all your contact information.

3. Under Edit Signature, add the text, graphics, and possible link you may want in the signature area, and then format it as needed.

4. Position the insertion point where you want the electronic business card, click **Business Card** in the toolbar, click the name of the person on the business card, and click **OK**.

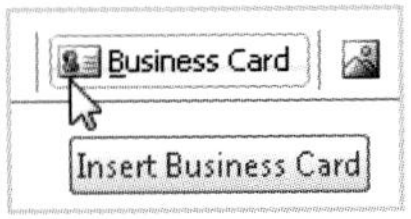

5. Select the e-mail account you want the signature to apply to and whether to apply it to either or both new and reply e-mails. Make any other adjustments to the signature, and click **OK**. Close the original message used to edit the signature.

6. In Outlook Mail, click **New** to open another message. If you chose to automatically add your signature to all new messages, you'll see your signature with the business card. Also, your business card .vcf file will be attached.

7. If you chose to not have your signature automatically added to your messages, you can add a signature. In the Message tab Include group, click **Signature** and click the name of your signature. Again, your signature with the business card and the attached .vcf file appears in the message.

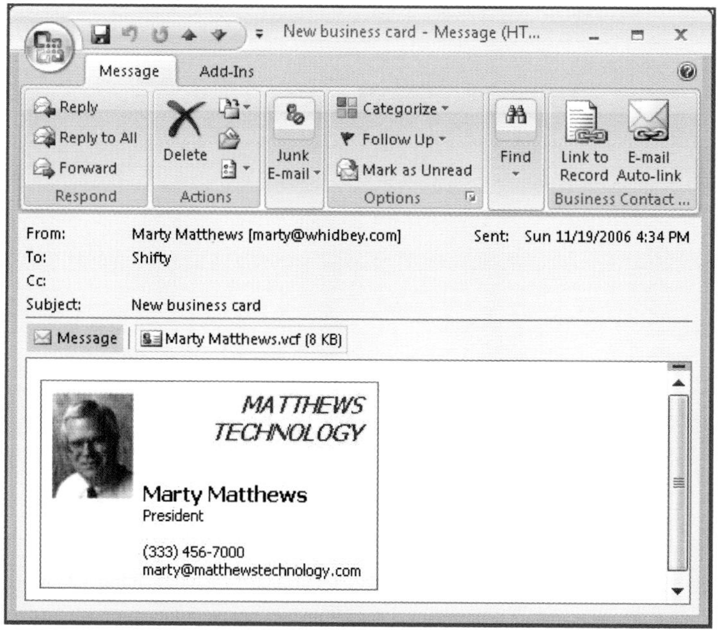

RECEIVE AND STORE AN ELECTRONIC BUSINESS CARD

When an e-mail message is received with an electronic business card attached, the recipient will see an image of the card, provided he or she is using Outlook 2007 or is using HTML to view the message in older versions of Outlook. The recipient will also receive an attachment with the card (see Figure 10-17). To store the electronic business card in Contacts:

1. In Outlook Mail, double-click the message in the Inbox to open the message window.

2. Double-click the attached .vcf file. A new Contact window will open with all the information on the electronic business card placed in the proper fields.

3. Make any needed changes or additions to the Contact form, and click **Save & Close**. Close the message that contained the electronic business card.

Figure 10-17: The recipient of an electronic business card can automatically add all the information on the card to his or her Contacts list.

Distribution List, 46, 75
  categorization of, 77
  creation of, 74–76
  removing name from, 76–77
  sending, 79
Domains, 29
Downloading e-mail information, 27–29
Dragging
  contacts and, 74
  to customize toolbars, 16
Driving directions, to contacts, 89–90
DSL. *See* Digital subscriber line

E

Electronic business card. *See* Business card
E-mail, 21–40, 71
  accounts, 24–25
  add contacts to, 77–78
  address for, 42–46
  archiving of, 40
  attached notes to, 154
  as attachment, 62
  bcc with, 46–47
  business cards in, 78
  calendars in, 109–110
  cc with, 46–47
  checking, 26
  compose page for, 182
  copying contacts from, 73–74
  creating, 41–65
  delay delivery of, 63–65
  deletion of, 37–38
  by distribution list, 74
  editing, 47–48

embedding pictures in, 53–54
follow-up flags for, 33–34
formatting, 49–50
forward of, 61–62
handling of, 32–40
headers in, 28
message body in, 42
with notes, 155
printing of, 39–40
priority of, 62
reading, 26–27
receiving, 25
recipient in, 42
reply to, 59–61
request receipts for, 63
ribbon with, 43–44
RSS in, 198–199, 202
security of, 169–172
sending, 59–65
sending calendar in, 109–110
setup for, 3
signature to, 54–55
sorting of, 36–37
spell checking of, 57–58
of status reports, 137
subject in, 42
themes in, 51
voting with, 55
E-mail Address, 75
Embedding pictures, in
  e-mail, 53–54
Encryption, 169–170
Envelopes, for mail merge, 192
Eudora, 165
Event banner, in calendar, 96

Events
  in calendar, 97
  entering of, 113–114
Excel, 205
Exchange Server, 101, 111
Export, of files, 165–167

F

Fields
  aligning, 178–179
  in forms, 173
  positioning, 178–179
File(s)
  as contacts attachment, 75
  copying, 163
  deletion of, 162–163
  export of, 165–167
  grouping, 164
  import of, 165–167
  management of, 157–172
  manipulation of, 162–167
  moving, 163
  sorting, 164–165
  viewing, 164
File As, 71
Filter
  in Business Contact Manager, 94
  of junk mail, 29–32
  for sorting tasks, 125
Find
  contacts, 83–85
  messages, 12–15
Find A Contact, 84
Find tool, with contacts, 84

Flags. *See* Follow-up flags
Folder(s)
 arranging messages in, 35–36
 copying, 160–161
 creation of, 158–159
 deleting, 160
 management of, 157–172
 moving, 160–161
 renaming of, 159–160
 setting properties of, 161–162
Folder List, 8–9
 setting folder properties from, 161
Folders pane, 6
Follow-up flags, 138–139
 for e-mail, 33–34
Fonts, for Notes, 151
Footers, in Business Contact Manager
  report, 94
Form(s), 173–192
 custom, 176–180, 184–185
 fields in, 173
 modifying, 174–176
 publishing, 183–184
Form Design window, 176
Formatting e-mail, 49–50
Forward
 of e-mail, 61–62
 of notes, 153
Free/busy indicator, in calendar, 96
Free/Busy Options, 106
Full Name, 71

G

Group files, 164
Group schedules, 119

H

Handling e-mail, 32–40
Handwriting recognition, 193
Headers
 in Business Contact Manager report, 94
 in e-mail, 28
Help, 11–15
Holidays, on calendar, 105–106
Hotmail, 22–24
HTML. *See* Hypertext Markup Language
HTTP. *See* Hypertext Transfer Protocol
Hyperlinks, 52
Hypertext Markup Language (HTML),
  47, 78
 with junk mail, 29–30
Hypertext Transfer Protocol (HTTP), 22

I

iCalendar, 166
IM. *See* Instant messaging
IM Address, 71
Image files, in junk mail, 30
Import
 in Certificates, 72
 of files, 165–167
Instant messaging (IM), 193–197
 activating, 195–196
 setup for, 194–195
Instant search, for messages, 12–13
International, in filtered address lists, 32
Internet Explorer, RSS with, 200
Internet Free-Busy, 71
Internet service providers (ISPs), 21
Invitations, to meetings, 120
ISPs. *See* Internet service providers

J

Job Title, 71
Journal, 141–156
 setup for, 4
 sharing of, 149
Journal entries, 4–9
 categorization for, 147–148
 changing, 145
 contacts to, 146–147
 creating, 4–5
 deleting, 145
 printing of, 149
 timeline for, 146
Journal folder, 142–143
Junk mail, 21
 filter of, 29–32
 HTML with, 29–30
 image files in, 30
 protection level from, 30–31
 sound files in, 30

L

Labels, for mail merge, 190–192
LAN. *See* Local area network
Link, contacts to tasks, 138
Local area network (LAN), 21

M

Macros, as viruses, 171–172
Mail merge, 173–192, 186–192
 contacts for, 186–188
 envelopes for, 192
 labels for, 190–192
 Word and, 187–189

Phone Numbers, 71
Phoning, contacts, 87–88
Pictures. *See also* Image files
  downloads of, 31
  embedding, 53–54
Plain text, 47
Planner Options, on calendar, 105
Planning meetings, 119–120
Podcasts, 197
POP3. *See* Post Office Protocol 3
Positioning fields, 178–179
Post Office Protocol 3 (POP3), 22
PowerPoint, 205
Preferences, 17–18
Print
  of calendars, 118–119
  of contacts, 85–87
  of e-mail, 39–40
  of journal entries, 149
  of notes, 156
Priority, of e-mail, 62
Privacy, options for, 167–169
Private tasks, 133–134
Programmatic Access, in Trust
  Center, 169
Proofing, in Show, 69
Properties, in Certificates, 72
Protection level, from junk mail, 30–31
.pst. *See* Personal Folders data files
Publisher, 205
Publishing forms, 183–184

Q

Quick Access toolbar, 45
Quick Click flags, 139

R

Read layout, 182–183
Reading e-mail, 26–27
Reading pane, 6, 101
  for Journal, 142–143
  for notes, 155
Real Simple Syndication (RSS), 2, 166, 197–205
  as attachment, 202
  cancellation of, 204–205
  in e-mail, 198–199, 202
  with Internet Explorer, 200
  subscription to, 198–200
  transfer of, 201–204
Receiving e-mail, 25
Recipient, in e-mail, 42
Recurring appointments, 101, 115–117
  in calendar, 96
Recurring tasks, 128–129
Reminders, 117
  for tasks, 128
Removing name, from Distribution List,
  76–77
Rename
  folders, 159–160
  tasks, 136
Reply, to e-mail, 59–61
Reports, in Business Contact Manager,
  93–94
Request Permission To View Recipient's
  Calendar, 111
Request receipts, for e-mail, 63
Requesting meeting attendance, 119–120
Responding, to meeting invitation, 120
Ribbon, 45, 68
  with e-mail, 43–44

Rich Text Format (RTF), 47
RSS. *See* Real Simple Syndication
RTF. *See* Rich Text Format
Rules and Alerts Wizard, 36–37

S

Safe recipients, in filtered address
  lists, 32
Safe senders, in filtered address lists, 32
Save & Close, 73
  in Actions, 68
Save & New, 73
  in Actions, 68, 72
Scales, on calendar grid, 98–99
Schedule
  of calendar, 95–120
  for groups, 119
Scheduling Assistant, 120
Scroll bar, with finding contacts, 84
Search Contacts, 85
Search folders
  creation of, 158–159
  for organizing mail, 159
  for reading mail, 159
Security, 167–172
  of e-mail, 169–172
  options for, 167–169
Select A Report Type, 93
Select Members, 75
Send A Calendar Via E-mail, 110
Send Me A Status When This Task Is
  Complete, 132
Sending e-mail, 59–65
Set As Default, in Certificates, 72
Setting folder properties, 161–162

SharePoint Services, 1
Sharing
  calendars, 109–111
  folders, 161
  journals, 149
  notes, 156
Show, 68
Show "Click To Add" Prompts On The
  Calendar, 105
Show Time Within My Working Hours
  Only, 110
Show Week Numbers In The Month View
  And Date Navigator, 105
Signatures. *See also* Digital signatures
  business card with, 211–213
  to e-mail, 54–55
Small Booklet Style, for printing
  contacts, 86
Smart Tags, 196
Snooze, 117
Sort
  of contacts, 82–83
  of e-mail, 36–37
  of files, 164–165
  removal of, 83
  of tasks, 125
Sound files, in junk mail, 30
Spam. *See* Junk mail
Specific Office Information, 71
Speed Dial, 88
Spell checking, 57–58, 69
Standard toolbar, in calendar, 101
Start Menu, 2, 3
Startup Wizard, 2

Stationery, 41, 48–52
Status reports
  e-mail of, 137
  for tasks, 136–137
Subject, in e-mail, 42
Subscription, to RSS, 198–200
Symantec, 167
Synonyms, 69

T

Tab, 71
Tab order, 181–182
Table Style, for printing contacts, 86
Task(s), 121–140
  assignment of, 131–132
  Automatic Formatting for, 126
  in calendar, 96, 97
  categorization of, 130–133
  creation of, 126–134
  deletion of, 136
  Detailed List for, 123–124
  display of, 135–136
  filter for, 125
  linked to contacts, 138
  managing of, 134–137
  Microsoft Exchange Server and, 133
  Outlook Data Files files, 124
  private, 133–134
  recurring, 128–129
  reminders for, 128
  renaming of, 136
  sorting of, 125
  status reports for, 136–137
  views of, 122–124

Task Recurrence dialog box, 129
Task Timeline, 124
Task window, 122–126
Templates, 184–185
Themes, in e-mail formats, 51
Thesaurus, 14
This Is The Mailing Address, 71
3DES encryption algorithm, 170
Time(s), conversion of, 113
Time bar, in calendar, 96
Time intervals. *See* Scales
Time zone, 106–107
  on calendar, 105
Timeline, for journal entries, 146
To-Do Bar, 6, 121, 139–140
  customization of, 11
Toolbars
  advanced, 7–8, 101
  customization of, 15–18
  deleting, 18
  for Journal, 142–143
  menus to, 18
  Quick Access, 45
Translation, 69
Trust Center, 167–168
Trusted Publishers, 168

U

Update Information Of Selected
  Contact, 74
Updates, 20
Use This Response When You Propose
  New Meetings Times, 105

V

vCalendar (.vcs), 166
vCARD (.vcf), 165
.vcf. *See* vCARD
.vcs. *See* vCalendar
View bars, 8–9
Views
  in calendar, 100–101, 102–104
  of contacts, 80–82
  customization of, 124–126, 154
  for Journal, 142–143
  for Notes, 153–155
  in Outlook window, 5
  of tasks, 122–124
Viruses, 168
  macros as, 171–172
  protecting against, 171
Voting, with e-mail, 55

W

WatchGuard, 167
Web browser, 193, 207–208
Web Page Address, 71
Week numbers, on calendar, 105
Window entry, for appointments, 112
Windows Live Messenger, 195
Windows SharePoint Services, 1
Word, 205, 208–210
  mail merge document in, 187–189
Work week, on calendar, 105

Z

Zone Alarm, 167